Probate Disputes and Remedies

Second Edition

Probate Disputes and Remedies

Second Edition

Dawn Goodman
Solicitor and Partner, Withers LLP

Brendan Hall
Solicitor and Partner, Laytons

Paul Hewitt
Solicitor and Partner, Withers LLP

Henrietta Mason
Solicitor, Withers LLP

JORDANS

Published by
Jordan Publishing Limited
21 St Thomas Street
Bristol BS1 6JS

British Library Cataloguing-in-Publication Data

A catalogue record for this book is available from the British Library.

ISBN 978 1 84661 040 0

Typeset by Letterpart Ltd, Reigate, Surrey

Printed in Great Britain by Antony Rowe Limited, Chippenham, Wiltshire

DEDICATION – BRENDAN HALL DECEASED

I have been asked by the surviving authors of the Second Edition of Probate Disputes and Remedies to say a few words about Brendan Hall, the co-author with Dawn Goodman of the first edition of Probate Disputes and Remedies in 1997. Brendan sadly died very suddenly in 2007. He is greatly missed not only by his fellow partners in Laytons but by colleagues across the profession, not least his collaborators at Withers.

Brendan made a significant contribution to the field of contentious probate and I know that he would be very proud to see this edition, which has been in preparation for some time, come to fruition.

Ian Burman, Laytons

PREFACE

The first edition of Probate Disputes and Remedies was published in 1997. The preface to that edition described probate disputes as a growing phenomenon. That growth continued as is witnessed by the growth of the Association of Contentious Trust and Probate Specialists, established shortly after the first edition was published.

Little said in the preface to the first edition does not ring as true ten years later. The introduction of the Civil Procedure Rules and in particular the emphasis on seeking to resolve disputes by alternative routes to a full trial means that the vast majority of probate disputes are undoubtedly resolved in one way or another without seeing court. Nevertheless, the number of disputed wills and other probate related disputes to which this work is addressed continues to grow.

We are very proud to associate ourselves with the words of Ian Burman of Laytons about Brendan Hall whose loss is felt keenly by many members of the profession.

We want to pay particular thanks to the contributors, Claire Blakemore (Appendix 1 – Ancillary Relief cases since *White v White*), Clive Cutbill (Tax Evasion, Foreign Taxes and Criminal Matters), Peter Leckey (Coroners' Inquests), Robin Paul (The Foreign Element) and Stephen Richards (Court of Protection), all of Withers LLP, and to Geraint Thomas (Fatal Accident Act Claims). Thanks are also due to Sophie Chapman, Isabel Moreton, Christopher Salomons and Rachel Wellman of Withers LLP, and Erin Hitchins of 24 Old Buildings for assisting on the text.

The law is correct as at 3 March 2008.

Dawn Goodman, Withers LLP

Paul Hewitt, Withers LLP

Henrietta Mason, Withers LLP

PREFACE TO THE FIRST EDITION

Probate disputes are a growing phenomenon. Although very few pure probate actions are tried each year, all practitioners dealing with private clients and professional personal representatives are conscious of the growing level of public interest and activity in this field.

There are a number of reasons why probate disputes are becoming a burgeoning area of practice. There has been a considerable build-up of wealth for a large section of the population. A higher proportion than ever before of those passing on to the next world leave behind a valuable asset in the form of their home. The generation which built up substantial wealth shortly after the Second World War is starting to die. And where there is money available for redistribution on death, there is often a dispute.

It is common for a deceased to leave assets in a number of jurisdictions. His or her lifestyle may have involved strong links with a number of jurisdictions, leaving difficult issues to be determined as to which law or laws apply to the devolution of his estate and what an executor should do about collecting assets scattered across the globe.

Family relationships have become more complicated. It is becoming more common for a deceased to have had a two- if not three-tier family with more than one failed relationship, whether within or out of marriage. The various members of the deceased's family may have, or believe they have, a claim on the deceased's bounty and disappointment may well lead to an Inheritance Act claim or a probate action.

There is a heightened awareness of people's rights and a willingness to pursue them through litigation if need be. Beneficiaries are no longer prepared to sit and wait while the administration may be conducted in a leisurely and/or less than perfect manner and will want to know what they can do about it.

Dealing with probate disputes is not easy. Emotions often run high, the underlying law is far from straightforward and the procedure is not the run-of-the-mill procedure familiar to most civil law or commercial litigators. Our aim in writing this book is to provide a first point of reference for an overlooked or disillusioned beneficiary, legal practitioner or personal representative faced with the potential for probate litigation or a problem arising during the course of the administration to enable them to consider the range of possibilities open to them and to provide some practical tips. We hope that, although not providing all the answers, it will provide a useful guide through the numerous remedies available for dealing with probate disputes.

We have based our exposition of the law on our understanding of the materials available to us at 1 April 1997.

Brendan Hall
Wedlake Saint

Dawn Goodman
Withers

CONTENTS

Part V
Disputes in the Estate Administration

Chapter 13
Claims against Personal Representatives

Chapter 14
Disappointed Beneficiary Claims: Proprietary Estoppel and Constructive Trust Claims

Chapter 16
Disappointed Beneficiary Claims: Fatal Accident Claims **175**

Chapter 17
Creditor Claims and Insolvent Estates **179**

TABLE OF CASES

References are to paragraph numbers.

TABLE OF STATUTES

References are to paragraph numbers.

TABLE OF STATUTORY INSTRUMENTS

References are to paragraph numbers.

Part I
PRE DEATH ISSUES

Chapter 1

DISPUTES ARISING OUT OF LIFETIME TRANSACTIONS

1.1   Various disputes can flow from personal representatives' (or beneficiaries') concerns about transactions involving the deceased pre-death which have the effect of diminishing the estate and require investigation. Such transactions can include (but are not limited to) gifts, contracts for sale at under value, registering of assets in joint names and death bed gifts.

1.2   Where personal representatives are on notice of such transactions (which will normally be relevant for completing HMRC formalities) and fail at least to investigate, they are potentially at risk of an allegation that they have failed in their duties to collect in all the assets of the estate.

VALIDITY OF LIFETIME GIFTS

1.3   An *inter vivos* gift may be open to challenge if it can be demonstrated that the donor lacked capacity at the time the gift was made.

Capacity to make a gift

1.4   Section 2 of the Mental Capacity Act 2005 (MCA 2005) defines a person who lacks capacity in relation to a matter as being: 'at the material time ... unable to make a decision for himself in relation to the matter because of an impairment of, or a disturbance in the functioning of, the mind or brain'. Section 3 defines inability to make a decision as being where a person is unable:

(1)   to understand the information relevant to the decision,

(2)   to retain that information,

(3)   to weigh that information as part of the decision making process, and

(4)   to communicate that decision (whether by talking, using sign language or any other means).

Existing case law offers guidance as to the appropriate test for capacity for various types of lifetime transactions. Although there is, at the time of writing, no case law on this test, commentators agree that the MCA 2005 and previous case law will complement one another.

1.5   *Re Beaney (Deceased)* [1978] 1 WLR 770 addressed the assessment of capacity to make a gift. Mrs Beaney was a widow aged 64 who lived in her own home with the eldest of her three adult children. Shortly after admission to hospital with advanced dementia, Mrs Beaney gifted her house to the elder daughter who had cared for her for a number of years. The following year she died intestate. The daughter's siblings applied for a declaration to have the deed of gift set aside on the basis that Mrs Beaney was mentally incapable of making the decision at the relevant time. On the basis of the medical evidence, the judge concluded that she was not capable of understanding that she was making an absolute gift of the property to her elder daughter. Accordingly the deed of gift was set aside.

1.6   The judge gave the following guidance on the validity of lifetime gifts ([1978] 1 WLR 770 at 774):

> 'The degree or extent of understanding required in respect of any instrument is relative to the particular transaction which it is to effect ... In the case of ... a gift inter vivos ... the degree required varies with the circumstances of the transaction. Thus at one extreme if the subject matter and value of a gift are trivial in relation to the donor's other assets a low degree of understanding will suffice. But, at the other extreme, if its effect is to dispose of the donor's only asset of value and thus ... to pre-empt the devolution of his estate ... then the degree of understanding required is as high as that required for a will, and the donor must understand the claims of all potential donees and the extent of the property to be disposed of.'

The *Re Beaney* test has been applied in subsequent cases involving the retrospective assessment of a lifetime disposal of property forming a large proportion of the donor's estate including in *Re Morris (Deceased), Special Trustees for Great Ormond Street Hospital for Children v Pauline Rushin* [2000] All ER (D) 598 where an elderly lady who suffered from Alzheimer's had transferred her house to her carer 2 years before death. The Court held that the requisite capacity for the transfer of the house was as high as that required for a will (as to which see Chapter 12 on testamentary capacity).

Practical considerations

1.7   The criteria contained in s 3 of the MCA 2005 provide a useful checklist for practitioners in relation to assessing capacity including the retrospective assessment that will be undertaken by personal representatives.

1.8   It was implied in *Re Beaney* that questions capable of a 'yes' or 'no' answer may be insufficient for the purpose of assessing capacity. In *Buckenham v Dickinson* [2002] WTLR 1083 the court advised solicitors to ask open questions to establish that the person could hear and understand what was being read to them. In *Williams v Williams* [2003] WTLR 1371 the solicitor asked 'closed' rather than 'open' questions, thus missing the fact that Mr Williams could not read.

Gifts made by an attorney or receiver/deputy

1.9   The powers of an attorney under an Enduring Power of Attorney to make gifts or maintain others and of an attorney under a Lasting Power of Attorney are set out at MCA 2005, ss 12(2), (3), Sch 4, para 3(3) (see also **2.22-2.24**).

1.10   Gifts may be made on customary occasions to those related to or connected with the donor, including the attorney. They may be made if they pass an objective reasonableness test.

1.11   The scope of customary occasions has been widened by MCA 2005, Sch 4 to include specifically the formation and anniversary of a civil partnership and on any other occasion on which presents are customarily given within families or among friends or associates. Effectively this is a very broad definition and enables a wide scope of gifts to be made without the need to seek the Court of Protection's consent.

1.12   Gifts may also be made to a charity which the donor has supported or which they might have supported, again provided the size of the gift is not unreasonable in relation to the size of the donor's estate.

1.13   The extent to which such gifts are vulnerable to retrospective challenges post death will depend on the circumstances. Whether a gift is void or voidable depends on the circumstances. If the donor still has capacity he can ratify the gift. The court also has a power to ratify.

OTHER LIFETIME TRANSACTIONS

1.14   Where both parties to a transaction have given consideration, the transaction will not be overturned merely on the grounds that one of those parties lacked capacity at the time of entering into the transaction. Such transactions may, however, be overturned on grounds of undue influence.

1.15   In *Hart v O'Connor* [1985] AC 1000 the Privy Council held that where one party had insufficient mental capacity to enter into a contract the contract was voidable at the instance of that party if the other party knew or ought reasonably to have known of that party's incapacity.

UNDUE INFLUENCE

1.16   Undue influence in the context of a lifetime transaction may be proved not only by evidence of actual undue influence but also by way of the doctrine of presumed undue influence.

Actual undue influence

1.17   An allegation of actual undue influence requires proof of coercion. The level of coercion required will depend upon the strength of will of the alleged victim of undue influence.

1.18   If actual influence is proved the transaction will be set aside even if the transaction is not clearly or obviously disadvantageous to the victim of undue influence. Actual undue influence in the context of the making of a will is discussed in Chapter 12.

Presumed undue influence

1.19   In contrast to wills, lifetime transactions may also be set aside by way of presumed undue influence.

1.20   A presumption of undue influence may arise out of the relationship between two persons where one has acquired influence over another.

1.21   The key decision in this area is that of the House of Lords in *Royal Bank of Scotland plc v Etridge (No 2)* [2002] 2 AC 773. Key principles distilled from that decision are:

(a)   The objective of the doctrine of undue influence is to ensure that the influence of one person, the donee, over another, the donor, is not abused.

(b)   Disadvantage to the donor is not a necessary ingredient of undue influence. However, it may have an evidential value.

(c)   Whether a transaction has been brought about by undue influence is a question of fact.

(d)   The legal burden of proving undue influence rests on the person alleging it.

(e)   Proof that the donor received advice from a third party before entering into the impugned transaction is one of the matters the court takes into account when weighing all the evidence.

(f)   The nature of the advice required is that someone free from the taint of undue influence should put before the donor the nature and consequences of the proposed transaction. It is not necessary for the adviser to recommend the transaction. An adult of competent mind is entitled to enter into a financially unwise transaction if he or she wants to.

1.22 There are two key elements in establishing a presumption of undue influence:

(1) a relationship of influence between the parties; and

(2) a transaction that calls for explanation.

If a relationship of trust and confidence is established and the transaction is such that an explanation is called for, a presumption of undue influence arises. It is for the defendant to show that nevertheless the donor entered into the matter with his or her will unconstrained.

Relationship between the parties

1.23 Where the relationship between the donor and donee comes within certain classes of relationship (such as parent and child, guardian and ward, trustee and beneficiary, solicitor and client) an irrebuttable presumption arises that there is a relationship of influence between the parties.

1.24 Where the relationship does not fall within a recognised category, the existence of a relationship of influence must be affirmatively proved.

Nature of the transaction

1.25 Once a relationship of influence has been established the claimant must demonstrate that the transaction is of a nature that calls for explanation. This will usually be evident from the face of the transaction.

1.26 Since *Etridge*, a significant number of reported decisions have considered undue influence addressing a variety of transactions. Substantial gifts obviously call for an explanation but other transactions set aside have included a deed of retirement, a trust deed, a loan on favourable terms, an option to purchase and an enduring power of attorney. The apparent trend towards court intervention should put all personal representatives on notice that they should be satisfied that there is no obvious reason to investigate lifetime transactions which substantially favoured a third party.

1.27 In *Hammond v Osborn* [2002] WTLR 1225 the court considered features of a transaction that would be likely to require explanation. The deceased, an elderly bachelor, had been befriended by a neighbour. In hospital he said that he wished to gift her investments.

1.28 Holding the gift to be invalid, the court found it to be particularly significant that:

- the transaction was substantial in relation to the donor's other liquid assets;

- the adverse tax implications of the gift were significant; and

- the gift was wholly out of proportion to the kindness shown to him.

Rebutting the presumption

1.29 Where a presumption of undue influence arises, the defendant may be able to rebut it by demonstrating that the donor entered into the transaction of his or her own free will. This is most obviously done by showing that the transferor received independent advice. The advice must have been of a sufficient standard such that the transferor was able to understand the nature and consequences of the transaction.

1.30 In *Pesticcio v Huet* [2004] WTLR 699 the Court of Appeal held:

'The participation of a solicitor is not ... a precaution which is guaranteed to work in every case. It is necessary for the court to be satisfied that the advice and explanation by, for example, a solicitor, was relevant and effective to free the donor from the impairment of the influence on his free will and to give him the necessary independence of judgement and freedom to make choices with the full appreciation of what he was doing. The judge was entitled to find that the role of [the solicitor] was wanting ... her advice was not such as a competent adviser would give, if acting solely in the interest of [the claimant].'

DEATH BED GIFTS

1.31 A person may attempt to make a gift which is not included in his will but which is intended to take effect upon his death. The gift is therefore not strictly a lifetime transaction, but nor is it a legacy. Such a gift is called a *donatio mortis causa*.

1.32 The requirements for a *donatio mortis causa* to be effective are:

(1) The gift must have been made in contemplation of death. Actual expectation of death is not a requirement.

(2) The gift must be made on the condition that it shall only take effect absolutely when the donor dies. It is therefore revocable during his lifetime.

(3) There must be delivery of the gift, or something representing the gift, which is accepted by the donee.

The last of these requirements is usually the most difficult to prove. Where there has been actual physical delivery of the property the donee must demonstrate that the donor intended to part with dominion over it and not just physical possession.

1.33 Where the property in question is capable of delivery, the donor must either have actually delivered it or delivered something which would give the donee access to the intended gift. For example, in *Re Lillingston* [1952] 2 All ER 184 the delivery of a key to a trunk which itself contained keys to safety deposit boxes containing jewellery was deemed to be sufficient delivery of the jewellery to constitute a *donatio mortis causa*.

1.34 Where the property is a chose in action transferable by delivery, the donor must deliver the document representing the chose. However, if the chose is not transferable by delivery the donor must deliver to the donee some document that would need to be produced in an action on the property in question. In such circumstances the legal title to the chose in action does not pass upon delivery of the document.

1.35 A trust analysis is used to explain the operation of a *donatio mortis causa*. If the transfer of the legal interest in the property is complete before the donor dies, the donee holds the property on trust for the donor during his lifetime, subject to a condition that upon his death the trust is extinguished and the donee owns the property absolutely. However, in the event that the donor revokes the gift during his lifetime then the donee holds the legal interest on bare trust for the donor absolutely.

1.36 If the transfer of the legal interest in the property is not complete before the death of the donor (for example, in the case of a chose in action not capable of being transferred by delivery) the whole title rests with the donor until he by his death perfects the gift. The personal representatives then hold the property on constructive trust for the donee and may be compelled to transfer legal title.

1.37 When faced with a possible *donatio mortis causa*, executors should ensure that the above conditions have been met and ascertain whether legal title to the property has passed before death. In the event that it has not the executors will be required to perfect an imperfect gift, as an exception to the usual equitable rule against this. They ought properly to keep the residuary beneficiaries abreast of substantive steps.

JOINT OWNERSHIP AND RESULTING TRUSTS

1.38 In most cases, the interest in jointly owned property will pass to the survivor upon the death of one of the parties. However, in some circumstances property held by the surviving joint owner, including the proceeds of jointly held accounts, is held on trust for the estate and passes under the terms of the will to the residuary beneficiaries rather than to the survivor.

1.39 Where property is owned jointly, the legal interest is held on a joint tenancy in equal shares. The beneficial interest, ie the right to the interest or benefit of the property, may be held on a joint tenancy or a tenancy in common.

1.40 Under a joint tenancy, the beneficial ownership belongs to the joint owners equally so that on the death of the first joint owner, the right of survivorship operates and the deceased's interest passes to the survivor(s) rather than to the deceased's estate.

1.41 Under a tenancy in common, the co-owners are entitled to specific shares in the beneficial ownership. When the first joint owner dies, his or her interest passes under his or her will, or alternatively on intestacy.

1.42 In some instances, the legal ownership of the property is in joint names but the beneficial interest is owned by one of the co-owners, for instance, a bank account on which the original owner has a carer added as a co-signatory in order to facilitate the operation of the account.

1.43 A resulting trust will exist where an asset is conveyed by one party to another but the equitable interest results back to the transferor or their estate. In other words, the new legal owner holds that asset on trust for the benefit of the original owner, or their estate.

1.44 A resulting trust can arise in a number of situations including:

- where property is transferred to trustees upon trusts which do not wholly dispose of the beneficial interest;

- where property is transferred to trustees upon trusts which are illegal;

- where, as a result of an ultra vires transaction, the legal title passes to a third party;

- where the property is purchased in the name of someone other than the person providing the purchase price; and

- in the operation of joint bank accounts.

1.45 By way of example, where the donor makes a gratuitous transfer to another and there are no express or inferred provisions about the nature of the beneficial ownership, there is a rebuttable presumption of a resulting trust. The presumption will be rebutted where:

- the presumption of advancement applies; or

- there is evidence that the transferor intended to make a gift.

Presumption of advancement

1.46 The presumption of resulting trust which normally arises where one party voluntarily transfers property to another will not arise in the case of certain transfers between parties where it may be readily inferred that A would have intended to make a gift to B (Snell's Equity, 31st ed, para 23-02). In such circumstances, there is a presumption of advancement, ie that A intended the transfer to be voluntary and gratuitous for the benefit of B.

1.47 The presumption applied traditionally to transfers made by a man to his wife or fiancée, or to his child, or to a person to whom he stands *in loco parentis*.

1.48 Changes in 'social and economic conditions have made the presumption a less reliable guide as to A's true intentions in providing the money than it might once have been' (Snell's Equity, 31st ed, para 23-05). Thus, in the authors' view, it is probable that if the issue is tested in the courts a rebuttable presumption of advancement will also arise in relation to transfers from a wife to husband or mother to child (or that only slender evidence would be required to rebut it).

1.49 The effect of this is that a gratuitous lifetime transaction may be held to be a valid gift and will not be held upon resulting trust by the donee for the donor's estate upon his death. In *Antoni v Antoni* [2007] UKPC 10 a father, Dr Antoni, ran a property business through a limited company. In 1991 he transferred one of the five shares in the company to each of his eldest sons and another share to a nominee, apparently to be held on trust for his third and youngest child.

1.50 In 1992 Dr Antoni made a new will leaving his entire estate to his new wife, Lena. This will expressly referred to lands in the name of the company 'of which I am president and principal owner'. Following Dr Antoni's death, Lena sought to argue that the two eldest children and the new nominee held the shares on resulting trust for Dr Antoni's estate because there was no evidence that he intended to part with the beneficial interest in these shares.

1.51 The Privy Council held that the youngest child was intended to be the beneficiary of the trust of the share, and that the presumption of advancement worked in favour of the two eldest children and that as Lena had failed to rebut this presumption she was not entitled to rely upon a presumption of resulting trust. Dr Antoni's reference in the will to his ownership of the company was inadmissible as evidence to rebut the presumption of advancement because the will post-dated the transfer of the shares. It was 'well established that evidence to rebut the presumption of advancement cannot take the form of denials of a transferee's beneficial ownership made by the transferor after the event'. The lifetime transactions were therefore upheld.

Real property held in joint names

1.52 Following recent case law, the presumption of resulting trust will not arise where real property is conveyed into joint names with no express declaration as to the respective shares held for each party. In *Stack v Dowden* [2007] 2 AC 432 a co-habiting couple conveyed a property into their joint names. Dowden contributed 65% of the purchase price and made a larger contribution to the mortgage payments. She sought to argue that a presumption arose that the beneficial shares were held under a resulting trust in proportion to the financial contributions made by each party.

1.53 The House of Lords concluded that where a property has been registered in the joint names of a married or cohabiting couple but with no express declaration of interest the presumption is that the parties have equal beneficial interests.

1.54 The burden is on the party asserting a different share to show that the couple did not intend their beneficial interests to be equal and that they intended that the property be shared in the manner contended for.

1.55 The parties' intentions are to be ascertained from the whole course of their conduct in relation to the property. This will include their respective financial contributions but will also extend to the nature of the relationship, the existence of any children, how the parties arranged their finances, discussions at the time of transfer and reasons why the property was transferred into joint names. Although the House found in that case that there was an intention to hold the beneficial interest in unequal shares, it expressed the view that the facts of the case were very unusual.

1.56 Consequently, in the absence of express intention to the contrary a property conveyed into joint names is presumed to be held in equal shares. Thus, in the majority of cases where the beneficial interest in a property is held as tenants in common, a half share will pass under the will of the first to die.

Joint bank accounts

1.57 Where a testator held money in a joint bank account the key question for the personal representatives is whether the surviving joint owner holds the account money for himself or on resulting trust for the estate. This may depend on any agreement between the joint owners, the terms of any bank mandate and the purpose for which the original owner opened the account.

1.58 The general rule is that where money is paid into a bank account held by the person who provided the money and another person, there is a rebuttable presumption of a resulting trust in favour of the person who provided the money.

1.59 The presumption can be rebutted by evidence that the person who paid into the account intended to confer a beneficial interest on the other account holder as was seen in *José Manuel Pitta de Lacerda Aroso v Coutts & Co* [2001] WTLR 797.

1.60 The question particularly arises in the context of accounts opened or transferred into joint names where funds originate from the deceased. It has to be established whether the original owner's intention was that:

(1)   the balance of the joint account should have been in the nature of a gift to the survivor, the survivor having become beneficial joint tenant with the original owner and accordingly entitled to succeed to the balance on the original owner's death by survivorship; or

(2)   only that the survivor should be able to sign on his or her behalf such documents and have access to the monies as might be necessary in the operation of that account for the purpose of paying the original owner's expenses during their joint lives.

Where the latter purpose is established the courts have normally found that the joint mandate was executed for the sole purpose of convenience. The beneficial interest in the monies remains with the original owner by way of a resulting trust and therefore forms part of the balance of the estate on death. HMRC will take the view that the balance is held by the personal representatives on resulting trust for the estate.

1.61 In *Marshall v Crutwell* (1875) LR 20 EQ 238 the husband, in ailing health, transferred his account into the joint names of himself and his wife. All the cheques were drawn at the husband's direction. It was held that the transfer had merely been a mode of convenience.

> 'Although a purchase in the name of a wife or child, if altogether unexplained, will be deemed a gift, yet you may take surrounding circumstances into consideration, so as to say that it is a trust, not a gift. So in the case of a stranger, you may take surrounding circumstances into consideration, so as to say that a purchase in his name is a gift, not a trust.'

In contrast, in *Young v Sealey* [1949] 1 All ER 92 money was transferred into a joint account in the names of an aunt and her nephew. The accounts remained under the aunt's effective control until she died. The nephew's evidence was that his aunt had told him he would benefit on her death. The presumption of advancement does not apply to the aunt/nephew relationship and the aunt's personal representatives claimed that the nephew held the funds on resulting trust for the estate. On the evidence the presumption of a resulting trust was rebutted.

Undue influence

1.62 It is usually difficult to prove that actual undue influence was exerted over the original owner in executing a joint mandate. However, it will often be the case that the survivor is someone in whom the original owner generally reposed trust and confidence and that any intention to pass the beneficial interest in monies in a bank account is to the manifest disadvantage of the original owner. Thus undue influence may well be presumed.

ROLE OF PERSONAL REPRESENTATIVES

1.63 The personal representative on notice of a potentially voidable lifetime transaction may make initial enquiries. For instance in relation to where there is a question as to capacity, obtaining medical records, contacting witnesses. Both mental and physical health issues are likely to be relevant to an undue influence challenge.

1.64 Personal representatives who turn a 'Nelsonian blind eye' to the potentially dubious nature of a lifetime transaction and, for instance, allow a limitation period to expire may face personal liability on a claim of devastavit (see Chapter 13) because they have failed or potentially failed in their duties to collect in (Administration of Estates Act 1925, s 25). However, personal representatives should be wary of too proactive a stance without agreement on the part of the residuary beneficiaries at whose expense such steps are ultimately being taken.

1.65 *Re Clough-Taylor* [2003] WTLR 15 is authority that it is no part of personal representatives' duty to take anything other than normal or routine steps to collect in an asset which is specifically bequeathed under the will (or passes to the surviving spouse or civil partner as part of the entitlement on intestacy). Lloyd J held that the executor could not be required to issue proceedings to recover a chattel allegedly removed from the deceased's house after her death by a person who claimed that the deceased had given it to him during her lifetime. The specific legatee argued that the executor did have such an obligation. The judge held that it was proper for the executor simply to assent in favour of the specific legatee and to offer an assignment of the cause of action in order to assist her title.

Chapter 2

COURT OF PROTECTION

2.1   The Court of Protection is the court that makes decisions concerning those who lack capacity to manage their own affairs. Following the coming into force of the Mental Capacity Act 2005 (MCA 2005) the Court of Protection's jurisdiction extends beyond property and affairs to welfare and health.

2.2   Although the Court's jurisdiction ceases on death, steps taken under its auspices often have an impact on the estate available post death.

STATUTORY WILLS

2.3   As part of the Court of Protection's supervisory jurisdiction it has the power to authorise the execution of a will (or codicil) (MCA 2005, s 18(1)(i)).

2.4   If a statutory will (or codicil) was authorised, the Court of Protection will have been satisfied (on the basis of the principles set out in *Re D(J)* [1982] Ch 237) that the statutory will represented what the person ('P') would have wanted to do if he or she had had testamentary capacity. P means a person who lacks (or is alleged to lack) capacity to make a decision in relation to the particular matter before the Court (The Court of Protection Rules 2007, r 6).

2.5   The Court of Protection's jurisdiction does not extend to determining the validity of an existing will, but a successful application for a statutory will is likely to obviate potential dispute over validity post death.

2.6   An Order of the Court of Protection authorising the execution of a statutory will is not itself dispositive. MCA 2005, Sch 2 sets out the formalities for the execution of a statutory will. Once the statutory will has been executed it takes effect as a valid will (MCA 2005, Sch 2, para 4(3)).

Failure to execute and seal

2.7   The executed statutory will must be sealed with the official seal of the Court of Protection (MCA 2005, Sch 2, para 3(2)(d)) but failure to seal before P dies will not invalidate the will (*Re Hughes*, (1999) The Times, January 8).

2.8   If P dies after the Court of Protection authorises, but before execution of, a statutory will, then the estate passes in accordance with any preceding will or under intestacy.

2.9 In such circumstances, the beneficiaries that would have received an interest under the statutory will had it been executed may, depending on the circumstances, have a negligence claim as a disappointed beneficiary in accordance with *White v Jones* [1995] 2 AC 207.

Challenge to the statutory will

2.10 It is unlikely that the validity of a statutory will can be challenged on any ground (failing improper execution).

2.11 In *Re Davey* [1981] WLR 164 a statutory will was made a matter of days before P died. After P's death her husband appealed against the order authorising execution of the statutory will. The appeal was rejected. It was stated *per curiam* that the court did not have jurisdiction to set aside a statutory will which complied with the provisions of the then Mental Health Act (1959).

2.12 Whether that can apply in circumstances where there is very convincing evidence that the statutory will was procured by means of fraudulent misrepresentations to the Court of Protection is untested.

2.13 The mere fact of a statutory will having been executed will not prevent a disappointed beneficiary pursuing alternative remedies for provision out of the deceased's estate, for instance pursuant to the 1975 Act as in *Robinson v Scott Kilvert* [2003] WTLR 529.

2.14 Heywood & Massey suggests (at para 14-037) that no application to rectify a statutory will post death could succeed on the basis that the jurisdiction to rectify is based on an assumption that the will fails to express the testator's intentions and a statutory will is made on a purely hypothetical basis. However, the authors do suggest that a clerical error might be dealt with under the slip rule.

DEATH INTERRUPTING PROCEEDINGS

2.15 The Court of Protection's jurisdiction comes to an end on P's death.

2.16 Costs are at the discretion of the court (MCA 2005, s 55(1)) and an order for payment of costs out of P's estate may be made within 6 years of P's death (Court of Protection Rules 2007, r 165).

2.17 Where proceedings concerning P's property and affairs have been interrupted because of P's death the court is likely to order that all parties' costs are paid out of P's estate.

2.18 As the Court of Protection no longer has jurisdiction, any dispute about costs will need to be addressed in another forum.

ACCOUNTS

2.19 The MCA 2005 is less prescriptive on duties to account giving the Court of Protection discretion to require a Deputy 'to submit to the Public Guardian such reports at such times or such intervals as a court may direct'. However, a Deputy must have regard to the Code of Practice (MCA 2005, s 19(9)(b)) which requires them to 'keep, and periodically submit to the Public Guardian, correct accounts ...' (Code of Practice para 8.66).

2.20 The death of P terminates the offices of Deputy and Attorney. There is no duty to submit final accounts to the Court of Protection. However, P's personal representatives will require an account so that they in turn can account for the estate administration, pre-death income tax and, subject to providing for reasonable expenses, can require an account to be provided.

2.21 The MCA 2005 does not contain any express provision allowing accounts to be reopened (either during P's lifetime or post-death). Where an application is made after P's death to reopen accounts then, given that the Court of Protection's jurisdiction has ceased, the appropriate forum will be the Chancery Division. However, any such application is only likely to be successful if fraud or misrepresentation can be established.

Authority to authorise gifts

2.22 The powers of an Attorney (either Lasting or under an Enduring Power of Attorney) or Deputy to make gifts or to maintain others are limited (MCA 2005, ss 12(2), (3), Sch 4, para 3(3)).

2.23 Again, during P's lifetime it is possible to apply to the Court of Protection for authority to make gifts out of P's estate (MCA 2005, s 18(1)(b)).

2.24 Where an order authorising a gift out of P's estate has been made but the gift was not implemented before P's death the gift does not take effect. In such circumstances the donee is a disappointed beneficiary and may have a claim as in accordance with the principle established in *White v Jones* [1995] 1 WLR 187.

Ademption

2.25 If an Attorney disposes of an asset specifically bequeathed under a will then that gift adeems because the subject matter of the gift is no longer in the estate (*Banks v National Westminster Bank plc* [2005] All ER (D) 159 (Apr)). A disappointed beneficiary is unlikely to have a cause for complaint unless it can be shown that property that would have formed the residuary estate should have been used in preference.

2.26 Where property specifically bequeathed under a will (or on intestacy) has been disposed of in accordance with MCA 2005, s 18 then the beneficiary who would have received the property under the will will, wherever possible, be treated as having an interest in the estate to the extent of that property (MCA 2005, Sch 2, para 8).

Part II
DEATH AND BURIAL DISPUTES

Chapter 3

CORONERS' INQUESTS

BACKGROUND

3.1   A Coroner is an independent judicial officer who is tasked with inquiring into certain types of death that must be reported to him. The deaths that need to be reported ('a reported death') are limited by statute (Coroners Act 1988, s 8(1)) and, in broad terms, are those where the deceased may have died an unnatural death; a sudden death of unknown cause; or died in prison.

3.2   The law governing coroners is set down in statute by the Coroners Act 1988 and Coroners Rules 1984. Until recently, the law was viewed as having significant limitations particularly in respect of the remit of a coroner's inquest to investigate certain types of death – death in state custody. However, the recent enactment of the Human Rights Act 1998 which gave effect to the European Convention on Human Rights, has led to the widening of the investigatory scope of a coroner's inquest for such deaths. (See for example *R (Sacker) v HM Coroner for West Yorkshire* [2004] 1 WLR 796; *R (Middleton) v HM Coroner for Western Somerset* [2004] 2 AC 182; *R (Takoushis) v HM Coroner for Inner North London* [2006] 1 WLR 461; and *R (Hurst) v Commissioner of Police for the Metropolis* [2007] UKHL 13.) Also, the coroner system in England and Wales has recently been subject to a comprehensive government review with the result that new legislation is hoped to provide a better response to bereaved families (see http://www.dca.gov.uk/corbur/ coron03.htm#cor_bill). It is anticipated that the new legislation will be brought into force in the next few years.

A REPORTED DEATH

3.3   In general, each coroner has a defined district over which he presides (Coroners Act 1988, s 1). In certain circumstances, a coroner may be approached to hold an inquest that falls outside his jurisdiction but such circumstances fall outside the remit of this work. When a death occurs in a coroner's district it does not follow that the coroner will be notified of it (see **3.1**).

3.4   However, in the event that he/she is notified, and depending on the circumstances, the death will be reported to the coroner's office either by a GP/hospital doctor or the police. Usually, it will be the coroner's officer who will liaise with the doctor/police and the next-of-kin in the first instance. The coroner's officer is often a police officer and works under the direction of the coroner.

3.5 The coroner will then consider the factual background to the death and if it is deemed appropriate, will direct that a post-mortem be made on the deceased's body (Coroners Act 1988, ss 19–21). The coroner will, unless it is impracticable to do so, inform the deceased's usual doctor and any relative who may have notified the coroner of their wish to be medically represented at the examination, amongst others, that a post-mortem will take place and the date, hour and locality of where this will happen (Coroners Rules 1984, r 7(2)). It is not necessary for the coroner to obtain the consent of the next-of-kin.

3.6 At the post-mortem, the pathologist is able to make provision for the preservation of material which in his opinion assists in determining the cause of death. This material could include, for example, blood and tissue samples. However, he must notify the coroner of this (Coroners Rules 1984, r 9(2)) who in turn is required to notify the-next-of-kin amongst others of this fact (Coroners Rules 1984, r 9(6)). On doing so, the coroner will inform them of how long the material is being preserved for and the options for dealing with the material when it is no longer needed. These options include disposing of the material by burial, cremation or other lawful disposal by the pathologist (Coroners Rules 1984, r 9(8)).

3.7 Following the post-mortem, the pathologist will prepare a post-mortem report (the 'Report') which will be sent to the coroner. It is then for the coroner to decide to whom the Report can be circulated (Coroners Rules 1984, r 10). It is usual that, on receipt of the Report, the coroner will release the body for burial. If the Report reveals that the death was due to natural causes and that an inquest is not needed, the coroner will release the body to the next-of-kin, his office will inform the Registrar of Births and Deaths and the death will be registered and a death certificate issued.

3.8 In the event that the death requires an inquest to be held, the coroner will usually open and then immediately adjourn the inquest after taking any available evidence of identity. A burial order/cremation certificate will be issued by the coroner and the body released to the next-of-kin. It is possible, however, that a second post-mortem will be required in consequence of, for example, the first post-mortem being inconclusive. This will delay the body's release but the coroner will endeavour to release the body within 28 days of death in any event.

3.9 When an inquest is to be held, while the body may be released, a death certificate cannot be obtained. In the interim, therefore, the coroner may issue an interim certificate of fact of death to assist in the administration of the deceased's estate (Coroners Rules 1984, r 30).

THE INQUEST

3.10 If one is required, the inquest will be held in public and the coroner will notify the deceased's spouse or a near relative or personal representative of the date, time and place of the inquest (Coroners Rules 1984, r 19). In broad terms, the inquest's purpose will be to find out who has died and how, when and where they died (Coroners Rules 1984, r 36).

3.11 The length of the inquest will be determined by numerous factors that include the following:

(1) the nature of the death;

(2) where the death occurred;

(3) whether expert evidence will be relied upon;

(4) whether the inquest will sit with a jury or without (a jury is usually only required if the death occurred in prison; in police custody; or in an incident at work – see Coroners Act 1988, s 8);

(5) the number of witnesses; and

(6) the public interest.

3.12 The venue of the inquest will vary for each coroner's jurisdiction and will in large part be dependent on the facilities available to the coroner's local authority. Some jurisdictions may have a designated coroner's court while others may use, for example, the local magistrates' court or a committee room belonging to the local authority.

3.13 At the beginning of the inquest, the coroner will publicly announce what documentary evidence relevant to the purpose of the inquest he is admitting to be examined (Coroners Rules 1984, r 37). Such evidence may be from any living person which in the coroner's opinion is unlikely to be disputed (Coroners Rules 1984, r 37(1)), or may have been made by the deceased (Coroners Rules 1984, r 37(5)). In doing this, the coroner will provide a brief account of each document as well as details of the maker of the document. Copies of any documentary evidence may be made available to any person who in the opinion of the coroner is within r 20(2) of the Coroners Rules 1984 – that is, properly interested persons who include; the deceased's parent, child, personal representative; any beneficiary under a policy of insurance issued on the life of the deceased; or any person whose act or omission (or their agent) may, in the opinion of the coroner, have caused or contributed to the death. Such persons may also object to any of the documentary evidence being admitted – this usually occurs when they dispute the substance of the evidence in such documents. The coroner will consider the reasons for the objection and then make a decision accordingly.

3.14 The coroner will then examine the witnesses on oath that have been notified to attend the hearing (Coroners Rules 1984, r 21). Such witnesses are those that assist the coroner/jury to determine how, when and where the deceased died and whose names may have been circulated beforehand to the properly interested persons attending the inquest (see *R v HM Coroner for Lincoln ex p Hay* (1999) JP 666), who in turn are entitled to examine the witnesses after the coroner. Such examination can be by the person in their personal capacity or by their legal representatives (if represented). While legal aid is generally not available in such instances, in view of the complexities of some inquests nowadays – in particular those where Art 2 of the European Convention on Human Rights is engaged (deaths in state custody) – the relevant minister in the Ministry of Justice may authorise the use of legal aid, particularly in respect of the deceased's family.

3.15 Upon hearing all the evidence (which the coroner shall have taken notes on (Coroners Rules 1984, r 39) and which properly interested persons may be entitled to copies of (Coroners Rules 1984, r 57)), the coroner will give his verdict and certify it by an inquisition (Coroners Act 1988, s 11(4)). An inquisition shall be in writing and prepared by the coroner. It will set out (i) who the deceased was, and (ii) how, when and where the deceased came by their death (Coroners Act 1988, s 11(5)). Within 5 days of the finding, the coroner will arrange to send to the Registrar of Births and Deaths information concerning the death which includes the cause of death and the time and place of the inquest (Coroners Act 1988, s 11(7)) so that it may be registered.

3.16 In the event that the inquest is heard with a jury, the process is similar to the above except that it will be for the jury rather than the coroner to certify the inquisition (Coroners Act 1988, s 11(3)). In both instances, however, when it relates to a person who came by their death by murder, manslaughter or infanticide the verdict will not include any finding of criminal liability on the part of a named person (Coroners Act 1988, s 11(6) and Coroners Rules 1984, r 42). Similarly, the verdict of an inquest will not determine any question of civil liability (Coroners Rules 1984, r 42).

3.17 While it falls outside the remit of this work, it should be noted that some inquests may be subject to significant adjournments (Coroners Act 1988, ss 16, 17A; Coroners Rules 1984, rr 23, 25–28). These can include when an inquest is held in which the death was caused by an accident or disease and the representative of the enforcing authority is unable to be present, or where the Director of Public Prosecutions requests the coroner to adjourn an inquest on the ground that a person may be charged with an offence committed in circumstances connected with the death. In the latter case, in the event that a criminal trial takes place and someone is convicted, it is unlikely that the coroner will resume the inquest, unless the criminal proceedings did not bring out the evidence of the circumstances of the death. Instead, the coroner will send to the Registrar of Births and Deaths a certificate stating the result of the criminal proceedings in order for the death to be registered (Coroners Act 1988, s 16(5)).

FURTHER INFORMATION

3.18 Further information on the role of coroners and inquest procedure can be found on the Ministry of Justice website and the Coroners' Society of England and Wales website (see http://www.dca.gov.uk/corbur/coronfr.htm and http://www.coroner.org.uk/).

Chapter 4

DISPUTES – BURIAL AND ASHES

RIGHTS AND RESPONSIBILITIES

4.1   The reality of the law governing the disposal of human remains is often at odds with the expectations of families and relatives who have lost loved ones. The law is based on stark rules which can be difficult for those grieving to accept.

4.2   Fundamental to the law governing ashes and burials is the premise that there is no property in a corpse (*Williams v Williams* (1882) 20 Ch D 659). A corpse is incapable of being the subject of property transactions or offences; for example, it cannot be bought or sold, stolen or criminally damaged, seized by the deceased's creditors as security for his debts (*R v Fox* (1841) 2 QB 246) and does not constitute 'goods and materials' for the purposes of the Income Tax Acts (*Bourne (Inspector of Taxes) v Norwich Crematorium Ltd* [1967] 2 All ER 576).

4.3   As a corpse does not constitute property, it does not form part of a person's estate and cannot pass under a person's will or under the intestacy rules (*Williams v Williams* (1882) 20 Ch D 659). Any direction in a will or codicil as to the disposal of a person's body is therefore unenforceable. (There are specific exceptions to this rule: the Anatomy Act 1984 and Human Tissue Act 1961 confer a statutory right to donate body parts for research or transplant purposes and the Human Fertilisation and Embryology Act 1990 permits a man to consent to the posthumous use of his sperm.)

4.4   Whilst it is not possible to have rights over a corpse, the law does impose responsibilities on certain categories of persons in respect of corpses. There is a hierarchy of persons who are under a duty to dispose of the deceased's body and for this purpose those persons have a right to possession of the corpse.

4.5   The normal methods of disposal are burial or cremation, but other methods are not forbidden (*Halsbury's Laws*, 10 (901)). Cremation, which has always been permitted provided it does not amount to a public nuisance (*R v Price* (1884) 12 QBD 247), now has a statutory footing under the Cremation Acts 1902 and 1952. The only restriction on cremation is that a local authority responsible for the disposal of a corpse may not sanction cremation where it has reason to believe that it would be contrary to the deceased's wishes or, in the case of a child in its care, cremation is not in accordance with the practice of the child's religious persuasion (*Halsbury's Laws*, 10 (958)).

DUTY OF DISPOSAL

4.6

(1) The primary duty to dispose of the deceased's body falls on the deceased's personal representatives where he or she died intestate. For this purpose the executors or personal representatives have a right to possession of the corpse and may determine the mode and place of burial. *Leeburn v Derndorfer* [2004] WTLR 867 confirmed that this right extends to the deceased's ashes, so as to enable the executors to properly dispose of the deceased's remains after cremation (see also *Robertson v Pinegrove Memorial Park Ltd* (1986) ACLD 496).

(2) Where there are no personal representatives, the person with the highest right to take out a grant (as set out in Non Contentious Probate Rules 1987 (NCPR 1987), r 20 and Administration of Estates Act 1925, s 46) can take possession of the corpse. In *Holtham v Arnold* (1985) 2 BMLR 123 the deceased's separated wife, being entitled to letters of administration of her late husband's estate, was entitled to possession of her husband's corpse above his cohabitee. In the Australian case *Smith v Tamworth City Council and ors* (unreported) 14 May 1997, the deceased's adoptive parents had the right to determine the burial rather than the biological parents.

(3) The parents of a child are responsible for the disposal of their child's body, provided they have sufficient means (*R v Vann* [1851], *Clarke v London General Omnibus Co Ltd* [1906] 2 KB 648, *Fessi v Whitmore* [1999] 1 FLR 767). In *Fessi v Whitmore*, married parents were held to be equally entitled to their deceased child's body. The right and duty to dispose of a child's remains may be an element of parental responsibility (as defined in Children Act 1989, s 3(1)), in which case a parent without parental responsibility would not have the right or duty to dispose of their child's remains, but there is no direct authority on this point (David Hershman, 'Parental disputes over a child's funeral', *Trusts and Estates Law Journal*, November 1999).

(4) If a child in the care of the local authority dies whilst in care, the right or duty to bury the child reverts to the child's parents (*R v Gwynedd County Council ex parte B* [1992] 3 All ER 317). Only if the parents cannot be found or are unwilling to take responsibility for the body, can the local authority exercise the right to arrange the child's burial.

(5) A householder is responsible for the disposal of any body on his premises (*R v Stewart* (1840) 12 Ad & El 773).

(6) If no other appropriate arrangements have been made for the disposal of a body in its area, the local authority bears the burden of disposal (Public Health (Control of Diseases) Act 1984, s 46).

4.7 The only exception to the above order is when a coroner is under a duty to inquire into the death of a particular person, he has a right to possession of the body for the purpose of those inquiries. This right overrides all others.

4.8 In carrying out the duty of burial, the personal representatives take possession of the body as trustees and should dispose of it in a way that seems to them to be appropriate having regard to any direction of the deceased in the will or otherwise and having regard to the claims of the relatives or others with an interest (*Leeburn v Derndorfer* [2004] WTLR 867, *Fessi v Whitmore* [1999] 1 FLR 767). However, this is only a moral and not a legal obligation, and executors can therefore act contrary to family members' or others' wishes. Furthermore, executors may act unilaterally, allowing, in the case of multiple executors, one executor to dispose of the deceased's body in a manner opposed by the others (*Leeburn v Derndorfer* [2004] WTLR 867).

4.9 The courts have proved reluctant to interfere with executors' decisions as to burial unless they are capricious, unreasonable or dishonestly made. In *Re Grandison* (1989) *The Times* July 10, strong grounds were required to interfere with the exercise of executors' discretion.

4.10 The testamentary appointment of executors is binding and testators should give careful consideration to this appointment if they wish their burial instructions to be respected.

CONFLICT

4.11 The above hierarchy provides a clear order of those responsible for the disposal of a body. Conflict can arise where two or more people who are equally entitled disagree as to the manner or place of disposal.

4.12 *Fessi v Whitmore* [1999] 1 FLR 767 concerned a dispute between divorced parents over where to lay their deceased child's ashes. Their 12-year-old son died during a visit to his father's home in Wales. The child's remains were handed over by the Welsh coroner to the father who, without consulting the mother, arranged for a cremation with a view to scattering the ashes off the Welsh coast. The mother wanted the ashes interred in the Midlands.

4.13 Judge Boggis held that as the parents were akin to trustees he was obliged to make a decision which did 'justice and fairness to both sides'. He concluded that the remains should be disposed of in accordance with the mother's proposals because there was a connection there with both sides of the family (being where the child's paternal grandparents were buried) and would thus provide a focus for all the family. The judge said that to divide the ashes, an option proposed by the mother, would be 'wholly inappropriate'. In contrast, in *Leeburn v Derndorfer* (see **4.14** et seq) Byrne J considered that division of the ashes was one option available to him. He decided against it in light of the strong opposition to it by one of the executors.

4.14 In the latter case the deceased appointed his three adult children as executors under his will. The executors agreed that their father should be cremated but could not reach consensus as to the disposal of his cremated remains: Ms Derndorfer and Ms Plunkett wanted the ashes interred at a cemetery, whereas Mr Leeburn wanted the ashes divided into three parts with each executor disposing of their one third share as they wished.

4.15 Without informing Mr Leeburn, Ms Derndorfer and Ms Plunkett had their father's ashes interred in their chosen cemetery. Mr Leeburn sought an order that one-third of the ashes be disinterred and given to him for disposal as he thought appropriate. Byrne J in the Supreme Court of Victoria refused to grant the order sought for the following reasons:

(1)   a significant length of time had elapsed since the death of the deceased and the commencement of proceedings by Mr Leeburn (2 years and 9 months). In his view the deceased's remains had been permitted to lie in the cemetery for over 4 years (by the time of the trial) and therefore should not be disturbed;

(2)   it was not appropriate to divide the ashes contrary to the wishes of Ms Derndorfer;

(3)   a majority of the executors had chosen to have the ashes interred at the cemetery; and,

(4)   he was not satisfied that the choice of the cemetery as the final resting place for the deceased was inappropriate.

4.16 In *University Hospital Lewisham NHS Trust v Hamuth & Ors* [2007] WTLR 309 the claimant, Lewisham Hospital NHS Trust, as the person lawfully in possession of the deceased's body following a post mortem examination, was granted an order that it could arrange for the disposal of the deceased's body in light of the ongoing dispute between the defendants (the first defendant being a nurse at the nursing home where the deceased was resident when he made his will, the remaining defendants being family members) as to the validity of the deceased's will and concomitant appointment of the first defendant as executor. Mr Justice Hart was assisted in his decision by the fact that there was no reason to believe that the Trust's proposal to bury the deceased in the family plot, in accordance with the family members' wishes, was not 'an entirely appropriate way for the deceased's body to be given its resting place.'

4.17 In *Calma v Sesar* [1992] 106 FLR 446, Martin J held that a dispute between parents as to the location of their deceased son's burial should be resolved 'in a practical way paying due regard to the need to have a dead body disposed of without unreasonable delay, but with all proper respect and decency'.

4.18 In resolving disputes between those equally entitled to dispose of the deceased's remains the court adopts a practical approach. It is accepted that it is often difficult to 'weigh the competing claims and arrive at what one would truly call a legal judgment' (*Dodd v Jones* [1999] SASC 458). Factors considered by the courts are the reasonableness of the (proposed) arrangements, the length of time which has elapsed since the disposal of the deceased's remains, the wishes of those entitled and the practical need for the disposal of the body without undue delay.

FUNERAL EXPENSES

4.19 Reasonable funeral expenses are payable out of the deceased's estate in priority to the payment of any debts or liabilities (Administration of Estates Act 1925, s 34). What is reasonable depends on the deceased's station in life, the manner in which he lived and, most importantly, the size of his estate. It is a question of fact to be decided in the circumstances of each case.

4.20 Where the estate is insolvent, only such expenses as are in the particular circumstances of the case absolutely necessary are payable out of the estate.

4.21 If the personal representatives exceed these limits they risk personal liability for the excess.

HEADSTONES

4.22 The personal representatives' right to choose the mode and place of burial includes the right to choose the headstone and inscription.

4.23 There are few English cases concerning disputes over the inscription on headstones. In *In re St. Mark's, Haydock (No 2)* [1981] 1 WLR 1167 a vicar petitioned the court for a declaration as to whether the widow or mistress of the deceased was entitled to choose the wording on the deceased's headstone. The inscription proposed by the widow contained no reference to herself, whereas that proposed by the mistress referred to the deceased as 'A dear friend of Myra [the mistress] and Family'. In directing that the headstone bear reference to neither woman, the judge said that,:

> '... there should not in cemeteries be any inclusion of one friend or relative to the pointed exclusion of another.'

4.24 The Australian case of *Smith v Tamworth City Council* (unreported), 14 May 1997, concerned, amongst other issues, an application by the claimants, who were the deceased's biological parents, to have a headstone of their choice erected on the deceased's grave. The deceased's adoptive parents strongly resisted the claimants' application. Under Australian law the right to erect the headstone is the right of the person who owns the burial plot, which in this case belonged to the deceased's adoptive parents. Young J in the Supreme Court of New South Wales rejected the claimants' contention that there was an equitable right for close blood relatives of the deceased to have themselves mentioned on the headstone or at least an additional headstone erected by them. He stated:

> 'If one were to ask would the community as a whole consider that a biological mother should have the right to have her name endorsed on the tombstone of a child who had been the adopted child of someone else for over 20 years when that other person did not consent to the biological mother's wishes, I could not see that the community would endorse the biological mother's claim.'

4.25 Only if the adoptive parents completely denied the biological parents' access to the grave or unreasonably removed flowers that the biological parents placed on it, might the biological parents be entitled to some relief.

4.26 Where there is a dispute over the cost of a tombstone, *Goldstein v Salvation Army Assurance Society* [1917] 2 KB 291 is authority for the proposition that it is a matter of fact in each estate as to whether or not the cost of a tombstone is a legitimate expense.

EXHUMATION

4.27 Except in certain specific cases (including where a body is removed from one consecrated place of burial to another by faculty), it is an offence under English law to exhume buried remains unless a licence has been issued by the Secretary of State (Burial Act 1857, s 25. See also DCA website http://www.dca.gov.uk/corbur/buriafr.htm for procedures for exhumation.). In the case of consecrated ground, it is an offence against ecclesiastical law to remove remains without a faculty, which is used to authorise the removal of remains from one consecrated burial place to another. A faculty will only be granted for good and proper reason (*Re Christ Church (Alsager)* [1999] Fam 142). Such reasons have included the extension of the church building, remedying a hasty decision after only a short interval, emotional disturbance, publicity at the burial and mistake (Williams Mortimer & Sunnucks, *Executors, Administrators and Probate*, 19th edn, 6-05). Before granting or refusing such a faculty the court will pay regard to the wishes of the deceased and his family. However, the relatives have no absolute right to insist on or object to the issue of the faculty.

4.28 In *Re Robin Hood Cemetery* [2006] All ER (D) 68 the court held that the petitioner (who sought disinterment of her late husband's cremated remains, so that they could be scattered on the garden of rest at the cemetery because she feared that due to her advancing years and deteriorating health she would be unable to maintain her husband's resting place in due course), had not successfully demonstrated the existence of exceptional circumstances justifying a departure from the general rule that a Christian burial is final. In coming to its decision the court was influenced by the fact that the petitioner's husband's remains had been buried for over 17 years. In this case the court applied the more stringent test of 'exceptional circumstances' over the 'good and proper reason' test applied in *Re Christ Church (Alsager)* [1999] Fam 142.

4.29 In *Re Mangotsfield Cemetery* (2005) *The Times*, April 26, the claimant petitioned for the exhumation of the cremated remains of his ex-wife from the burial plot she shared with their deceased son. His ex-wife had been buried there in the mistaken belief that the plot belonged to her. In fact, the plot was the property of the claimant. The claimant's petition was dismissed on the basis that a contractual right to burial in a plot of consecrated land in a local authority cemetery did not of itself entitle the owner of the right to insist on disinterment of ashes mistakenly buried in his plot.

4.30 If a body is to removed other than from one consecrated burial place to another, the licence of the Secretary of State may be necessary in addition to any faculty and without such faculty the removal is unlawful in civil law.

4.31 In *R v Jacobson* (1880) 14 Cox CC 522 Counsel suggested that:

> 'A time may come when the bones are not recognisable as human remains, when the bones have become dust and the ground might be built upon. To disturb remains of Druids who had been buried on Salisbury Plain, for instance would not be indictable. This must always be a question of degree ...'

4.32 This approach is supported by the Scots case of *HM Advocate v Coutts* (1899) 3 Adam 50, in which Lord McLaren said:

> '... the crime [ie violating sepulchres] is committed by the act of disturbing a body which is in a condition to be regarded as an object of reverential treatment ... I should have thought that if the indictment had only disclosed a case of disturbing bodies after the elapse of ten or more years from their burial in the common ground of a cemetery it would be very difficult in a case of that kind to satisfy a jury that a crime had been committed.'

4.33 Therefore it would seem that the more remains decompose in the ground the less likely is a conviction for disinterring and removal to succeed.

PRACTICE AND PROCEDURE

4.34 There has been some confusion over how to apply for determination in relation to burial disputes under the Civil Procedure Rules.

4.35 In *Holtham v Arnold* (1985) 2 BMLR 123, the claimant sought directions under RSC Ord 85, r 2 asking a court to direct that she be entrusted with the burial, or alternatively under s 116(1) of the Supreme Court Act 1981 (SCA 1981) for appointment as administrator of the estate solely for the purpose of securing the burial.

4.36 RSC Ord 85, r 2 is replaced by CPR Part 64. Part 64.2 applies to claims for the court to determine any question arising in the administration of the estate of a deceased person or for an order for the administration of the estate of a deceased person to be carried out under the direction of the court.

4.37 In *Holtham v Arnold* the court stated that ordinarily an order under RSC Ord 85, r 2 would take the form of direction to the executors or administrators concerning the carrying out of their duties in the estate. They did not see how they could direct an administrator to hand over the duty of burial to someone else under that power. Similarly, in *Fessi v Whitmore* [1999] 1 FLR 767, the judge held that questions regarding the disposal of remains could not fall within the definition of the administration of an estate and that the matter was not properly brought under RSC Ord 86. Instead, the judge concluded that he was being asked to determine a dispute between like entitled parents, akin to trustees. It seems most likely that such a claim should be brought under CPR Part 8.

4.38 The claimant in *Holtham v Arnold* also submitted that under SCA 1981, s 116(1), the court could appoint the claimant administrator solely for the purpose of conducting a burial. The section allows the court, in special circumstances, to appoint as administrator someone other than the person who would be entitled under the ordinary probate rules. Again, the judge felt that s 116 concerned the proper and efficient administration of the estate and was not really 'adapted to dealing with the sort of question which is raised in this case'. In the event, the judge presided over the procedural issue and decided in the favour of the defendants.

4.39 As regards headstones, it is conceivable that the executor could ask for directions under CPR Part 64 and that the placing or inscription of a headstone would be considered to be part of the administration of the estate.

4.40 As regards exhumation, in the first instance one would need to apply to the burial authority for a licence to exhume. The written consent of the grave owner must be attached to the application. The application form states that it should normally be completed by the spouse, civil partner, child or sibling of the deceased (in that order). Other relatives with the same or closer degree of kinship as the applicant must confirm their consent by countersigning the application. If the removal will disturb the remains of another person, the nearest surviving relatives of that other person's consent will be required. Those to whom notice is given can raise objections at this point. If proceedings are necessary, again we suspect that the CPR Part 8 procedure is most suitable in resolving an issue of this type.

4.41 If the remains are in consecrated ground, an application will need to be made to the relevant diocese for a faculty. Decisions relating to exhumation from consecrated ground are dealt with by the Chancellor, the judge of the consistory court. The petitioner must rebut the presumption that the remains should be left undisturbed by presenting evidence and potentially also legal argument to the Chancellor. If necessary, the matter will be determined at a sitting of the consistory court. (See Annex LI of *Guidance for best practice for treatment of human remains excavated from Christian burial grounds in England, 2005* (http://www.english-heritage.org.uk/upload/pdf/16602_HumanRemains1.pdf). This guidance booklet contains general information, although its main focus is on the excavation of human remains for archaeological purposes.)

Part III

OBTAINING THE GRANT – DISPUTES AND RESOLUTIONS

Chapter 5

OBTAINING THE WILL

SECURING THE WILL

5.1   If a will is not found among the deceased's papers but is believed to exist, extensive inquiries should be made and particulars advertised where appropriate. If the original is lost or destroyed and there is no evidence of revocation, application may be made by notice with supporting affidavit to the probate registrar to obtain a grant in respect of a copy. If no complete copy is available, a grant may be issued based on an accurate draft or reconstruction (by someone with detailed knowledge of the contents). Evidence of due execution may also be required. Where a will has been returned to the testator at his request and cannot be found on death then, in the absence of evidence to the contrary, there is a presumption that it was revoked by destruction (see Non Contentious Probate Rules 1987 (NCPR 1987), r 54 and **12.25**).

WITNESS SUMMONS

Last will or codicil

5.2   If an original will or codicil is believed to be in the possession, custody or power of a person who refuses to release it, an application without notice may be made to the probate registrar supported by an affidavit for an order under the Supreme Court Act 1981 (SCA 1981), s 123. The registrar authorises the issue of a witness summons (technically still called a '*subpoena*' under NCPR 1987, r 50) requiring that person to lodge the document at the registry within eight days, or such other period as the registrar considers reasonable. The affidavit must set out in detail the grounds for the application, although it may be sworn by either the person issuing or his solicitor. The service copy of the witness summons is endorsed with a penal notice, which threatens imprisonment in the event of disobedience and must be served personally. If the person served does not have the document in his possession or control, he should file an affidavit (although this is not mandatory) stating the current whereabouts of the document (if known) and such other information as is likely to assist the court. (A precedent form subpoena and affidavit in support is set out in Appendix 2.)

Previous documents

5.3   An application under SCA 1981, s 123 can also be very useful where it is doubtful whether the last will is a valid will and previous testamentary documents are in the possession of a person who refuses to produce them on the assumption that they are irrelevant as having been revoked by the later will. The issue of a witness summons will also be required:

- where the court directs a document to be produced before issuing a citation; or

- where a caveator needs to know the extent of his entitlement under an earlier document so as to enter an appearance.

5.4   If the probate registrar is satisfied by the affidavit evidence that there is real doubt about the validity of the last will, he will order the penultimate will to be produced to the registry and will then provide a copy to the person issuing the witness summons. If the issue as to validity may also affect earlier wills (such as where the deceased may have lacked testamentary capacity for some time) the probate registrar may be prepared to order production of a series of previous testamentary documents.

Proceedings already issued

5.5   The above procedure applies prior to the commencement of a probate action. If proceedings have already been issued, the application for an order under SCA 1981, s 123 is to the Chancery master or to a District Judge either at the directions hearing or by application notice (see CPR 57 PD para 7). In this case, the rules require only 'written evidence' in support, ie not a sworn affidavit. Anyone outside the jurisdiction may first have to be joined as a defendant in the action before a witness summons can be validly served on that person.

Professional executors and advisers

5.6   If a will is held by an executor's professional adviser (whose client may or may not have renounced probate), a co-executor wishing to prove may issue a witness summons. In that situation the adviser's representative is required to swear an affidavit but is unlikely to be required for examination as to the Will's contents. If the document is held by a firm of lawyers or accountants the witness summons should recite the full name of the senior partner upon whom it must be served personally. Where there is a dispute about the circumstances in which the will was made, the solicitor draftsmen should make available certain documents, as determined by the Court of Appeal in *Larke v Nugus* [2000] WTLR 1033 (see **12.72-12.75**).

EXAMINATION BY THE COURT

5.7   If a person fails to comply with a witness summons or if there are reasonable grounds for believing that a person has knowledge of a purported testamentary document, that person may be required by witness summons to answer specific questions and/or to attend for examination on oath, under SCA 1981, s 122. If such a person fails to attend, he/she is guilty of contempt. Again, where proceedings have already been commenced an order will be sought at the directions hearing or by application notice.

5.8   This procedure is most often used where attesting witnesses have declined to swear affidavits of due execution, although anyone with relevant information can be required for examination. If a person to whom an order under s 122 is directed is outside the jurisdiction, a separate order is necessary appointing the British Consul or his representative to take evidence on oath for this purpose.

5.9   Where a person to whom a witness summons was directed has responded by affidavit or witness statement to the effect that the testamentary document which is the subject of the witness summons is not in his possession, custody or control, but it is clear from the affidavit that he has some knowledge of the whereabouts of the document, an order for examination can be sought to enable him to be cross-examined on his affidavit or statement.

5.10   The procedure under SCA 1981, s 122 may also be useful if the deceased's solicitor who has knowledge of the will and/or codicil(s), refuses to provide a *Larke v Nugus* statement (see **12.72–12.75**).

Chapter 6

ENTITLEMENT TO THE GRANT

WHO MAY APPLY?

6.1   A grant of probate may be obtained by any of the executors appointed in the will who are not under any legal disability, subject to giving notice of the application to all co-executors. Persons entitled to letters of administration where there is no executor able or willing to act, or on intestacy (as to which see Non Contentious Probate Rules 1987 (NCPR 1987), r 20 and Administration of Estates Act 1925, s 46), may apply without notice to other persons entitled in the same degree. In respect of deaths on or after 1 January 1996, a spouse must first survive for 28 days before being entitled to take a grant on intestacy. A living person or one of full age will respectively have priority to the personal representatives of a deceased applicant or a child's legal guardian.

6.2   If a co-executor is notified of an application for probate and wishes to object, or if there is a dispute between administrators as to who should apply, the matter may be determined in either case on application by summons to the district judge or probate registrar. The objector's supporting affidavit should give details of reasons why he/she believes the grant should not be issued, e g because the applicant is not of sound mind or not entitled to apply. A stop notice is placed on the pending application until the summons is disposed of (NCPR 1987, r 27).

ACTIONS AGAINST THOSE CLAIMING ENTITLEMENT

6.3   An action can be commenced against a person claiming to be entitled to letters of administration or contesting the validity of a will where this is disputed. The person bringing the claim under CPR 57 must make it clear in the statement of case the interest or entitlement which is in dispute and give full reasons (CPR, r 57.7(2)). In the case of entitlement to a grant, if the allegation is substantiated, the statement of case must demonstrate that the applicant would be the person next entitled in that event. If a grant has already been obtained, it will be necessary to issue revocation proceedings.

6.4   Although persons born illegitimate or adopted by the deceased are entitled to share in the estate and obtain letters of administration on intestacy, an interest action might be used to disprove the alleged entitlement of a stepchild who was not so adopted. The Chancery courts have no power to make declarations of legitimacy under the Family Law Act 1986, s 56, as amended. Such applications must be dealt with by the Family Division.

CITATIONS

6.5   A citation is a notice in writing issued by the District Judge or Probate Registrar requiring the person to whom it is directed to take some step intended to accelerate the probate process. The citation will state what it is that the person cited is required to do and the time limit, as well as the consequences of failing to comply.

6.6   The person entitled to a grant may be dilatory in obtaining it and yet not willing to renounce his/her right to do so. Anyone entitled in a lower capacity (ie with an interest in the estate) can cite those persons with a prior right to either accept or refuse a grant. This entitlement must be demonstrated in the citation and supporting affidavit. The citation will operate so as to 'clear off' anyone with priority.

6.7   There are three types of citation, a citation to take probate, a citation to accept or refuse a grant of probate and a citation to propound a will:

(1)   A citation to take probate requires an executor (including one who has intermeddled in the estate (see below)) to show why he should not be ordered to apply for a grant. There must be no current proceedings concerned with the will's validity and such a citation cannot be issued for six months after the death. Note that the court has general discretion to appoint a person of its choice to take a grant, as opposed to the person next entitled (Supreme Court Act 1981 (SCA 1981), s 116 – see below).

(2)   A citation to accept or refuse a grant may be issued at any time. If the person cited does nothing, or fails to apply for a grant within a reasonable time of being ordered to do so by the court, his right to apply ceases. Anyone who is entitled to apply, if persons with priority do not renounce, can issue such a citation (see generally NCPR 1987, r 47(1)). As an alternative, the court can require an executor to prove or renounce on application by summons in the Principal Registry (SCA 1981, s 112).

(3)   If there is some doubt as to the validity of a testamentary document, anyone entitled on intestacy or under an earlier document may require the executors or beneficiaries in respect of the later one to propound (ie prove) it, or stand aside and accept that it is invalid. It must be directed to and served upon all persons with an interest under the document (NCPR 1987, r 48(1)). Since the person issuing this citation may be adversely affected if the later document is proved, a probate action is likely to be the result – either validity proceedings are commenced by the citor or the executor issues and asks for a declaration by the court in solemn form in favour of the document upon which he relies. A grant

obtained following such a declaration will give additional protection to the executor – it is irrevocable in the absence of fraud, or unless a further conflicting testamentary document comes to light.

6.8 As a preliminary step, a caveat must first be entered (see Chapter 7). This will prevent another interested party applying for a grant before the citation has been dealt with. If the will is available this is lodged with the application. The citation should be prepared in draft to be settled by the probate registrar; the settlement fee is £10 at the time of writing. The affidavit is completed once the citation is settled.

6.9 Personal service is required and the document once served must be endorsed with a certificate to that effect. If, despite extensive inquiries, the person to be cited cannot be traced, reference should be made to this and an order for substituted service (e g by advertisement) requested in the affidavit. The person cited has eight days to enter an appearance (in person or by post) and if he fails to do so, the registrar may grant the relief requested, eg:

(1) An order directing the person cited to take a grant within a specified time.

(2) An order in favour of the citor, i e allowing him to take a grant. This may or may not be in default of the person cited applying as directed in (1) above.

(3) An order against an intermeddling executor – this requires a further application to be made by summons to the district judge or registrar (NCPR 1987, r 47(5)).

(4) An order treating a will as invalid (NCPR 1987, r 48(2)).

6.10 If the person cited enters an appearance and is willing to take a grant, he applies without notice by affidavit for an order in his favour. If he does not apply with reasonable diligence, a summons is issued and served on him and an order obtained as in (1) to (4) above.

6.11 If a co-executor was notified of an application for probate and has power reserved to him to take a grant, he may subsequently be cited to accept or refuse, e g by the personal representatives of an executor who proved the will but has since died. Note that if the proving executor died testate, the chain of representation would apply and such an application would be unnecessary.

6.12 If an appearance is entered by the citee, a note is placed on the original grant to the effect that his executorship rights have lapsed. If he appears but does not proceed to take a grant of double probate, a summons is issued for an order striking out the appearance and for noting of the grant (NCPR 1987, r 47(2) and (7)(b)).

APPLICATIONS UNDER SCA 1981, S 116

Introduction

6.13 Section 116 of the SCA 1981 gives the court power, where it considers it to be 'necessary or expedient', to appoint as administrator someone other than the person(s) entitled. Such grant may be limited in any way the court thinks fit. The application, also under NCPR 1987, r 52, is made to the probate registrar in the Registry where it is intended to apply for a Grant, or to a District Judge at the Principal Registry.

Main uses

(1) The person entitled to a grant is considered unfit or inappropriate to act or the estate may be at risk, e g because of previous financial dealings or bankruptcy.

(2) Where that person has been found guilty of murder or manslaughter against the deceased.

(3) Where a grant is required to enable proceedings to be issued against the estate or under the Inheritance (Provision for Family and Dependants) Act 1975.

(4) The person(s) entitled have renounced probate and there is no-one else who is able and willing to act.

(5) The person(s) entitled cannot be traced despite extensive enquiries.

(6) The person(s) entitled are in dispute with one another or have a conflict of interest – in this situation the court may 'pass over' their entitlement in favour of someone independent – see *Iliffe v Trafford & Another* [2002] WTLR 507.

(7) Where an executor has intermeddled in the estate – see *In the estate of Biggs deceased* [1966] I All ER 358 where a citation to take probate had been issued, but the citee failed to do so within a reasonable time.

Procedure

6.14 The application is made without notice, preferably with a draft affidavit in support for settling by the Registrar. This gives the Registrar the opportunity to direct that further evidence be obtained and included in the affidavit, or that the matter should be dealt with on notice, by the issue of a summons. A precedent affidavit can be found at Appendix 2.

6.15 Depending on the particular circumstances, the grant issued under s 116 can be limited (e g to enable proceedings to be commenced or pending resolution of a dispute) or general. The District Judge or Probate Registrar has complete discretion in selecting an appropriate person to take the grant, having regard to the interests of all persons entitled to the estate.

6.16 If the deceased died domiciled outside England and Wales the appropriate application is under NCPR 1987, r 30(1)(c) rather than s 116.

INTERMEDDLING

6.17 Anyone who, by taking steps in relation to the deceased's assets leads a creditor or beneficiary to believe that he is authorised to administer the estate can be personally liable for the consequences of his actions and in particular may be required to make good any loss suffered. Third parties in their dealings with such a person are entitled to assume that he has authority to act (see *Parker v Kett* (1701) 1 LD Raym 658).

What constitutes intermeddling?

6.18 The question of liability will depend upon the type of activity undertaken: it must be significant. Making enquiries as to the extent of the assets and liabilities or taking items into safe custody will be insufficient as will arranging the funeral. However, clearance of furniture or discharging debts will constitute intermeddling. Instructions from the testator to non-executors should therefore be discouraged when taking will instructions. Funeral directors or valuers will look for payment to the person giving them instructions, whether or not they are entitled to instruct them. Liability to account for inheritance tax on assets within the control of a person who intermeddles is imposed by IHTA 1984, ss 199(4) and 200(4).

6.19 A person appointed as an executor who intermeddles in the estate loses his/her right to renounce probate and may be cited to take a grant (see above). Although authority to act derives from the will, he/she may still be liable if that authority is not confirmed by the issue of a grant to him/her.

Extent of liability

6.20 Liability will extend only to the assets received or coming into that person's hands or, if he/she has released debts due to the estate, to the value of those debts. He/she is entitled to offset any payments he/she has made which 'might properly be made by a personal representative' and any legitimate sums due to him/her from the deceased. There is a further exception where full valuable consideration was given in respect of any assets in the estate. Section 28 of the Administration of Estates Act 1925 requires a fraud on the deceased's creditors to be demonstrated by an intermeddling executor but it is submitted that negligent activity may well suffice. A person receiving instructions as agent and acting accordingly may be held accountable. This will apply even if he/she believes that the person instructing him had authority to do so unless he/she can demonstrate that he/she acted honestly and reasonably, ie was misled (see *Sharland v Mildon* (1846) 5 Hare 469 and *Thomson v Harding* (1853) 2 E & B 630).

6.21   The court's discretion under SCA 1981, s 116 (see above) extends to passing over an appointed executor who has acted in the administration but failed to take a grant. A person appointed under a limited grant (eg administration *ad colligenda bona* – see Chapter 8 below) may be held liable if he/she exceeds the authority given to him by that grant; however, the court has an overriding power to extend his/her authority if it considers it appropriate to do so.

Chapter 7

BLOCKING THE GRANT: CAVEATS

ENTERING A CAVEAT

7.1   If a person interested in a deceased's estate wishes to prevent a grant of probate or letters of administration issuing, he/she can do so by entering a caveat at the Leeds District Probate Registry. Under r 44 of the Non Contentious Probate Rules 1987 (NCPR 1987) the Registrar will not allow any grant to be sealed (other than a grant *ad colligenda bona* or grant of administration pending suit under SCA 1981 s 117) until the caveat has been lodged. The caveat will be effective from the day after it is entered.

7.2   The caveat is entered by sending the relevant form (see Appendix 2) to any probate registry together with the appropriate fee (£15 at the time of writing). The caveat can also be entered by taking the form and fee in person to any district probate registry. Details of the deceased's full name including all alternatives on his/her name should be provided, together with his/her date of death.

EXPIRY AND RENEWAL

7.3   A caveat is effective for six months. It can be extended on an ongoing basis for six months at a time by application in writing made during the last month before it is due to expire. A fee of £15 will be required each time it is renewed. The registry will not send a reminder and therefore if the caveat is not renewed it will expire and any interested party is free to extract a grant.

WARNING AND APPEARANCE

7.4   If those propounding the will believe there is no real reason for preventing a grant, they may enter a warning to the caveat. The procedure for warning a caveat is dealt with under NCPR 1987, r 44. The warning is filed at the Registry and served on the caveator stating the interest of the person warning and requiring the caveator within eight days of service (including the date of service) to enter an appearance at the Leeds District Probate Registry. The caveator must give particulars of any contrary interest in the estate. If he/she does not have a contrary interest to the person warning but wishes to

show cause against the sealing of a grant to that person he/she should issue a
summons for directions, as to which see NCPR r 44(6).

7.5 It is worth noting that the appearance must be entered within eight
calendar days – not eight business days. Once an appearance has been entered
the question can only be resolved through proceedings in the Chancery
Division, or, if agreement is reached between the parties before proceedings are
issued, before the district probate registrar.

7.6 The form of warning and appearance can be found at Appendix 2.

7.7 If no appearance is entered to a warning, an affidavit of service of the
warning on the caveator can be filed at the Leeds District Probate Registry on
the eighth calendar day after service of the warning (see Appendix 2). The
caveat will then cease to have effect. It is important to act swiftly in filing the
affidavit of service as the caveator can enter an appearance after the eight day
period so long as no affidavit of service has been filed.

WITHDRAWING THE CAVEAT

7.8 A caveat can be withdrawn at any time before entering an appearance by
writing to the district probate registry at which the caveat was entered. The
caveator must give notice of the withdrawal to anyone who has warned the
caveat.

STANDING SEARCH

7.9 A standing search can be entered for a £5 fee. When entered the person
who arranged the standing search will receive an office copy of any grant which
was issued not more than 12 months before the entry of the standing search or
which issues in the period of six months after the standing search. It can be
useful where an action for rectification or under the Inheritance (Provision for
Family and Dependants) Act 1975 is contemplated as these actions must be
issued within six months from grant (see Chapters 10 and 15). The standing
search expires after 6 months but can be renewed in the same way as a caveat.
The relevant form is at Appendix 2.

WHEN TO LODGE A CAVEAT

Doubt about validity of a testamentary document

7.10 The usual reason for lodging a caveat is that the caveator has some doubt
about whether the last will of the deceased is indeed the last valid will and
wishes to make enquiries to establish its validity or otherwise. If he/she fails to

prevent the issue of a grant and then discovers that the will is invalid, he/she will have to issue proceedings for the revocation of the grant. This can have disadvantages:

(1) some steps may have been taken in the administration before the proceedings for revocation are commenced;

(2) the would-be caveator is forced into the position of claimant and does not have the option of sitting back and obliging those who wish to take out the grant to issue the proceedings;

(3) the opportunities for settling the dispute may not be as great as if the potential claimant had been able to block the grant.

7.11 If enquiries establish that the caveator has little or no chance of proving that the last will is invalid, the caveat should be withdrawn. If a caveat is lodged or continued vexatiously, then, if the matter comes before a probate registrar on an application for directions or to strike out following an appearance having been entered, the caveator could be ordered to pay the opposing party's costs.

Dispute about who should be personal representative

7.12 A caveat can be lodged to give a person interested in the estate the opportunity of making representations as to who should take out the grant. A residuary beneficiary may have good reason to suppose that an executor named in the will would be unsuitable to take out the grant because of criminal conduct, irresponsibility with money, mental illness, conflict of interest or some other reason. One of a number of people entitled to take out a grant of letters of administration may be unhappy about the grant being taken out by another. An application could be made through appropriate channels as set out in Chapter 6 above, and a grant prevented in the interim by lodging a caveat.

Where a citation is to be taken out

7.13 If the caveator wishes to issue a citation to require another person to accept or refuse a grant, to take out a grant or to propound a will, he must enter a caveat beforehand (see NCPR 1987, r 46(3)). The caveat remains in place until the citation proceedings have been disposed of, as to which see Chapter 6 above.

WHEN A CAVEAT SHOULD NOT BE LODGED

7.14 A caveat should not be lodged:

(a) Where the caveator is an outsider who has no real interest in the estate. If a complete outsider lodges a caveat he will be unable to enter an appearance (because he will be unable to state what is his interest contrary to that of the person warning) and, unless he can establish good reason why the grant should not issue to the person entitled, could be at risk of an adverse costs order made by a probate registrar.

(b)   Where the caveator intends to make an application for provision to be made out of the estate under the Inheritance (Provision for Family and Dependants) Act 1975 (the 1975 Act). It is counter-productive for a would-be applicant under the 1975 Act to lodge a caveat; the caveat will prevent the issue of the grant and the applicant will be unable to bring an application under the 1975 Act until a grant is issued (see *Re McBroom* [1992] 2 FLR 49 where an application made before the grant was struck out as being premature).

7.15   The potential applicant under a 1975 Act claim will wish to know when the grant has issued in order to avoid missing the six month time limit under the Act, and can do so by entering a standing search, as explained at **7.9** above.

Chapter 8

LIMITED AND DISCRETIONARY GRANTS

INTRODUCTION

8.1   If a caveat has been lodged a grant will not be sealed until the caveat expires or is removed, or upon application by summons or following a court order disposing of a probate action. However, the Non Contentious Probate Rules 1987 (NCPR 1987), r 44 allows a grant to be obtained under the Supreme Court Act 1981 (SCA 1981), s 117 notwithstanding the caveat. In addition, r 52 permits a grant of administration under SCA 1981, s 116 (see Chapter 6 above) or *ad colligenda bona*. SCA 1981, s 113 gives the court power to issue a grant in respect of part of the deceased's estate.

ADMINISTRATION PENDING DETERMINATION OF A PROBATE CLAIM

8.2   A party to a probate action may apply under s 117 for appointment of an administrator pending determination of that action. This enables the estate to be administered in the interim, assets collected in and tax and other debts paid. Subject to the consent of the parties to the action, the administrator may also take such other steps as are consistent with his appointment; this could include a partial distribution, eg payment of legacies which are not in dispute. However, s 117 requires leave of the court to be given before a distribution is made, unless the terms of the appointment prescribe otherwise.

8.3   The court will sometimes appoint joint administrators (eg a solicitor acting for each party), in which case they will have to agree as to which of them will undertake the work required, although all of them should be authorised to charge. Increasingly the court prefers to appoint someone not connected with the action and in that event the parties should agree on and nominate a suitable person (eg an independent solicitor) who should produce a letter consenting to act. A sole administrator can act despite a life or minority interest arising on intestacy. An order under s 117 is usually made at a case management conference or otherwise by application notice. Once the order is made the s 117 grant can be issued only by the Principal Registry. Section 117(3) of the SCA 1981 gives the court discretion to allow such reasonable remuneration as it thinks fit from the deceased's estate. It is advisable to secure an order for payment of the administration fees, if any, and costs at the time of the application. The s 117 grant remains in force until the final order is made, either by consent or following trial. If a full grant is subsequently obtained, it will refer to the order.

ADMINISTRATION AD COLLIGENDA BONA

8.4   If the delay in obtaining a grant is such that the preservation of the deceased's estate is put at risk, an application may be made for an order for a grant of letters of administration *ad colligenda bona*. The grounds for the application must be set out in the supporting affidavit (NCPR 1987, r 52). This may be required because:

(1)   there is a probate dispute but the parties are unable or unwilling to commence proceedings;

(2)   the estate requires administration and/or protection pending the issue of a full grant;

(3)   a person is refusing to disclose information which would enable the value of the estate to be obtained in the absence of a grant;

(4)   specific action is required in default of which the estate will suffer loss, e g an asset must be sold or shares transferred immediately;

(5)   assets cannot be utilised to pay tax due without a grant.

8.5   In *IRC v Stype Investments* [1982] 3 All ER 419 the Inland Revenue requested that a grant *ad colligenda bona* should be issued to the Official Solicitor in the estate of Sir Charles Clore. This was authorised by the Senior Registrar and upheld by the Court of Appeal on the basis that the Revenue stood to lose capital transfer tax on assets of £20m transferred to a Jersey company shortly before death. The executors, who were also directors of that company, had, not unnaturally, declined to obtain a grant.

8.6   It is submitted that an application without notice should be made only in circumstances where there is a real risk to the estate and not merely to secure some tactical advantage (see *Ghafoor v Cliff* [2006] 2 All ER 1079). The overriding obligation is to give full and frank disclosure to the court and if serious allegations are made in the supporting affidavit the defendants should be given an opportunity to answer them before a grant *ad colligenda bona* is made. In addition, David Richards J commented that a solicitor for one of the parties would not reasonably be regarded as independent or impartial (and an appropriate person to take such a grant) in a highly contentious case.

8.7   A precedent affidavit in support of an application for a grant *ad colligenda bona* is at Appendix 2.

GRANT TO PART OF THE ESTATE

8.8 Section 112 of the SCA 1981 allows a grant to be issued to part of an estate, upon application to the probate registrar. An affidavit should be lodged with other relevant documents (eg renunciations). The affidavit must 'clear off' persons entitled in priority and state whether or not the estate is thought to be insolvent (see Chapter 17). This procedure may be used in conjunction with a s 116 application, allowing a grant to part of the estate to a nominee at the court's discretion.

8.9 An application under CPR Part 69 may be made by application in the Chancery Division for appointment of a receiver in whom property in the estate vests. The receiver can authorise a sale or other transaction or act so as to prevent a beneficiary or third party from dealing with that property. Similar remedies are available under CPR Part 64 (see Chapter 13). The receiver's remuneration is fixed by the court and he may be directed to file accounts in relation to his dealings. CPR Part 69 proceedings are heard by a Chancery Master in chambers.

Chapter 9

THE FOREIGN ELEMENT

INTRODUCTION

9.1   The English estate of an English domiciliary will normally be governed by English law (for English read English or Welsh throughout this part) for all purposes, but where there is a foreign element then consideration must be given to the relevant foreign law and its interaction with English law.

9.2   The difficulty is that one country's legal system may not fit together happily with another's. There are very significant differences, for instance, between common law and civilian or Shari'a law systems and indeed between those systems themselves. Each system is comprehensive and logical when taken in isolation but when elements of each are mixed there are likely to be anomalies and fertile conditions for disputes to arise.

9.3   The foreign element may be present in two circumstances: where there are foreign assets; or where the deceased was domiciled or resident in, or was a national of, a foreign country.

9.4   In both cases the key questions are:

(1)   Who is responsible for collecting in the assets?

(2)   What should they do with the assets when they have collected them?

9.5   Where English domestic law alone is concerned the answers are straightforward. The validity of the will is governed by the Wills Acts. The executors named in the will take out the grant of probate, administer the estate in accordance with English law and distribute it in accordance with the terms of the will. If there is no will, then the Non-Contentious Probate Rules 1987 set out who should take out the grant of letters of administration, and the Administration of Estates Act 1925 governs the distribution of the estate.

9.6   Where foreign law comes into the equation matters are not so simple.

ENGLISH DECEASED: FOREIGN ASSETS

English wills and foreign wills

9.7   Testators with foreign assets are usually advised to make separate wills in each country where assets are held. Such local wills will conform with the domestic law of the country of situs. Problems do arise, however, where insufficient care has been taken to limit the scope of the will to the relevant assets.

9.8   All too frequently, for instance:

(1)   the local will revokes an earlier English 'worldwide' will in its entirety rather than just so far as the local assets are concerned; or

(2)   a later English will is executed that fails to exclude the foreign assets and thereby unintentionally revokes the foreign will.

9.9   The Jersey Court held in *Re the Estate of Vickers* [2001–02] 4 ITELR 584 that if in these circumstances the obvious facts militated against an intention as expressed in the will then the court could act on the real intention as found by the court (and see also *Lamothe v Lamothe* [2006] WTLR 1431). Nonetheless, such careless drafting will usually be expensive to cure and a beneficiary who loses out as a result may have a claim for negligence against the lawyer who drew up the will – although often it is the testator's fault for being too secretive (maybe for tax reasons) about the existence of the foreign assets.

9.10   If the estate is dealt with in an English form worldwide will, then it will still usually be formally valid in the foreign country. An English form will of an English domiciliary is recognised in most jurisdictions, and certainly where the assets are situated in a country that has ratified the 1961 Hague Convention on Conflicts of Laws Relating to the Form of Testamentary Dispositions (which includes most of the major jurisdictions) there is unlikely to be a problem.

English executors and foreign assets

9.11   If there is a foreign will and an English will which is limited to the English estate, then the English executors are concerned only with the English estate and have no duties in respect of foreign assets. Where there is an English will that purports to deal with the worldwide estate the situation is less clear.

9.12   Section 25 of the Administration of Estates Act 1925 imposes a general duty on personal representatives to 'collect and get in the real and personal estate of the deceased and administer it according to law'. However:

(1)   As regards foreign assets the English grant will be effective only insofar as these assets are brought to England before anyone has acquired good title in the country of situs.

(2)   The English grant may assist the English executors to institute succession proceedings abroad (especially in common law countries, eg USA) but civil law and Islamic jurisdictions do not recognise the concept of executorship in its English sense and the estate will usually vest in the heir direct. The English executors may therefore be unable to take any effective steps to acquire title to the foreign assets.

(3)   The revised s 25 of the Administration Estates Act 1925 was substituted with effect from 1 January 1972 by s 9 of the Administration Estates Act 1971, and this part of the 1971 Act is headed 'rights and duties of personal representatives in England and Wales' – the implication being that the personal representatives' duties are limited to dealing with property in England and Wales. There is a distinct paucity of case law on the subject. *Re Fitzpatrick* [1952] Ch 86 indicates that an executor may be under a duty to recover foreign assets where there are insufficient assets in England to pay off creditors – but where there are no such creditors then there may well be no obligation on the executors to make any attempt to 'collect and get in' foreign assets.

9.13   The practical point is that executors should think very carefully before instituting succession proceedings abroad. They may well have the right, but they probably do not have the obligation, to do so and they should consider carefully what they may be letting themselves in for.

A formally valid will in a foreign jurisdiction

9.14   Where a will is formally valid in a foreign jurisdiction where the testator held assets the concept of forced heirship – easily the most common source of dispute arising out of the foreign element – may come into play. English law permits full freedom of testamentary disposition subject only to the discretionary power of the court under the Inheritance (Provision for Family and Dependants) Act 1975 where the deceased died domiciled in England and Wales. Many foreign jurisdictions, however, particularly civil law and Islamic ones, dictate minimum shares that must pass to certain close relatives. Indeed, this is often extended to lifetime gifts (but not generally by Islamic law jurisdictions), so that any attempt to avoid the rules by making lifetime gifts to, say, a mistress (or even a spouse) at the expense of a child's entrenched share may well leave the child with the right to claw back a proportion of the gifts on the parent's death.

9.15   The key question is whether these entrenched rights will apply even where the deceased was domiciled anywhere in the UK.

9.16   Many jurisdictions apply their own domestic law to immovables and the law of the country of domicile (or habitual residence) to movables. Where, for instance, a UK domiciliary leaves a house and bank accounts in France, France will apply its own forced heirship rules to the devolution of the house but will refer back to English (private international rather than domestic) law as regards movables. England in turn will apply its own domestic law, being the law of domicile. The effect is that France will accept freedom of testamentary disposition as regards the French movable property of an English domiciliary but not for French immovables.

9.17   Other countries, for example Italy and Spain, refer the succession to both movables and immovables to the law of country of the deceased's nationality. Such countries may or may not then accept a referral back from English law.

9.18   Take, for instance, the holiday home in Italy of a British national. Italy refers the succession to England as the country of the deceased's nationality (assuming a closer connection to England than Scotland or Northern Ireland). Under English private international law, the succession to immovables is governed by the lex situs. As the property is in Italy, English law refers back to Italian law.

9.19   Until 1995, Art 30 of the Italian Civil Code rejected the referral back – so that Italian domestic law (with its forced heirship rules) did not apply to Italian immovables left by a British national, irrespective of domicile. However, this changed in 1995 when Art 13 of Law 218 of 31 May 1995 came into effect; Art 13(1) now provides that references to foreign law should take account of the reference made by that law to that of another state where either the latter accepts the reference to it, or where that reference is to Italian law.

9.20   There is, however, an exception under Art 46(2) which provides that the law of the deceased's last country of (habitual) residence will govern the succession where the deceased makes a declaration to that effect in his will. Where this applies, although Italian law refers to English law and English law refers back to Italian law as the *lex situs*, Italian law rejects the renvoi and its domestic forced heirship rules will not apply.

9.21   Spain is another country that applies the law of the deceased's nationality. Again, in the case of a holiday property in Spain owned by a British national, Spanish law would apply English law as the law of nationality and English law would refer back to Spanish law as the law of the situs of the immovable property.

9.22   The question is whether this renvoi would be accepted by Spain; this was reviewed in 1996 in the *Lowenthal* case and again by the Spanish Supreme Court in Appeal No 3086/1995, Judgment No 436/1999. In both these cases the court recognised that on a literal reading of Art 12.2 of the Civil Code, Spanish law would accept the renvoi. However, it went on to say that to accept the renvoi in those cases would have the effect of applying a different legal treatment of inheritance rights to movable property and immovable property. The purpose for which the Civil Code existed was the harmonisation of the legal systems of different states and the court did not feel that this would be achieved by allowing a different treatment for movable property and immovable property.

9.23 The upshot of these cases is that Spanish domestic forced heirship rules will probably not apply to the Spanish holiday house of a British national domiciled in England. Having said that, at a practical level much will depend on the Spanish notary and Land Registry, and indeed, on the affidavit of English law prepared by the English lawyer and whether that affidavit just deals with English domestic law or goes into the ramifications of private international law.

9.24 Where, therefore, there are foreign assets dealt with by an English will, consideration should always be given to:

(1)   whether the country of situs has entrenched heirship rules that are not reflected in the will;

(2)   whether that country will apply these rules to the local:
      (a)   immovables, or
      (b)   movables,
      of an English domiciliary.

9.25 It was acknowledged in *Al-Bassam v Al-Bassam* [2004] WTLR 757 that there was some force in the argument that the English court would be wasting its time making any order in favour of the beneficiary of an English domiciliary where the assets were outside the jurisdiction if such an order would not be enforced in the jurisdiction where the assets were located. However, the judge, at paragraph 18, said that whatever the realpolitik of the situation, the argument was not acceptable in English law: if the deceased died domiciled in England, the English court would apply English law to the material validity of the will with the result that the claimant would be held entitled to the entire worldwide moveable estate. That was a separate matter from how the English court would treat a foreign judgment to the contrary. Such a judgment would be taken into account by the English court in working out the consequences of its own ruling, provided the foreign judgment complied with the basic requirements of English private international law. Unless and until the English court was faced by a foreign judgment which it recognised, it would simply apply its own choice of law.

9.26 As wealth management becomes increasingly international, disputes over forced heirship claims will inevitably increase. The growing recognition, too, of the uses and abuses of asset protection trusts for protecting family assets from forced heirship claims, and possibly to try to defeat claims under the Inheritance (Provision for Family and Dependants) Act 1975, is likely to give rise to an increased volume of litigation. Many offshore jurisdictions such as Cayman, Bahamas and Jersey have introduced anti-forced heirship provisions to defeat claims by disaffected heirs in jurisdictions which recognise entrenched inheritance rights.

Other problems with foreign estates

Situs

9.27 The situs of the assets is of fundamental significance in any dispute as it is the situs that will determine the choice of law involved.

9.28 The increasing sophistication of asset holding structures can, however, make it difficult to identify the situs of an asset, and it will often be relatively easy to change the situs by changing the structure. The situs of land will, of course, be obvious; but where, for instance, that land is held through a company with shares in bearer form the effective situs will be the place where the bearer shares are held.

9.29 It should be appreciated that the Brussels and Lugano Conventions on Jurisdiction and Enforcement of Judgments specifically exclude matters of succession, although of course attempts may be made to circumvent this by framing the claim as relating to something other than succession.

Identifying the assets and ownership structure

9.30 Civil law countries may not recognise trusts but they have a full range of their own structures – such as establishments and foundations – that will be unfamiliar to English practitioners and will need analysing to determine what, if anything, passes under the will. In extreme cases it may be that the structure is merely illusory and that a claim can be mounted – that what appears to be, for instance, a trust is a mere sham or nomineeship and that the assets devolve as free estate.

9.31 Again, foreign matrimonial property regimes may mean that the estate comprises only a proportion of the assets in the deceased's name – the rest being held by the testator effectively as nominee for the spouse.

Tax

9.32 The UK executors of an English domiciliary will be liable for inheritance tax on the worldwide estate under s 200 of the Inheritance Tax Act 1984 (IHTA 1984). However, inheritance tax on foreign property is not a 'testamentary or administration expense' (IHTA 1984, s 211(1)) and 'shall, where occasion requires, be repaid to [the personal representatives] by the person in whom the property to the value of which the tax is attributable is vested' (IHTA 1984, s 211(3)).

9.33 Whatever the strict legal position, however, the executors may find it difficult to recover the tax from a foreign beneficiary. They may also have real problems with the effect of double tax treaties and the interplay between the wording of the will and the incidence of any foreign tax.

9.34   There is also the issue of whether UK executors can be liable for, and should pay, foreign tax. It is a long-standing principle that the UK courts will not directly or indirectly enforce the penal, revenue, or other public laws of another country and for so long as foreign taxes are not enforceable in the UK, executors who do pay them without the agreement of the beneficiaries concerned are likely to be acting in breach of trust and may be unable to recoup the tax from the estate. This may be so even where there is a clause in the Will authorising them to pay foreign tax. In the Barbados case of *The Bank of Nova Scotia v Tremblay* [1998/9] 1 ITELR 673, the trustees were not permitted to pay foreign tax even though a clause empowering them to do so was included in the trust deed. In that case, the power was limited by the provision that an exercise of it had to be bona fide and the court held that it was 'difficult to envisage any circumstances in which the trustees can be said to be acting bona fide if the trustees satisfy any claims which (on the authority of the *Government of India v Taylor* case) they are not obligated by law to satisfy'. It may be different if the UK executors refund foreign beneficiaries for tax that they have already paid, or if they pay foreign tax that has to be paid so that the foreign beneficiaries may receive and keep their legacies under the will (see for example *Scottish National Orchestra Society Limited v Thomson's Executor* 1969 SLT 325).

9.35   Although the case of *QRS1 ApS & Others v Frandsen* [1999] STC 616 was authority for the proposition that this unenforceability survived the UK accession in 1972 to the EEC treaty, there was concern that the Finance Act 2002, s 134, opened the floodgates and enabled an EU Member State to request another Member State to attempt recovery where it appeared that the debtor resided or had assets there. The section itself, and the Mutual Assistance Recovery Directive referred to in the section, were unclear as to what taxes were covered by the mutual assistance procedures, but HMRC have subsequently confirmed that they do not consider that s 134 covers inheritance, estate or gift taxes.

9.36   Another development, the impact of which has yet to be considered by the court, is the effect of the anti-money laundering legislation previously in the Criminal Justice Act 1988 and now in the Proceeds of Crime Act 2002 (POCA 2002).

9.37   Under POCA 2002, s 329, a person commits an offence if he has possession of criminal property. Under POCA 2002, s 340(3) property is criminal property if it constitutes a person's benefit from criminal property, or it represents such a benefit (in whole or part and whether directly or indirectly) and where the alleged offender knows or suspects that it constitutes or represents such a benefit. Under s 340(2) criminal conduct is conduct which constitutes an offence in any part of the UK or would constitute an offence in part of the UK if it occurred there (subject to certain minor exceptions which will not be relevant for these purposes).

9.38 It seems to follow that where the non-payment of inheritance tax would be an offence in the UK, the non-payment of estate tax abroad would similarly constitute an offence for the purposes of POCA 2002.

9.39 It is of course a defence to have made an authorised disclosure (to the Serious Organised Crime Agency (SOCA)) under POCA 2002, s 338 and to have received the appropriate consent from SOCA before going ahead. Nonetheless, the fact that dealing with an estate on which foreign tax has not been paid may (technically or otherwise) constitute a criminal offence might well be an important factor in persuading a court to authorise executors to pay the foreign tax, notwithstanding that it would not be directly enforceable in England.

FOREIGN DECEASED: ENGLISH ASSETS

9.40 Just as an English grant has limited application abroad (but note that if England is the country of domicile many US States will accept an English grant, in the same way as they would accept a domiciliary grant from another US State), a foreign grant (or local equivalent) will usually be ineffective here, and to establish the right to receive or recover English situs assets there has to be an English grant of probate or letters of administration. Much the same questions arise with the UK estates of foreign based deceaseds as they do in respect of foreign estates.

A valid will that can be proved in England

9.41 Section 1 of the Wills Act 1963 is very wide and in general terms provides that a will is treated as properly executed if it was made in accordance with the internal law of a country where the will was executed, or where the testator was domiciled or habitually resident, or of which he was a national at the time the will was executed, or at his death.

9.42 Section 2 of the Wills Act 1963 adds some more ways in which a will may be validated, of which perhaps the most useful is s 2(b) which validates a will 'so far as it disposes of immovable property, if its execution conformed to the internal law in force in the territory where the property was situated'.

9.43 Section 2(b) is especially valuable in the not unusual situation where a foreign testator is persuaded that he needs an English form will to deal with English assets, but executes it abroad. Such a will may be invalid under s 1, but s 2(b) allows it to be at least partially effective.

Who can take out the grant

9.44 Possession being at the very least a substantial advantage in any succession dispute, it will often be crucial that the claimant, rather than the opposition, takes out the grant (but bear in mind that the person taking out the grant will be putting himself in a vulnerable position if he goes on to administer the UK estate or to distribute it in too partial a manner).

9.45 In the case of a foreign domiciled deceased the normal order of priority does not apply; instead the order set out in the Non Contentious Probate Rules 1987 (NCPR 1987), r 30 applies as follows:

(1) If the will is in English or Welsh, to the executor named therein or, if the will describes the duties of a named person in terms sufficient to constitute him executor according to the tenor of the will, to that person (NCPR 1987, r 30(3)(a)).

(2) Where the whole or substantially the whole of the estate in England and Wales consists of immovable property, a grant in respect of the whole estate may be made in accordance with the law which would have been applicable if the deceased had died domiciled in England and Wales (NCPR 1987, r 30(3)(b)).

(3) With a registrar's order:
    (a) the person entrusted with the administration of the estate by the court having jurisdiction at the place where the deceased died domiciled (NCPR 1987, r 30(1)(a));
    (b) where there is no such person so entrusted, to the person beneficially entitled to the estate by law of the place where the deceased died domiciled or, if there is more than one person so entitled, to such of them as the registrar may direct (NCPR 1987, r 30(1)(b));
    (c) such person as the registrar may direct (NCPR 1987, r 30(1)(c)).

9.46 Where there is a life or minority interest, the usual requirement for two administrators still applies and a grant made under NCPR 1987, r 30(1)(b) or (c) may be issued jointly with such person as the registrar may direct (NCPR 1987, r 30(2)).

9.47 In practice, where there is a will and the testator was domiciled in a common law jurisdiction then the will will normally appoint an executor so that NCPR 1987, r 30(3)(a) will operate. In the case of a civil or Islamic law jurisdiction, or an intestacy, r 30(1)(b) is usually applicable and evidence will be adduced that the applicant is one of the persons beneficially entitled to the estate under the law of the deceased's domicile.

Material validity of the will

9.48 The same factors as were discussed earlier in this chapter will be relevant. English law will apply to English immovables so that a foreign domiciliary may leave English realty to whomever he wants – although if this results in a smaller proportion of the worldwide estate passing to a reserved heir than he is entitled to, then the country of domicile may adjust the distribution of the home estate to compensate.

9.49 As regards movables, however, English conflict rules will apply the law of the testator's domicile at the date of death, so that a will that purports to ignore a reserved heir will be only partially effective.

9.50 As will be appreciated there are all kinds of complications that may arise, and disputes over material validity involving, as they may well do, both the domestic and private international laws of several jurisdictions can be complex and expensive to resolve – which perhaps explains the paucity of recent reported cases.

Matrimonial property

9.51 It must not be assumed that a foreign domiciliary – especially from a civil law jurisdiction – can deal with all his assets by will. The will can only bite on property that passed on the death, and this in turn is determined by the system of matrimonial property.

9.52 English law recognises the effect of a marriage contract or settlement (express or implied) enforceable under the law of the matrimonial domicile (the husband's domicile at the time of the marriage). It may well be, therefore, that a half share of the movables in the name of a civil law domiciliary spouse will not pass under the will at all but will remain the property of the other spouse.

9.53 The position in respect of English immovables is less clear. *De Nicols v Curlier* [1900] AC 21 applied the law of matrimonial domicile to English immovables but there is a view that the law of situs, ie English domestic law, might apply and it is surprising that there have been no recent reported cases on the point.

Part IV
PROBLEMS WITH THE WILL

Chapter 10

RECTIFICATION

10.1 Rectification is a long-standing equitable remedy allowing the court to reform or correct a document which does not give effect to the true intentions of the parties to it. However, apart from a limited power to omit words (see *Re Morris* [1971] P 62) included by fraud or mistake on the basis that there was a want of knowledge and approval of such words, rectification has been applicable to wills only since the Administration of Justice Act 1982 (AJA 1982), s 20(1) came into force on 1 January 1983.

10.2 AJA 1982, s 20(1) states that:

'If a court is satisfied that a will is so expressed that it fails to carry out the testator's intentions, in consequence –

(a) of a clerical error; or
(b) of a failure to understand his instructions,

it may order that the will shall be rectified so as to carry out his intentions.'

10.3 The jurisdiction is narrowly defined, and is not available where the draftsman's error is one of legal understanding (see **10.19**).

WHAT THE COURT IS REQUIRED TO ASK

10.4 Three distinct questions arise (per Chadwick J in *Re Segelman* [1996] 2 WLR 173).

(1) What were the testator's intentions (if any) with regard to the dispositions in respect of which rectification is sought?

(2) Does the will fail to carry out those intentions?

(3) If so, is that failure due to:
   (a) clerical error; or
   (b) a failure on the part of the draftsman to understand those instructions?

CLERICAL ERROR

10.5 In *Wordingham v Royal Exchange Trust Company* [1992] 2 WLR 496 the draftsman of an updating will inadvertently left out a clause exercising a testamentary power of appointment in favour of the testatrix's husband. The clause had appeared in two earlier wills. The omission 'was an error made in the process of recording the intended words of the testatrix and ... constituted a clerical error within AJA 1982, s 20(1)(a)'. Similarly, in *Chittock v Stevens* [2000] WTLR 643 which was argued solely on the preliminary issue of applying out of time, a gift in favour of the surviving spouse of all real and personal property had been omitted.

10.6 To establish that a clerical error has been made it needs to be shown that the draftsman failed to apply his mind to the significance and effect of offending words.

10.7 The failure can extend to the inclusion of an entire clause. In *Re Segelman* the testator had wished to set up a trust fund for needy members of his family. The will contained relatively complicated provisions that were themselves the subject of a construction summons. When preparing a draft, the solicitor had added a proviso whose effect was that issue of certain family members could not benefit during the lifetime of their parent. The proviso should have been deleted in the light of the testator's further instructions. Chadwick J was satisfied that rectification was available in those circumstances to delete the offending words. The court's jurisdiction is not limited to transcribing errors, but:

> 'extends to cases where the relevant provision in the will, by reason of which the will is so expressed that it fails to carry out the testator's intentions, has been introduced, or, as in the present case, has not been deleted, in circumstances in which the draftsman has not applied his mind to its significance or effect.'

10.8 Nicholls J stated in *Re Williams* [1985] 1 WLR 905 that rectification is available for homemade wills. Although his comments were *obiter* there appears no reason to consider they are incorrect.

FAILURE TO UNDERSTAND INSTRUCTIONS

10.9 Where a solicitor applies his mind to the meaning and effect of words used but achieves the wrong result because he misunderstood the testator, AJA 1982, s 20(1)(b) may apply.

10.10 The wording of sub-section (b) clearly envisages third-party intervention, and therefore will not avail those seeking to rectify a homemade will.

10.11 To succeed an applicant should be able to show:

(1) what the testator's intentions were with regard to the dispositions in respect of which rectification is sought;

(2) that the will fails to reflect those intentions;

(3) what were the testator's instructions;

(4) that the draftsman misunderstood those instructions; and

(5) that the failure of the will to reflect the testator's intentions was due to a failure on the part of the draftsman to understand those instructions.

10.12 *Goodman v Goodman* [2006] WTLR 1807 is the first reported decision where rectification was ordered on the basis of failure to understand the testator's instructions. The testator and his wife, Jennifer, had entered into an arrangement with the testator's father, Geoffrey, whereby Jennifer purchased the latter's property and, inter alia, paid Geoffrey £3,000 per month (from which a monthly rent of £1,000 was deducted).

10.13 The testator's will contained provision for a monthly payment of £2,000 to his father until such time as the latter ceased to reside at the property. After the testator's death in a car accident Jennifer applied to delete the legacy, claiming the intention was merely to record the lifetime transaction she had entered into with Geoffrey. Geoffrey did not advance a positive case but, unsuccessfully, opposed the claim on the basis that Jennifer could not establish the 'convincing' evidence required to rectify the will.

10.14 The relevant time for determining the testator's intention is the time of execution of the will, not the time the instructions were given. In *Goodman* a crucial part of Geoffrey's case was that Jennifer could not show that at the point when the testator executed his will he did not intend to leave his father a legacy (*Goodman v Goodman Presentation to Withers LLP*, 23 August 2006, Richard Wilson, 9 Stone Buildings). There had been considerable delay between instructions for the will, its preparation and execution and Geoffrey argued that there was sufficient basis to infer that the testator may have changed his mind.

BURDEN OF PROOF

10.15 The probability that a will, executed in circumstances of some formality, reflects the testator's intentions is 'usually of such weight that convincing evidence to the contrary is necessary' (per Chadwick J in *Re Segelman* [1996] 2 WLR 173 (at 184)).

10.16 The usual civil burden of proof, ie on the balance of probability, applies. However, the circumstances of formality surrounding execution mean that, generally speaking, the testator will be deemed to have ensured that the will records what was intended. The more obvious the error, the more convincing the evidence will need to be in order to persuade the court that rectification is appropriate, as in *Bell v Georgiou* [2002] WTLR 1105 where Blackburne J referred to the 'blindingly obvious' nature of the alleged error.

10.17 In *Re Grattan* [2001] WTLR 1305, where husband and wife had made mirror wills incorporating a life interest in favour of the survivor, the widow contended that the instructions had been that the survivor was to take outright. Behrens J preferred the draftsman's evidence to that of the widow, making reference to the deceased's reputation as an intelligent businessman, the relatively straightforward nature of the will, and the draftsman's reputation as an experienced solicitor, who had made contemporaneous notes of his meeting with the couple and prepared the wills within a short time of receiving instructions.

10.18 A review of the will-drafting file may reveal records of discussions or correspondence with the testator regarding the will which reinforce the presumption that the testator had read the document, thus raising the barrier that any applicant needs to overcome. The importance of retaining careful records of discussions and correspondence with the testator cannot be overstated.

THE DIVIDING LINE WITH NEGLIGENCE

10.19 Virtually every case of rectification of a professionally drafted will involves an original negligent act by the professional. In *Wordingham v Royal Exchange Trust Company* [1992] 2 WLR 496, without the power to rectify, the draftsman would have faced a very considerable claim from the disappointed husband. However, not every negligently drafted will is capable of being rectified.

10.20 *Bell v Georgiou* [2002] WTLR 1105 is a classic example of a draftsman, under pressure and conscious of the prevalent professional negligence claim culture, for whom rectification initially at least appears preferable.

10.21 *Walker v Medlicott* [1999] 1 WLR 727 is authority for the proposition that where rectification is available it should be pursued in preference to an action in negligence (avoiding the risk of double recovery). It is also an example of where there was a possibility of rectification (the issue was not decided), but the draftsman was not considered to have been negligent.

10.22 The claimant, the testatrix's favourite nephew, sought damages in negligence from the solicitor for the alleged omission of a specific devise of house and contents. The Court of Appeal upheld dismissal of the negligence claim. Sir Christopher Slade stated that, despite strong hearsay evidence about the deceased's intentions which led him to conclude that on the balance of probabilities there had been a misunderstanding, the evidence was insufficient to uphold any allegation of negligence. (See R Kerridge and AHR Brierley, 'Mistakes in Wills: Rectify and be Damned', *Cambridge Law Journal* 2003, 62(3), 550 at 575 et seq for criticism of the decision.)

10.23 The appeal also failed because the nephew had not mitigated his damages (if any) by first issuing proceedings for rectification, although Simon Brown LJ made clear that there may be circumstances where an action in negligence can be preferred to a rectification claim. In *Horsfall v Haywards (a firm)* [1999] 1 FLR 1182 the defendant solicitors had drawn up a will containing an absolute devise of the home to the testator's second wife, rather than a life interest as instructed. By the time the disappointed remaindermen realised the position, the time limit for rectification had long expired, the property had been sold and the proceeds remitted abroad, and the second wife was resistant to any claim for return of the funds. Accordingly, rectification would not have been an effective remedy.

10.24 Section 20(1) does not avail the draftsman who, understanding the testator's instructions, misunderstands the significance of words chosen, particularly through a misunderstanding of the law. Thus the court's power is narrower than was envisaged by the Law Reform Committee in its Report on the Interpretation of Wills (1973, Cmnd 5301, at paras 20–21), and contrasts with the position concerning inter vivos instruments which may be rectified where there has been a mistake over the legal effect of language used.

10.25 The contrast cited by Evans-Lombe QC in *Wordingham v Royal Exchange Trust Company* [1992] 2 WLR 496 between 'clerical error' and 'an error made in carrying [the testator's] intentions into effect by the drafter's choice of words' marks a boundary beyond which the disappointed beneficiary's remedy lies in negligence and rectification is not available.

COSTS AND INDEPENDENT LEGAL ADVICE

10.26 Where a professional fails to record a testator's intentions accurately, those adversely affected by any proposed rectification may wish to take their own independent legal advice. In the context of a professionally drafted will, it can invariably be argued that rectification arises either through a clerical failure on the part of the draftsman, or a failure to take proper instructions and is then negligent. Clearly (per Sir Christopher Slade), where fault can be established the costs of rectification proceedings may be recovered from the draftsman.

10.27 The draftsman will often be involved in the estate administration and thus will indeed be the first to realise an error has occurred. In that event, a reasoned letter containing all the facts, with an offer to pay reasonable legal costs for the beneficiary (or for a representative beneficiary) to take independent legal advice, may well be the most cost effective route.

10.28 The strategy for anyone advising the potential beneficiary of a rectification claim must be to argue that the error requiring rectification was negligent, in order to maximise the probability of a contribution to legal costs. However, those who fight a weak claim in the expectation that indemnity policies will in any event pick up the costs may be heading for disappointment.

10.29 In *Goodman v Goodman* [2006] WTLR 1807 (see **10.12**) the judge ordered that, as between Jennifer and Geoffrey, there be no order as to costs. The defendant had deliberately chosen not to advance a positive case to minimise the risk of an adverse costs order. In addition, the judge ordered that the firm responsible for the drafting show cause why it should not pay the costs of the claim.

PROCEDURE

Uncontested

10.30 If no probate action has been started, an application for rectification supported by affidavit may be made to the Probate Registrar (Non-Contentious Probate Rules 1987 (NCPR 1987), r 55). The affidavit should set out the grounds of the application, exhibit the will in its original form and an engrossment in the proposed rectified form, provide evidence of the testator's intentions, and identify the relevant sub-section of AJA 1982, s 20. Unopposed applications may be made before or after issue of the grant.

10.31 Notice should be given to everyone whose interest may be prejudiced, and any written responses exhibited to the affidavit. As a matter of good practice the notice should set out clearly the facts on which the application is based, state the intended course of action, and expressly invite written replies; the notice itself should be exhibited. The Registrar has authority to waive the requirement for notice to be given, which may be of practical benefit, for instance, where inadvertently included beneficiaries are hard to trace. If the application is unopposed, rectification may be ordered.

10.32 Where the will is rectified before the grant issues an engrossment of the rectified version should accompany the application for probate (or letters of administration with will annexed); see NCPR 1987, r 11(2).

10.33 Where the grant has already issued, the original grant should be lodged at the Principal Registry of the Family Division for filing and a memorandum of the order endorsed on, or permanently annexed to, the grant under which the estate is administered (see CPR 57 PD 11.1).

Contested

10.34 A claim will need to be issued. CPR, r 57.12 applies. Part 57 does not specify which form should be used to issue the application, or whether Part 7 procedure applies. It is submitted that, in common with probate claims, with which Part 57 deals in more detail, Form N2 should be used and Part 7 procedure applies. Applications should be issued in the High Court, Chancery Division, or (if the net estate does not exceed £30,000) a county court where there is also a High Court Chancery District Registry (currently Birmingham, Bristol, Cardiff, Leeds, Liverpool, Manchester, Newcastle Upon Tyne and Preston), and in the Central London County Court.

10.35 Every personal representative must be joined as a party to a claim for rectification (CPR, r 57.12(2)) although their role is likely to be one of neutrality (see below).

10.36 The practice direction directs that if the claimant is the person to whom the grant was made he must, unless the court orders otherwise, lodge the probate or letters of administration with will annexed with the court when the claim form is issued. If a defendant has the probate or letters of administration in his possession or under his control, he must, unless the court orders otherwise, lodge it within 14 days after service of the claim form on him.

10.37 The claim will then follow the normal procedure set out at CPR Part 7. A precedent claim form and witness statement in support can be found at Appendix 2.

10.38 CPR PD 2B 5.1 excludes a Master or District Judge from hearing a rectification claim without the consent of the Vice Chancellor.

10.39 Rectification is hostile litigation and it is not for the personal representatives to actively pursue rectification unless they accept the risk of personal liability for costs.

COMPROMISE AND INHERITANCE TAX

10.40 Litigation is always uncertain, and parties are often well-advised to compromise a claim for rectification as much as any other dispute. The usual expectation that parties will seek to resolve disputes before litigating applies.

10.41 It may be advantageous to embody the terms of compromise in a Deed of Variation to avoid the expense of an application although where all parties are of age and capacity that degree of formality may be an unnecessary expense. Rectification by court order is retrospective. Where non-exempt beneficiaries bring a rectification claim which has merit, and to which the defendant beneficiaries are exempt, there is a particular benefit to reaching agreement outside the formal court process so as to preserve inheritance tax advantages.

TIME LIMITS AND PROTECTION FOR PERSONAL REPRESENTATIVES

10.42 AJA 1982, s 20(2) provides that an application shall not be made after 6 months from the grant of representation without permission of the court. In *Chittock v Stevens* [2000] WTLR 643, on an application under s 20(2), Donaldson QC held that the court should follow the principles laid down by Megarry VC in *Re Salmon* [1981] Ch 167 when considering an application out of time under the Inheritance (Provision for Family and Dependants) Act 1975.

10.43 The court's discretion is unfettered and the burden is on the claimant but the time limit is a substantive provision rather than a procedural time limit. Therefore the claimant must make out a substantial case for the time limit to be extended. The promptness of the application and whether negotiations have commenced within the time limit will be material. What appears to be particularly relevant is the question of distribution – where the estate is yet to be distributed defendants will have much greater difficulty in arguing that unfair detriment is caused by the court exercising its discretion positively.

10.44 AJA 1982, s 20(3) provides personal representatives with protection against liability for wrongful distribution where a will is rectified subsequent to the court giving permission for an application brought after the end of 6 months from the issue of the grant. That protection does not prevent recovery from the original beneficiaries by any person benefiting under rectification (subject of course to a change of position based defence).

10.45 A claim can be validly issued within the six-month period, but not served for a further 4 months (CPR, r 7.5). Of course it is possible for further extensions to be allowed but it is difficult to envisage a court not coming to the aid of a personal representative who has distributed the estate in ignorance of a validly issued claim that has yet to be served.

PERSONAL REPRESENTATIVES' DUTIES AND DISCLOSURE OF WILL DRAFTING FILES

10.46 Although personal representatives are necessary parties to an application, rectification is hostile litigation, and the authors' view is that the personal representatives should not take an active role unless they accept the risk of personal liability for costs (although, if all beneficiaries agree to such a course, a more cost-effective route is probably for the personal representatives to bring the application since they are likely to have all the information to hand).

10.47 The authors consider that, where there is a dispute over whether or not a will should be rectified, disclosure of the original file should be made by personal representatives to any party having an interest in the outcome, and, where appropriate, a statement provided detailing the instructions and drafting. This is in line with the principles espoused by the Court of Appeal in *Larke v Nugus* [2000] WTLR 1033 where Brandon LJ commented that 'when there is litigation about a will, every effort should be made by the executors to avoid costly litigation' (see **12.72–12.75**)

10.48 A personal representative who played no role in the will-drafting may reasonably believe that a rectifiable error has been made. It may be going too far to suggest that an executor has a positive duty to notify third parties who do not appear in the will that they may have the right to seek rectification. However, on taking out the grant an executor swears that he is exhibiting not merely the last will of the deceased but also the true will, and that he will administer the estate according to law. Paying out to the wrong beneficiaries or in the wrong amounts, whether deliberately or because of mistakes, may constitute devastavit (a breach of duty to administer the estate) (see also **13.1–13.9**). There is a lack of case law on the point, but a personal representative who fails at least to investigate in appropriate circumstances may incur, not merely criticism, but also a liability to disappointed beneficiaries or costs penalties in resulting litigation.

10.49 A belief that a will should be rectified may be used by a disappointed beneficiary who is also a personal representative to delay the issue of a grant for a perceived advantage in negotiation. In the authors' experience, no prejudice can be read into an application for probate made by that personal representative who has notified other parties, and the registrar, of their belief that the will should be rectified but where the application for probate is being brought to facilitate estate administration whilst discussions between the affected parties on any rectification application take place.

SIGNING THE WRONG DOCUMENT

10.50 The English court expressly refused to save a will in *In the Estate of Meyer* [1908] P 353. Here two sisters had executed codicils in similar terms but by mistake each sister executed the codicil intended for, and purporting to be, that of the other. That however predates the AJA 1982 and the modern court may be prepared to be creative. There is Canadian and, more recently, in *Re Vautier's Estate* (2000–01) 3 ITELR 566, Jersey precedent allowing rectification in such circumstances.

HM REVENUE & CUSTOMS

10.51 HM Revenue & Customs should be invited to join in proceedings which may affect it but cannot be joined without its consent.

Chapter 11

CONSTRUCTION

11.1 The key principle of construction is that effect must be given to the intention of the testator.

11.2 The intention (subject to rules regarding extrinsic evidence) must lie in the will itself.

BACKGROUND

11.3 When construing a document to determine its effect the Chancery Division acts as a court of construction (whereas when considering which of the deceased's papers are his last testamentary instruments the court is acting as a court of probate, historically the Ecclesiastical Courts).

11.4 In construing the will, the testator's intention is ascertained from the will itself and the words 'used'. In *Perrin v Morgan* [1943] AC 399, Viscount Simon LC stated that:

> 'the fundamental rule in construing the language of a will is to put on the words used the meaning which, having regard to the terms of the will, the testator intended. The question is not, of course, what the testator meant to do when he made his will, but what the written words he uses mean in the particular case – what are the "expressed intentions" of the testator.'

RESOLVING NON-CONTENTIOUS CONSTRUCTION ISSUES

11.5 Section 48 of the Administration of Justice Act 1985 enables the High Court to authorise action to be taken in reliance on counsel's opinion. The section provides that:

> '(1) Where –
> (a) any question of construction has arisen out of the terms of a will or a trust; and
> (b) an opinion in writing given by a person who has a 10 year High Court qualification, within the meaning of section 71 of the Courts and Legal Services Act 1990 has been obtained on that question by the personal representatives or trustees under the will or trust,

the High Court may, on the application of the personal representatives or trustees and without hearing argument, make an order authorising those persons to take such steps in reliance on the said opinion as are specified in the order.

(2)   The High Court shall not make an order under subsection (1) if it appears to the court that a dispute exists which would make it inappropriate for the court to make the order without hearing argument.'

11.6   The procedure is governed by CPR Part 64 and is set out at paras 26.37 to 26.42 of the Chancery Guide (see www.hmcourts-service.co.uk/cms/1231. htm). A CPR Part 8 claim form is issued without naming a defendant (under CPR, r 8.2A) and no separate application for permission to serve on anyone is required. The claim should be supported by a witness statement or affidavit attaching:

(1)   copies of all relevant documents;

(2)   instructions to a person with a 10-year High Court qualification;

(3)   the qualified person's opinion; and

(4)   draft terms of the desired order.

11.7   The witness statement should state:

(1)   the names of all persons who may be affected by the order sought;

(2)   all admissible surrounding circumstances relevant to construing the documents;

(3)   the date of qualification of the qualified person and his or her experience in the construction of trust documents;

(4)   the approximate value of the fund or property in question; and

(5)   whether it is known to the applicant that a dispute exists and, if so, details of such a dispute.

A precedent claim form and witness statement in support are at Appendix 2.

11.8   The papers will first be considered by the Master who, if he considers the evidence is complete, will send the file to the judge.

11.9   The judge may direct service of notices under CPR, r 19.8A (power to make judgments binding on non-parties) or request further information as required.

11.10 If, following service of any CPR, r 19.8A notice, any acknowledgement of service is received, the claimant must apply to the Master (on notice to the acknowledging party) for direction and, ordinarily, the matter will proceed as a CPR Part 8 claim.

11.11 If, on hearing, the judge considers any party who entered an acknowledgement of service has no 'reasonably tenable arguments contrary to the qualified person's opinion' in exercise of his discretion the judge may order that party to pay any costs thrown away, or part thereof.

RESOLVING CONTENTIOUS CONSTRUCTION ISSUES

11.12 CPR Part 64 governs any contentious construction disputes applying to claims for the court to determine any question arising in 'the administration of the estates of a deceased person' and must be made by issuing a CPR Part 8 claim form.

11.13 The CPR Part 8 procedure is followed because, usually, there is no (or no substantial) dispute of fact. It may be required where agreement of all beneficiaries cannot be obtained as to how the will is to be interpreted (because there are conflicting views or because there are minor, unborn or unascertained beneficiaries whose agreement is unobtainable).

11.14 Usually the representatives bring the claim with at least one beneficiary interested in each possible answer to the question of construction joined as defendant. It is usual, pursuant to CPR, r 19.7(2), for a representative order to be made and similarly where persons are unborn, cannot be found or cannot easily be ascertained.

11.15 The defendants must acknowledge service and state whether the defendant contests the claim (CPR, r 8.3(2)) and, if wishing to rely on written evidence, file it when filing the acknowledgement of service (CPR, r 8.5(4)). The Practice Direction provides for agreement or applications for an extension of time at CPR PD8, 7.4 and 7.5.

11.16 The Master or district judge, when satisfied that the evidence is complete, will adjourn the case to a judge for decision, having no jurisdiction to determine questions as to the construction of a document (CPR Part 2 PD2B, 5.1).

GENERAL RULES AS TO EVIDENCE

11.17 Extrinsic evidence, including evidence of the testator's intention, may be admitted to assist in the interpretation of a will under s 21 of the Administration of Justice Act 1982 only:

(1)   insofar as any part of the will is meaningless;

(2)   insofar as the language used in a part of it is ambiguous on the face of it;
      and

(3)   insofar as evidence, other than evidence of the testator's intention, shows
      that the language used in any part of it is ambiguous in the light of
      surrounding circumstances.

Chapter 12

VALIDITY DISPUTES

12.1 The will making process is an area ripe for dispute – the key witness, the deceased testator, being no longer available.

VALIDITY: ESSENTIAL ELEMENTS

Due execution

Basic principles

12.2 The formal requirements for executing a will are set out at Wills Act 1837, s 9 as amended by Administration of Justice Act 1982 (AJA 1982).

'No will shall be valid unless –

(a) it is in writing, and signed by the testator, or by some other person in his presence and by his direction; and

(b) it appears that the testator intended by his signature to give effect to the will; and

(c) the signature is made or acknowledged by the testator in the presence of two or more witnesses present at the same time; and

(d) each witness either -
  (i) attests and signs the will; or
  (ii) acknowledges his signature, in the presence of the testator (but not necessarily in the presence of any other witness),

but no form of attestation shall be necessary.'

Signature

12.3 The signature of the testator can be merely a mark (for example a thumb print as in *Borman v Lel, In the Estate of Parsons* [2002] WTLR 237). The key requirement is that the testator intended by his signature to give effect to the will.

12.4 A will or codicil no longer needs be signed 'at the foot or end thereof' (after the AJA 1982, s 17) and a testator's writing of his name as part of the attestation clause has been held to be a signature intended to give effect to a will (*Weatherhill v Pearce* [1995] 1 WLR 592).

Witnesses and attestation

12.5 Two or more witnesses must be present at the same time when the testator signs his will.

12.6 The witnesses must then attest or acknowledge the will in the presence of the testator but not necessarily in each other's presence.

12.7 'Acknowledge', introduced by the AJA 1982, is liberally interpreted. In *Couser v Couser* [1996] 1 WLR 1301, one of the witnesses to the will was deemed to have acknowledged that she had witnessed the will by her protests as to its validity at the time of execution.

12.8 A formal attestation clause is not required by law but will assist in proving the will if there is any dispute at a later stage. For example, in *Re Denning, Harnett v Elliott* [1958] 2 All ER 1 two names, in different handwriting from each other and from the testator's signature, on the reverse side of a will, were found to be there for the purpose of attesting the will.

Presumption of due execution

12.9 Where 'on its face' a will is properly attested and executed there is a presumption of due execution.

12.10 The presumption is rebuttable only by the strongest evidence. In the absence of the strongest evidence, the intention of the witness to attest is inferred from the presence of the testator's signature on the will, the attestation clause and the signature of the witness. The court's stance on this issue has recently been reinforced in *Sherrington v Sherrington* [2005] WTLR 587 and *Channon v Perkins* (a firm) [2006] WTLR 425.

12.11 In *Sherrington v Sherrington* the first instance judge found that the witnesses signing the will had not intended to attest the will (neither knowing that the document they were signing was a will, nor understanding why they were signing the will). The Court of Appeal overturned the first instance decision on the basis that the witness evidence was 'open to serious doubt'.

12.12 In *Channon v Perkins* both witnesses were sure that they had not signed a document in the testator's presence. The first instance judge held that the requirements of the Wills Act 1837, s 9 had not been satisfied. The Court of Appeal overturned the judge's decision and characterised the evidence of the witnesses as a mere failure to recollect.

12.13 These cases show that challenges on technical grounds based on due execution are not finding favour with the Court of Appeal without very strong positive evidence in support. Other recent cases where the challenge has failed are *Borman v Lel, In the Estate of Parsons* [2002] WTLR 237, *Sohal v Sohal* [2002] EWCA Civ 1297 and *In the matter of the estate of Yvonne Cynthia*

Sholto-Small (unreported) 2002. The message of the Court of Appeal appears to be that witnesses need to positively remember a specific event where something went wrong with the execution.

12.14 In the case of *Murrin v Matthews* [2006] EWHC 3419, Guy Newey QC found the presumption was rebutted. The case involved a will in which everything was left to one beneficiary. Although signed by two witnesses, there was no address given for them, nor could they be found. Guy Newey QC considered that the beneficiary of the contested will was 'overwhelmingly likely' to have been involved in the preparation of the will. No evidence was produced by the attesting witnesses as to its execution and therefore the will was found to be invalid.

Revocation

12.15 Only marriage or civil partnership automatically revoke a will (Wills Act 1837, ss 18, 18B).

12.16 Wills Act 1837, s 19 states that no will is to be revoked by presumption from altered circumstances.

12.17 Other than as a result of marriage or civil partnership, a will may only be revoked in accordance with Wills Act 1837, s 20, namely:

(1) by another will or codicil;

(2) by some writing declaring an intention to revoke and executed in the same manner as a will; or

(3) by burning, tearing, or otherwise destroying by the testator, or by someone in his presence and by his direction, with the intention of revoking.

12.18 Whether a subsequent testamentary document revokes a will is a matter of construction.

12.19 Similarly, the question with a subsequent will is whether the requisite intention to revoke existed. There is long-standing authority (*Lowthorpe-Lutwidge v Lowthorpe-Lutwidge* [1935] P 151) that the courts can reject an express clause of revocation if there is evidence that the deceased did not know and approve of it or did not in fact intend to revoke the earlier will.

> '... it is a heavy burden upon a plaintiff who comes into this Court to say: "I agree that the testator was in every way fit to make a will, I agree that the will which he has made is perfectly clear and unambiguous in its terms, I agree that it contains a revocatory clause in simple words: nevertheless I say that he did not really intend to revoke the earlier bequests in earlier wills."'

12.20 In *Lamothe v Lamothe and Others* [2006] WTLR 1431, the court preferred evidence that a 1995 will executed in Dominica had been intended to revoke the earlier 1993 will.

12.21 In examining acts of destruction, the court must consider whether the act was accompanied by the requisite intention to revoke.

12.22 The testator must have had capacity at the point of revocation in accordance with the tests in *Banks v Goodfellow* (1869-70) LR 5 QB 549 (see *Re Sabitini* (1970) 114 SJ 35) (see **12.28**).

Burden of proof and presumptions

12.23 Where there is proof of due execution, the burden lies on the person challenging the will to prove revocation.

Destroyed will

12.24 However, where a will is found destroyed after the testator's death, it is presumed that the testator destroyed it with the intention of revoking it, and the onus is on those seeking to propound the will to prove there was no intention to revoke.

Missing will

12.25 Similarly, where an original will was known to have existed and was last seen in the hands of the testator, but is missing on death, there is a rebuttable presumption that the will was destroyed by the testator with the intention of revoking it. The onus is on the propounder to show that there was no intention to revoke.

12.26 *Rowe v Clarke* [2006] WTLR 347, reiterates that 'the strength of the presumption depends on the level or degree of security with which the testator had custody of the will during his lifetime'. In that case, the judge found that the will, known to be in the hands of the testator during his lifetime but missing after his death, was not carefully looked after and that the testator was disorganised. The presumption of revocation was weak and was rebutted. However, in *Wren v Wren* [2007] WTLR 531 the presumption was held to have been rebutted by the production of a copy will even though the judge found that the testator was 'a hoarder' and took considerable care with 'what he regarded as important documents' and in spite of the findings of the joint handwriting expert that there was strong support for the conclusion that the signature on the copy will was not genuine and was a simulation.

12.27 A missing later will only revokes a valid earlier will if there is 'stringent and conclusive' evidence either of an express revocation clause in the later will or of inconsistency between its provisions and those of the earlier will (*Re Wyatt deceased* [1952] 1 All ER 1030). This was applied in *Broadway v Fernandes* [2007] EWHC 684 (Ch).

Testamentary capacity

12.28 The testator/testatrix must be of sound mind, memory and understanding when the will or codicil was made. In making a will he/she must, in accordance with the requirements formulated in *Banks v Goodfellow* (1869–70) LR 5 QB 549:

(1)   understand the nature of the act and its effects;

(2)   understand the extent of the property of which he/she is disposing;

(3)   be able to comprehend and appreciate the claims to which he/she ought to give effect;

and must not be affected by any 'disorder of the mind' that shall:

> 'poison his affections, pervert his sense of right, or prevent the exercise of his natural faculties—that no insane delusion shall influence his will in disposing of his property and bring about a disposal of it which, if the mind had been sound, would not have been made.'

Presumption of capacity

12.29 If the will appears rational and contains no irregularities it will be presumed that the testator had testamentary capacity.

12.30 If the testator has a history of mental illness, or there is evidence of confusion or memory loss, it will be for those persons seeking to rely on the document to establish capacity (see *Vaughan v Vaughan* [2005] WTLR 401).

12.31 Mere eccentricity does not rebut the presumption of capacity but an irrational disposition will. In *Sharp and Bryson v Adam and Others* [2006] WTLR 1059 the judge held that the presumption of capacity was rebutted as a result of the severe damage suffered to the testator's brain and the 'unusual' decision to leave nothing to his children. Once rebutted, the judge found that the propounders of the will were not able to prove that the testator had capacity. Although the two solicitors and GP who attended the execution agreed that the testator was lucid, the absence of explanation for his decision to exclude his daughters from his will meant that the judge found his decision to be so remarkable that he could not have had the capacity to come to a rational decision. The Court of Appeal upheld the decision despite their finding that the solicitor draftsman did 'everything conceivably possible ... to satisfy herself that [the testator] had testamentary capacity'.

12.32 It is presumed that the testator has capacity to revoke an existing will by destruction or otherwise unless evidence is produced to the contrary. The tests in *Banks v Goodfellow* apply equally to revocation (see *Re Sabatini* (1970) 114 SJ 35).

Proof of actual understanding or inference of capacity

12.33 Where the presumption has been rebutted, proof of actual understanding of the nature of the *Banks v Goodfellow* factors is not required. In *Hoff v Atherton* [2005] WTLR 99 the testatrix was suffering from mild to moderate Alzheimer's dementia. The Court of Appeal held that it would be absurd for the law to insist on proof of actual understanding in every case. If there was evidence of such understanding this would suffice but often there would not be and the court should look at all the evidence to see what inferences should be drawn.

12.34 Therefore the question is not whether a person actually understands the nature of the act of making a will, the nature and extent of property disposed of and the people who might be expected to benefit but whether he/she has the mental capacity to do so.

12.35 The complexity of the estate will be taken into account in deciding whether an inference of capacity can be drawn. In *McClintock v Calderwood* [2005] EWHC 836 the testator's confusion was held to be intermittent and not sufficient to preclude his having mental capacity. The judge noted that the testator's estate was not complex and would not have been difficult for the testator to understand.

Capacity at execution

12.36 Capacity should be proved both when instructions (if any) were given and when the document was executed. The degree of capacity required on execution is less than that required when instructions are given. The case *Clancy v Clancy* [2003] WTLR 1097 reaffirmed the principle in *Parker v Felgate* (1883) LR 8 PD 171 that if a testator does not have testamentary capacity when executing a will it will be valid so long as the testator had testamentary capacity when instructions were given and, on execution, had the capacity to understand that he was executing a will he believed to have been prepared in accordance with those instructions.

The effect of drugs or alcohol

12.37 In *Chana v Chana* [2001] WTLR 220, the judge found that for drunkenness to vitiate the execution of a will it must have such an effect on the testator that he does not know the nature and quality of the act which he is carrying out. As the testator had capacity when giving instructions for the will, his drunkenness at the point of execution was not enough to affect his ability to execute the will.

Knowledge and approval

12.38 The court must be satisfied that a testator knew and approved the contents of his will. Where a testator possessed testamentary capacity and the will was duly executed there is a presumption of knowledge and approval of its contents.

12.39 In certain circumstances, for example, where the testator is blind or where a beneficiary has been involved in the preparation or execution of the will, the court will require affirmative proof of knowledge and approval. *Barry v Butlin* (1838) 2 Moo PCC 480 dealt with the latter situation. The court held that:

> 'If a party writes or prepares a will, under which he takes a benefit, that is a circumstance that ought generally to excite the suspicion of the court, and calls upon it to be vigilant and jealous in examining the evidence in support of the instrument, in favour of which it ought not to pronounce unless the suspicion is removed, and it is judicially satisfied that the paper propounded does express the true will of the deceased.' (at 481, Mr Baron Parke)

12.40 Once the suspicion of the court is excited, it will be for those propounding to will to prove knowledge and approval.

12.41 The greater the suspicion, the greater the burden on the proponent of the will to dispel that suspicion. In *Hoff v Atherton* the degree of suspicion raised by virtue of the *Barry v Butlin* principle was considered low and to have been dispelled by the propounder. In *Vaughan and Others v Vaughan* [2005] WTLR 401 the judge found that the case 'bristle[d] with suspicious circumstances'; instructions for the will were given by the proponent; the testatrix took no advice in relation to the will; the proponent chose to ignore the suggestion that a medical opinion should be obtained as to the testatrix's capacity; and the will was not read over to the testatrix at execution. The proponent did not prove the righteousness of the transaction and the judge refused to grant probate.

12.42 Knowledge and approval will be easier to prove if the will is a simple document. In *Hart v Dabbs* [2001] WTLR 527 the will was not a complicated document and thus the burden of positively proving knowledge and approval was discharged (even though the coroner's jury had returned a verdict of unlawful killing in respect of the testator's death and the beneficiary of the will, who had also prepared the will, was the prime suspect). The simplicity of the will was an important point in *Sherrington v Sherrington* leading the Court of Appeal to reject the first instance decision that the deceased had lacked the requisite knowledge and approval.

Solicitors benefiting under a will

12.43 The Solicitors' Code of Conduct 2007 sub-rule 3.04 states that, where a client wishes to make a gift to his/her solicitor and the gift is significant having regard to the size of the client's likely estate and the reasonable expectations of prospective beneficiaries, the client must take independent advice. A 'significant amount' is defined for the purposes of 3.04 as 'anything more than a token gift' and the Code states that 'if … anything more than a token amount is accepted without the client having separate advice (other than where … acting for a family member as permitted by 3.04) [the solicitor] may be exposed to allegations of misconduct' (Solicitors' Code of Conduct 2007, sub-rule 3.04, p 52, para 59).

12.44 Sub-rule 3.04 allows a solicitor to prepare a will for a family member under which that solicitor receives a significant gift without requiring the client to seek independent advice on that gift. However, the Code states that 'extreme caution should always be exercised in these circumstances as your ability to give independent dispassionate advice could easily be undermined by your relationship with others within, and outside, the family'. If, having considered the risk of conflict and the reasonable expectations of other prospective beneficiaries, it seems that the benefit to the solicitor is in any way disproportionately large, the solicitor should ensure that the client is separately advised on the gift. The Code states that in the event of a complaint an objective test is applied. The Code notes that it may be 'far easier for a close family member to talk through their proposals for their will with someone with no personal interest in its contents' and that the 'relative's bequests are secure from allegations of undue influence if their will is drawn by someone totally independent and who does not take benefit from it' (Solicitors' Code of Conduct 2007, sub-rule 3.04, pp 51–52, paras 57 and 58).

12.45 Case law has also shown that solicitors benefiting under a will prepared for a relative should prove knowledge and approval. The safest course of action would be to insist on a relative receiving independent advice. In *Franks v Sinclair* [2007] WTLR 439, a will drafted by the solicitor son of the deceased was overturned. The alleged new will was obviously controversial, and the judge felt the son was 'incapable of impartial discussion of his mother's instructions'. Further, he had not kept a note of instructions, and had simply read the will out to his mother verbatim instead of explaining the complex clauses.

Undue influence

12.46 Unlike in transactions that take effect during life (see Chapter 1), no presumption of undue influence can apply in the context of wills and, therefore, actual undue influence has always to be proved.

12.47 Actual undue influence requires coercion; the testator is coerced into making a will that he does not want to make. In *Hall v Hall* (1865-69) LR 1 P & D 481 this was defined as 'Pressure … so exerted as to overpower the volition without convincing the judgment.'

12.48 What amounts to coercion varies with the strength of will of the testator and if that will is weak due to mental or physical frailty, less force is required to overpower it.

12.49 Sir James Hannon said in *Wingrove v Wingrove* (1885) LR 11 PD 81:

> 'Coercion may be ... of different kinds, it may be in the grossest form, such as actual confinement or violence, or a person in the last days or hours of life may have become so weak and feeble that a very little pressure will be sufficient to bring about the desired result.'

12.50 It is possible to be influenced to do something without that act being against one's will.

12.51 In *Hansen v Barker-Benfield* [2006] WTLR 1141, Bernard Livesey QC considered whether the defendant's influence over the deceased in relation to a disposition of property to the defendant during the deceased's lifetime had been 'undue' in that it amounted to coercion. Although he agreed that the testator would have been vulnerable to pressure because of his physical dependence, the fact that the defendant expressed her objection to the testator's intention to benefit his daughter under his will did not amount to pressure which was undue or coercion.

12.52 The burden of alleging undue influence is on the person making the allegation. It is not enough to show that someone has the power to overbear the testator's will. The person making the allegation must show that the power was exercised and the will obtained as a result. As per James Munby QC, giving judgment in *Killick v Pountney* [2000] WTLR 41:

> 'No amount of evidence of bodily or mental infirmity will of itself establish undue influence in the absence of some independent evidence tending to show the exercise of an improper influence.'

Standard of proof in undue influence

12.53 The nature of undue influence is the overpowering of the testator's will. Convincing and direct evidence is therefore required, although the standard of proof is the civil standard and therefore the court is to be satisfied on the balance of probabilities.

12.54 In *Carapeto v Good* [2002] WTLR 801, Rimer J said,

> 'In my view, the wholesale overbearing of a testator's will by coercion is an inherently more improbable event than, for example, the bringing to bear on the testator of legitimate persuasion of the type referred to in the Hall case, and I bear that in mind in assessing whether, on the evidence, the defendants have discharged the burden of proving coercion.'

12.55 In *Killick v Pountney*, James Munby QC said:

'Any allegation of undue influence is plainly a serious one. Thus, although the standard of proof is the ordinary civil standard of proof on a balance of probabilities, one has to bear in mind that "The more serious the allegation, the more cogent is the evidence required to overcome the unlikelihood of what is alleged and thus to prove it"; see the speech of Lord Nicholls of Birkenhead in *In re H (Minors) (Sexual Abuse; Standard of Proof)* [1996] AC 563 ...'

Fraud

12.56 Fraud is rarely pleaded in validity claims, probably because, as established in *Re H and Ors (Minors) (Sexual Abuse: Standard of Proof)* [1996] AC 563, a civil court when considering a charge of fraud will require a higher degree of probability than usual. This was reiterated in *Parks v Clout* [2003] EWCA Civ 892 in which Mr Clout appealed against a strike out of his claim that his deceased sister's husband had obtained letters of administration by fraudulently destroying the deceased's will.

12.57 Instead want of knowledge and approval is often pleaded, particularly in the situation where persons benefiting under a will have been instrumental in its preparation. It may be that there was an element of dishonesty in the preparation or execution of the will, and if want of knowledge and approval is pleaded, the rule in *Barry v Butlin* (1838) 2 Moo PCC 480 helpfully puts the burden onto the propounder in this situation. Fraud is sometimes pleaded as forgery, for example in the case of *R v Spillman and Russill* (unreported) July 1999 (Basildon Crown Court) where the mother of the 'beneficiary' dressed up as the testatrix so as to forge the will. Needless to say the beneficiaries were subsequently tried in the criminal courts for conspiracy to defraud and theft and sentenced to imprisonment (*R v Spillman (David Stephen)* [2001] 1 Cr App R (S) 139).

Forgery

12.58 Forgery is rarely pleaded on its own but often coupled with want of knowledge and approval. It is a serious allegation and, as with fraud, although the standard of proof is the balance of probabilities, a higher level of proof will be required.

12.59 Civil courts seem to have been reluctant to find forgery. In *Fuller v Strum* [2002] 1 WLR 1097, although the joint expert found there was 'very strong positive evidence' of a forgery, the first instance court held it was not a forgery but rather that the testator lacked knowledge and approval. This decision was set aside in the Court of the Appeal and the will upheld.

12.60 However, in *Supple v Pender & Another* [2007] WTLR 1461 where there was overwhelming evidence of forgery, the judge found for the claimant. In *Vaccianna v Herod* [2006] WTLR 367 the judge found the alleged last will of the testator had been forged because the defendant filed no defence and adduced no evidence from the attesting witnesses.

12.61 Generally forgery is hard to prove. Handwriting experts rarely give a conclusive answer and one must usually prove the attesting witnesses were involved in the forgery (unless, as in *R v Spillman* the 'beneficiary' dressed up as the testatrix in order to execute the false will (see **12.57**)). Because it is a serious allegation, there is a considerable cost risk alleging it (see *Re Barton* [1977] CLY 3182 in which the widow was only awarded costs to a certain point as allegations of forgery were almost incredible thereafter).

PRACTICE AND PROCEDURE

Pre-claim investigations

Standing search

12.62 If your client is concerned as to the validity of an alleged will, a standing search will establish whether a grant has already issued in the estate.

12.63 If the grant was issued some time ago, it may be that the personal representatives have already distributed the funds. If that is the case, it may be unwise to embark on an action for revocation of an existing grant unless he has a good case.

Caveat

12.64 If a grant has not been extracted a caveat should usually be entered as soon as possible. As detailed in Chapter 7, a caveat will block a grant, is easy to enter and costs only £15. It will provide time for the collation of evidence.

12.65 Clearly if seeking to prove the will, extracting a grant quickly (so long as your client feels able to swear the required oath on a grant) may be a tactical move to knock out the challenger's claim or to bring him/her to the table.

12.66 If a caveat is entered, as a matter of courtesy those named as personal representatives under the challenged will and their solicitors should usually be informed.

Collating evidence

12.67 There are a number of essential steps that anyone considering challenging a will should take.

The will itself

12.68 The will itself may be a source of evidence. If your client has not been able to obtain a copy of the alleged last will that is in the possession of the personal representatives or their solicitors, they should be asked to provide this. Enquiries should also be made as to whether or not a copy of any previous will is still available. If a person believed to be in possession of such a copy document refuses to reveal it, an application for the issue of a witness summons can be made under the Supreme Court Act 1981, s 123 (see Chapter 5).

12.69 Once the will is before you, it should be carefully reviewed.

(1)   How consistent is the will? Any irregularity on its face may assist in establishing lack of knowledge and approval or lack of testamentary capacity.

(2)   How complex is the will? If it is simple it will be easier to establish that the deceased knew and approved of its contents. If it is lengthy, with complex administrative powers and trusts, it may be more difficult.

(3)   Was the will handwritten? If the will was written in the handwriting of the person who takes a substantial benefit, a suspicion will automatically be raised. A handwritten will is likely to suggest no lawyers were retained.

(4)   Who were the attesting witnesses? Were they in any way suggestible? If alleging forgery, you will most likely need to show that the attesting witnesses were involved in the fraud.

(5)   How was the will executed? It is important to review the order of attestation and whereabouts on the paper the various parties signed.

(6)   It is useful to examine the testator's signature. Was it shaky? Is it similar to any other examples of the testator's signature? If the signature is very different from the signature on other documents it may be an indication of dementia or possibly forgery.

(7)   Has the defendant made a previous will? The deceased's previous will making patterns should be examined. Any radical change, for example, to benefit a comparative stranger or someone with no connection whatsoever with the deceased, may indicate want of knowledge and approval, undue influence or lack of capacity.

The attesting witnesses

12.70 An approach should be made to the attesting witnesses regarding the deceased's state of mind and health at the time of executing the will. Such an approach may reveal further concerns, for example suggestions of influence, or that the will was not properly executed.

12.71 If the request for a statement is refused, an application may be made under s 122 of the Supreme Court Act 1981 for examination of a witness before the court.

The will draftsman

Larke v Nugus statement

12.72 An application should be made to the will draftsman for a *Larke v Nugus* statement.

12.73 In 1959 the Law Society recommended that in circumstances where a will that a solicitor has drawn up becomes the subject of a dispute, the solicitor should make available a statement of his evidence regarding the execution of the will and the circumstances surrounding it to anyone who asks for it, and that no issue of confidentiality arises. This recommendation was endorsed by the Court of Appeal in the case of *Larke v Nugus* [2000] WTLR 1033.

12.74 In that case the deceased's solicitor declined to produce a statement in accordance with the Law Society's recommendation and a probate action ensued. The Court of Appeal confirmed that not only should the statement have been given relating to the execution of the will, but also that, where the solicitor's knowledge made him a material witness, the statement of his evidence should have been extended to deal with the surrounding circumstances leading up to the preparation and making of the will. The Court of Appeal's decision was reflected in the Guide to the Professional Conduct of Solicitors 1996 (8th edn, 1999) but is not included in the new Solicitors' Code of Conduct 2007, which replaces the old Guide. Guidance is now incorporated in the Law Society's Practice Note 'File Retention: records management – retention and wills, deeds and documents together with supporting data', which was published in September 2007. The guidance states, at paragraph 1.8:

> 'Prior to destruction of papers [solicitors] should consider *Larke v Nugus* [2000] WTLR 1033 and established guidance from Professional Ethics that where there is a dispute about the circumstances in which a will was made, and where requested, a solicitor should make available a statement of evidence regarding the execution of the will and the circumstances surrounding it, to anyone who asks the solicitor for such a statement'.

At the time of writing this contradicts paragraph 1.13 of the Practice Note which states that the statement should be made available to 'anyone who is a party to probate proceedings or whom the solicitor believes has a reasonable claim under the will'.

12.75 A precedent request for a *Larke v Nugus* report can be found at Appendix 2. Statements should be taken from all persons who took instructions for the preparation of the will.

Weight of will draftsman's evidence

12.76 The weight of a will draftsman's evidence will vary depending on his level of experience, how long he knew the testator, and whether he complied with Lord Templeman's 'golden rule'.

12.77 The golden rule, set out in *Kenward v Adams* (1975) *The Times* November 29 1975 states that, where a testator is elderly and infirm, the making of a will by such a testator ought to be witnessed and approved by a medical practitioner who satisfies himself as to the capacity and understanding of the testator and makes a record of his examination and findings.

12.78 The observation of the golden rule will add weight to the solicitor draftsman's evidence. However, in *Allen v Emery* [2005–6] 8 ITELR 358, Sonia Proudman QC stated that the golden rule, whilst a 'desirable precaution', is 'no more that prudent guidance for a solicitor' and not 'determinative'. In *Hansen v Barker-Benfield* [2006] WTLR 1141, the Deputy Judge found that the claimant did not prove the deceased had testamentary capacity. He was not convinced that the two trainees who took instructions for the will separately on 27 and 28 January, were experienced enough to make a proper assessment of capacity.

The will file

12.79 The deceased's file belongs to the estate (subject to a limited number of documents belonging to the firm including documents prepared for the firm's benefit and not charged to the client, and original letters sent by the client intended to become the firm's property). Therefore the solicitor draftsman can be asked to hand it to the personal representatives. The Law Society's Practice Note 'File Retention: records management – retention and wills, deeds and documents together with supporting data' states that 'with wills the limitation period does not start to run until the testator has died' so will files and related material should be retained bearing this in mind. References to the preparation of the will in a *Larke v Nugus* statement (see **12.72—12.75**) should annex the relevant notes from the will file as part of the exhibit. On the issue of a probate claim, all parties will be required to prepare evidence of testamentary documents which includes a statement and provision of the will file and all relevant documents.

Medical records

12.80 A further avenue of investigation is the deceased's medical records. The Access to Health Records Act 1990 at s 3(1)(f) provides that an application for access to health records may be made by 'the patient's personal representative and any person who may have a claim arising out of the patient's death'.

12.81 There may be a delay in providing the deceased's medical records if they have already been transferred from the relevant surgery to the Area Health Authority. Therefore it is sensible to obtain the medical records as quickly as possible. A letter requesting medical records can be found at Appendix 2.

GP's report

12.82 If the medical records suggest loss of capacity or mental or physical vulnerability, it would be sensible to write to the deceased's GP requesting a report. The GP will generally be happy to provide this report so long as his reasonable fee is covered. It is often helpful to telephone the GP in advance.

12.83 Not every medical practitioner automatically understands what is required when asked to provide a report as to the deceased's testamentary capacity. It is helpful to outline the *Banks v Goodfellow* test. It may also assist if a copy of the will and basic information about the estate, if known, is provided.

12.84 The medical report should provide details of:

(1)   the medical practitioner's qualifications and experience;

(2)   the deceased's dates of birth and death;

(3)   the length of time the medical practitioner knew the deceased and the capacity in which he knew him;

(4)   the times the medical practitioner saw the deceased and the date when instructions were given for preparation of the will, when it was executed, bearing in mind that the level of testamentary capacity required when executing a will is less than that on giving instructions;

(5)   any medical conditions suffered by the deceased which might have affected his testamentary capacity and susceptibility;

(6)   whether there were any indications of influence or susceptibility to pressure;

(7)   what treatment was given, what drugs were being taken at the relevant time and what effect those might have had on his mental state;

(8)   the medical practitioner's opinion as to whether or not the deceased had testamentary capacity within *Banks v Goodfellow* to make a will of the type in question.

12.85 It is helpful to include a paragraph in the letter giving comfort to the GP regarding the difficult task of a retrospective assessment of capacity.

12.86 If there is any question that the medical records have already been sent to the Area Health Authority, it should be borne in mind that the GP is unlikely to have retained a copy and therefore it can be helpful to send him a copy of those records, if available, to jog his memory.

12.87 A precedent letter to a GP for a report can be found at Appendix 2.

Social Services records

12.88 These are not included within the Access to Health Records Act 1990 and it is likely that access to these records will only be obtained once proceedings have been issued, at which point an interim application can be made for an order that they be released.

Further investigations

12.89 It may be sensible to approach neighbours, pecuniary legatees, other beneficiaries in the will and any other people who knew the deceased well to establish testamentary capacity or susceptibility to influence. Diaries and address books maintained by the deceased and left at their property after death can be a valuable source of information and a means of contacting friends of the deceased who might otherwise be difficult to trace. Residential or nursing home records are likely to set out daily activities and doctors' visits.

Joint or sole approach

12.90 The ACTAPS Practice Guidance Notes for the Resolution of Trust and Probate Disputes suggests that applications to the draftsman for a *Larke v Nugus* statement and to the medical records holder for medical notes should be made by the parties jointly. However, this may not always be practical.

12.91 Either way, it is sensible to frontload investigations. This way you will discover the merits of your client's case as soon as possible in order to avoid unnecessary costs.

Proceedings

Jurisdiction

12.92 Validity actions are generally brought in the Chancery Division of the High Court. An action can be brought in the county court where the value of the net estate does not exceed £30,000.

Limitation

12.93 There is no specific limitation period in probate claims, although the equitable defences of laches and acquiescence may apply.

Commencement and procedure

12.94 A validity action is a 'probate claim' under the Civil Procedure Rules and as such is dealt with by CPR Part 57.

12.95 Probate claims follow the CPR Part 7 procedure with slight modifications:

(1)   the time limit for acknowledging service is 28 days after service of the Particulars of Claim;

(2)   the time limit for filing the defence is also 28 days after service of the Particulars of Claim.

Precedent claim forms requesting the court to decree probate of a will in solemn form and to pronounce against the purported last will of the deceased in favour of an earlier will are at Appendix 2.

12.96 Once the action has begun, the relevant office will send notice to Leeds District Probate Registry requesting that all testamentary documents, grants, representation and any other relevant documents currently held at any probate registry, be sent to the relevant office.

12.97 The commencement of the probate claim will, subject to a court order, prevent any grant of probate or letters of administration being made until the probate claim has been disposed of.

Evidence about testamentary documents

12.98 In addition, testamentary documents and evidence about testamentary documents should be filed by the claimant when issuing the claim and by the defendant when acknowledging service.

12.99 A testamentary document is defined as 'a will, a draft of the will, written instructions for a will made by or at the request of, or under the instructions of, the testator, and any document purporting to be evidence of the contents or to be a copy of a will, which is alleged to have been lost or destroyed'. A 'will' includes a codicil.

12.100 The form of evidence about testamentary documents is annexed to the Practice Direction to Part 57. A precedent witness statement of testamentary scripts is at Appendix 2.

12.101 Once both parties have filed their evidence and documents, they can be inspected by any party.

12.102 If there are reasonable grounds for believing that a person has knowledge of a testamentary document but refuses to lodge it, Supreme Court Act 1981, s 122 empowers the court to question that person or to order him/her to attend court for examination or to bring in documents. Supreme Court Act 1981, s 123 (as set out at **5.2**) enables the court to issue a subpoena requiring him/her to bring in documents.

Parties or persons who may be affected

12.103 Those who are entitled under the will at issue or a previous will or on intestacy, together with anyone claiming entitlement to administer the estate as personal representative, should be joined as parties to the action. In giving case management directions in probate claims, courts will give consideration to whether any further parties should be joined or given notice of the claim under CPR, r 19.8a and whether to make a Representation Order under CPR, r 19.6 or 19.7 (for example where minor children are involved).

Service of the claim form

12.104 Once proceedings are issued, the claim form must be served within 4 months.

Defence and counterclaim

12.105 The defence is often combined with a counterclaim seeking to set up a different (normally earlier) will or claiming that letters of administration should be obtained on the basis of intestacy.

12.106 If not, CPR, r 20.5 states that if there is to be a counterclaim against a person other than the claimant, the defendant must apply to the court for an order that that person be added as an additional party.

Revocation of existing grant

12.107 Where a probate claim is issued seeking the revocation of a grant, whoever has the probate or letters of administration under his control must lodge it at the court either when the claim form is issued (if the claimant has control) or when the defendant acknowledges service (if the defendant has control).

Judgment in default

12.108 Judgment in default cannot be obtained in a probate claim. Instead, if no defendant acknowledges service or files a defence the claimant may apply to the court for an order that the claim proceeds to trial. The court can then direct that the claim be tried on written evidence.

Discontinuance

12.109 Once a probate action has started, under CPR, r 57.11 the court's approval is required to discontinue and there is discretion for the court to discontinue the claim on such terms as to costs as it thinks just. The court may refuse to discontinue if it considers there is a serious question for the courts, a principle that was restated in *Wylde v Culver* [2006] 4 All ER 345. In this case George Bompas QC held that the grounds for questioning the will did not raise a serious issue for the court and therefore permission to discontinue was granted. (See **12.120** for an analysis of the costs position).

Compromise

12.110 Probate actions can be very acrimonious and parties to the dispute may become entrenched even at an early stage. The door should always be left open to the possibility of compromise and legal advisers must be encouraged to facilitate this. It may be that your client's objectives can be achieved in ways other than by going to trial. In suggesting the alternatives considered below, it is important that the client understands precisely what is involved and the limitations.

Mediation or conciliation

12.111 An independent third party may be asked to facilitate a compromise between the parties although such a person has no authority to make any binding determination. Both sides must be willing to take part and the mediation process will end if one of them subsequently withdraws from the negotiations. The mediator's objective should be to assist in the parties' negotiations rather than to conduct those negotiations himself. At the initial meeting all parties will be present and as the process develops, the mediator holds separate sessions with each side, regularly reporting back as to progress. It is at these sessions that areas of dispute can effectively be narrowed, hopefully to the extent that a solution is arrived at which is palatable to everyone.

12.112 Although alternatives to litigation should be considered with the client at an early stage, mediation in particular might run alongside the court action and be used as the basis of an agreed draft consent order.

Settlement before trial

12.113 If the parties agree before trial to settle a probate claim the court has the option either to (1) order the trial of the claim on written evidence, (2) order that the claim be discontinued, or (3) pronounce for or against the validity of one or more wills without a trial if every relevant beneficiary has consented to the proposed order. The latter is a power under s 49 of the Administration of Justice Act 1985, is only available in the High Court and must be supported by evidence identifying the relevant beneficiaries and exhibiting each of their written consents.

Costs

12.114 The general rule is that the costs of a contentious probate claim, as with any other civil claim, are within the discretion of the Court and CPR 43 and 44 apply. Thus, the general rule is that costs follow the event.

12.115 There are two exceptions to that general rule which were stated in *Spiers v English* [1907] P 122 at 123:

> 'In deciding questions of costs one has to go back to the principles which govern cases of this kind. One of those principles is that if a person who makes a will or persons who are interested in the residue have been really the cause of the litigation a case is made out for costs to come out of the estate. Another principle is that, if the circumstances lead reasonably to an investigation of the matter, then the costs may be left to be borne by those who have incurred them. If it were not for the application of those principles, which, if not exhaustive, are the two great principles upon which the Court acts, costs would now, according to the rule, follow the event as a matter of course. Those principles allow good cause to be shown why costs should not follow the event. Therefore, in each case where an application is made, the Court has to consider whether the facts warrant either of those principles being brought into operation.'

The two exceptions to the general rule are therefore that:

(1) where the testator or those interested in the residue have been the cause of the litigation: in such a case the costs of the unsuccessful party will usually be ordered to be paid out of the estate; and

(2) where the circumstances lead reasonably to an investigation in regard to a propounded document: in such a case the costs will usually be left to be borne by those who respectively incurred them.

12.116 In *Kostic v Chaplin and Others* [2007] EWHC 2909, Henderson J noted that it has been the trend of more recent authorities to scrutinise carefully any case in which the first exception is said to apply, there being less importance attached today than formerly to the court's duty to investigate independently the circumstances in which a will was executed and to be satisfied as to its validity, whilst, conversely being alert to the dangers of encouraging litigation.

12.117 In *Kostic*, Henderson J found that, in the highly unusual circumstances of the case, the testator's conduct might properly be regarded as the primary cause of the initial dispute. The defendants' investigation of the testator's testamentary capacity had been 'fully justified' and they were allowed their costs from the estate up to the stage at which a realistic assessment of the merits of the claim could first properly be made. However, the court was of the view that this assessment could have been made at an early stage and the period for which the defendants recovered their costs was therefore limited to the initial stages of the proceedings.

12.118 The rationale of the second exception was explained in *Mitchell v Gard* (1806) 3 SW and TR 275:

> 'It is the function of this court to investigate the execution of a will and the capacity of the maker, and having done so, to ascertain and declare what is the will of the testator. If fair circumstances of doubt or suspicion arise to obscure this

question, a judicial inquiry is in a manner forced upon it. Those who are instrumental in bringing about and subserving this inquiry are not wholly in the wrong, even if they do not succeed. And so it comes that this court has been in the practice on such occasions of deviating from the common rule in other courts, and of relieving the losing party from costs, if chargeable with no other blame than that of having failed in a suit which was justified by good and sufficient grounds for doubt.'

In *Kostic* the unsuccessful defendants argued the second exception should apply making an adverse costs order against them inappropriate.

12.119 Each side was ordered to bear its own costs from the date upon which the costs order under the first exception expired up to the exchange of expert reports, on the grounds that from this date on the defendants had taken a stand on the basis of their own expert's opinion.

12.120 Where an action is discontinued, the usual rule is that costs follow the event so that the party who unsuccessfully opposes a grant pays the other parties' costs. However, the court has discretion to discontinue on such terms as to costs as it thinks fit and generally it is accepted that costs will be borne by the estate if the testator is at fault or there will be no order as to costs where there were reasonable grounds for an enquiry by the losing party. This was reiterated in *Wylde v Culver* [2006] 4 All ER 345 as set out in **12.109** in which the judge held that the grounds for questioning the will did not raise a serious issue for the court and permission to discontinue was granted. However, even though he stated that no serious issue had been raised, the claimant was not penalised in costs because, following CPR, r 57.7(5)(b), the judge stated that a reasonable, but nevertheless mistaken, belief in a state of affairs which, if not mistaken, would lead to a will being pronounced against, did amount to reasonable grounds for opposing a will. In *Jarrom v Sellars* [2007] WTLR 1219 the judge made no order as to costs on the basis that the winning party had acted unreasonably in refusing to attend a without prejudice meeting to resolve the issues.

Part V

DISPUTES IN THE ESTATE ADMINISTRATION

Chapter 13

CLAIMS AGAINST PERSONAL REPRESENTATIVES

DEVASTAVIT, BREACH OF TRUST AND FIDUCIARY DUTY

Devastavit

13.1 Disaffected beneficiaries may wish to consider proceedings against their trustees to seek restitution to the trust fund or equitable compensation on the basis that the trustees have acted in violation of their duty as trustees towards the beneficiaries. Before so doing there are numerous points which the beneficiaries must consider, not least whether:

- the act complained of constitutes *devastavit*, or a breach of trust or fiduciary duty;

- the breach has occasioned quantifiable loss and there is no difficulty establishing the causal link between the breach and the loss;

- the personal representatives are covered by professional indemnity insurance, trustee indemnity insurance (relatively unusual), or have sufficient assets in their own right to render making a claim against them commercially worthwhile;

- the claim is statute-barred or a defence of *laches* is likely;

- the personal representatives are able to rely on a widely drawn exculpatory clause;

- the trustee is likely to be relieved from liability pursuant to s 61 of the Trustee Act 1925;

- the claim may rebound on the beneficiary by the personal representative alleging acquiescence, instigation or waiver and seeking to impound the beneficiary's interest.

13.2 *Devastavit* is the breach by an executor or an administrator of his duty to administer the estate. It has been described as 'mismanagement of the estate … squandering and misapplying the assets contrary to the duty imposed on them'. A personal representative is bound to do what is in his power for the benefit of the estate; he must be diligent, exercise the appropriate standard of care and act as a prudent man of business would in relation to his own affairs.

13.3 The breach of the duty to administer is, in effect, breach of the duty imposed by s 25 of the Administration of Estates Act 1925 to:

(a) collect and get in the real and personal estate of the deceased and administer it according to law;

(b) when required to do so by the court, exhibit on oath in the court a full inventory of the estate and when so required render an account of the administration of the estate to the court;

(c) when required to do so by the High Court, deliver up the grant of probate or administration to that court.

Every executor or administrator swearing the oath in support of the grant swears that he will administer the estate in accordance with the provisions of s 25.

13.4 A personal representative may also be liable for breach of trust or fiduciary duty. Assets are given to personal representatives on trust and they may breach not only their duty to administer but also the express or implied trusts on which they hold the estate and their duty of loyalty to the beneficiaries. Under s 68 of the Trustee Act 1925 the definition of trustee is extended to include the duties of a personal representative who will be personally liable for all breaches of the ordinary trusts which arise from his office.

13.5 A claim for *devastavit* or for breach of trust/fiduciary duty is a claim against a personal representative personally and not against the estate. If there has been a breach of trust/fiduciary duty or *devastavit* a personal representative cannot escape liability by pleading that the estate has been fully administered and that he has no assets left in his hands. If he is found liable he will have to make good the loss to the estate out of his personal resources.

Examples of devastavit

13.6 *Devastavit* can either be deliberate/reckless or negligent. The degree of culpability associated with the act or omission which gives rise to a *devastavit* claim will influence the court in deciding whether the personal representative liable to account to the estate should also have to account for interest and, if so, whether at a fixed court rate or a commercial rate and whether simple or compounded.

13.7 Examples of failing to collect in the assets of the deceased are:

- selling property in the estate at an undervalue (which is also a breach of trust);

- failing to dispose of wasting assets before they lose value;

- taking the assets of the estate and using them for the personal representative's own purposes;

- leaving the assets in an inappropriate form of investment not authorised by the will or general law.

13.8 Failure to discharge debts may well give rise to a claim for *devastavit*. Examples are:

(1) Non-payment of a debt which is regarded as a remote contingent liability. If the contingency arises later and either the personal representatives have not obtained an order from the court that they should distribute the estate without regard to that contingency or protected themselves by means of an advertisement under s 27 of the Trustee Act 1925 (and the contingent liability was not known and did not come to light in response to the advertisement), the personal representatives will be personally liable to pay the debt when the contingency occurs.

(2) If personal representatives discharge a moral obligation which is not, in fact, a debt which they are bound to pay they will generally be liable for *devastavit*. Personal representatives do, however, have wide powers to compromise claims in good faith under s 15 of the Trustee Act 1925 (as amended by the Trustee Act 2000, Sch 2, Pt II, para 20).

(3) Personal representatives will be liable if they pay a statute-barred debt which has been judicially declared statute-barred (see *Midgley v Midgley* [1893] 3 Ch 282).

(4) Personal representatives will be liable if they discharge debts in an insolvent estate out of order such as by paying ordinary debts before funeral, testamentary and administration expenses or preferential debts: for the order for payment of debts see the Administration of Insolvent Estates of Deceased Persons Order 1986 (SI 1986/1999).

13.9 Examples of failing to administer in accordance with the law are:

(1) Payment to beneficiaries (whether under the will or in accordance with the intestacy rules) when there are inadequate funds to pay the funeral, testamentary and administration expenses and the deceased's debts.

(2) Paying out to the wrong beneficiaries or in the wrong amounts whether deliberately or because of mistake, misunderstanding or misinterpretation of the provisions of a will or the effect of the intestacy rules. A failure to adhere to the terms of the will or the application of the intestacy rules as to beneficial entitlement will be a *devastavit* unless the personal representatives are authorised to depart from those terms by all beneficiaries (being of full age and unimpaired mental faculties), such as under a deed of variation or family arrangement; or by order of the court (such as the Variation of Trusts Act 1958) or the consequence of the court's exercise of its discretionary powers under the Inheritance (Provision for Family and Dependants) Act 1975.

The identity of all beneficiaries entitled on intestacy may not have been established and although personal representatives will usually escape personal liability if they have advertised under the Trustee Act 1925, s 27 at least two months prior to distributing, this does not exonerate them from making the usual searches and enquiries so as to establish who the beneficiaries are. If a beneficiary is missing, enquiries can usefully be made to the Department of Social Security in Newcastle (which will forward a letter addressed to the lost beneficiary) and the Salvation Army. Personal representatives should also consider enlisting the help of genealogists who will charge beneficiaries in relation to sums recovered. The Law Society recommends that, before employing such firms, solicitors should be satisfied that it is appropriate to do so in view of the size and nature of the estate and the circumstances of beneficiaries affected.

If all enquiries are inconclusive, an application may be made to the court for an order based on the jurisdiction invoked in the case of *Re Benjamin* [1902] 1 Ch 723. Such an order affords the personal representatives the protection of authority from the court to distribute the estate based on certain assumptions and, if those assumptions prove subsequently to be incorrect, the personal representatives will not themselves be liable. This does not mean that a successful claimant is prevented from following assets into the hands of a beneficiary.

(3) Applying the assets of the estate in the wrong order in discharge of debts. Funeral, testamentary and administration expenses, debts and liabilities are to be met out of the assets of the estate in the order set out in the Administration of Estates Act 1925, Sch 1, Pt 2. If debts are met out of order (such as using pecuniary legacies to discharge debts before property specifically devised) any beneficiary adversely affected can make a personal claim against personal representatives.

Breach of trust

13.10 In *Armitage v Nurse* [1998] Ch 241 Millett LJ said that the duty of trustees was to perform the trusts honestly and in good faith for the benefit of the beneficiaries and that this was 'the minimum necessary to give substance to the trusts'.

13.11 Most of the responsibilities ascribed to trustees can be reduced down to this statement subject to the embellishment of those responsibilities by case law and statute.

13.12 Section 1 of the Trustee Act 2000 imposes a duty of care on trustees: to exercise such care and skill as is reasonable in all the circumstances (including whether the trustee is a professional or holds himself out as having particular skills) when performing particular trustee duties set out in Sch 1, such as when investing trust funds or buying land. Under Trustee Act 2000, s 35, this same standard applies to personal representatives.

13.13 The duty of care may be specifically excluded by the trust deed.

13.14 The Act also imposes specific obligations on trustees in connection with investment, such as having regard to standard investment criteria, review of investments and diversification.

13.15 A breach of trust may also arise from circumstances which give rise to proceedings seeking to set aside action taken by trustees on the basis that the action complained of is beyond the scope of their powers. If the transaction is void no limitation period will apply to an action to set it aside.

Common breaches of trust

13.16 The range of acts which may constitute breach of trust is very wide but will usually involve personal representatives acting in excess of their powers, acting improperly when exercising powers (such as not exercising their powers in good faith or reasonably for the legitimate purposes of the administration of the estate) or, by act or omission, breaching a core duty, such as the duty to act as a prudent man of business would towards those for whom he has a moral obligation to provide (*Learoyd v Whiteley* (1887) 12 App Cas 727). Examples of common breaches are:

(1) A personal representative failing to acquaint himself thoroughly with the terms of the will/intestacy rules and the extent of the estate assets and, where there has been a loss, to investigate.

(2) Failure to account for profits made by the personal representatives on the deceased's assets.

(3) Failure, where trust assets include shares in a private or public company, to exercise all the rights of a shareholder and take such further steps as the personal representative can (including appointing nominees as directors if possible) to ensure that he receives sufficient information about the management of the company's affairs to enable him to intervene if necessary (*Bartlett v Barclays Bank Trust Co Ltd (No 2)* [1980] 2 WLR 430).

(4) Failure to invest within the powers given by the will or by general law.

(5) Failure to act impartially between beneficiaries, particularly when making investment decisions which might benefit one class of beneficiaries more than another. This does not mean that they must treat all beneficiaries equally (even if such were permitted under the terms of the will or the application of the intestacy rules) but they must balance the interests of the beneficiaries fairly and not bow to pressure from one beneficiary or group of beneficiaries.

(6) Failure to invest assets in the estate: a long line of eighteenth and nineteenth century cases has established that if personal representatives keep the estate's money without investing it for in excess of a reasonable period they will be liable for the income which could have been earned on that money.

(7) Failure to invest prudently. If personal representatives enter into speculative property deals and the estate suffers loss as a result the court may conclude that they have not discharged their obligation to act prudently and they may be liable to make up the loss as in *Bartlett v Barclays Bank Trust Co Ltd* [1980] 2 WLR 430. The powers in relation to investment must be exercised in the best interests of the beneficiaries as a whole (*Cowan v Scargill* [1985] Ch 270).

(8) Failure to have regard not only to the suitability of prospective investments but also the need for diversification (Trustee Act 2000, s 4 and *Nestle v National Westminster Bank Plc* [1993] 1 WLR 1260).

(9) Delegating powers or duties where not authorised by the settlement or by statute. It used to be the case under s 23 of the Trustee Act 1925 that personal representatives could not, as a collective body, delegate their duties to distribute estate property to those entitled to it or their fiduciary discretions without authority under the will. The position under s 11 of the Trustee Act 2000, read with s 26, is that personal representatives may delegate their powers of administration in relation to the estate but (if there is a discretionary trust in the will) do not have authority to delegate their decision-making powers in relation to the distribution of income or capital for the benefit of the beneficiaries.

(10) Charging the trust fund in circumstances where neither the settlement nor the court authorised the trustees to charge. (Trustee Act 2000, s 29 provides a mechanism for trustees to be paid in most circumstances.)

Additional duties have been imposed pursuant to the Trusts of Land and Appointment of Trustees Act 1996. Where there are trusts of land, personal representatives will be in breach of their duties if they fail to consult beneficiaries of full age entitled to an interest in possession insofar as it is practicable for them to do so in the exercise of any function relating to land subject to the trust (s 11(1)), or fail to allow beneficiaries with an interest in possession to occupy the land subject to the trust, provided that the land is available for occupation (s 12(1)).

Breach of fiduciary duty

13.17 A personal representative is a fiduciary and as such is not allowed to put himself in a position where his personal interest and his duty conflict, unless that conflict is authorised by the instrument governing the estate.

13.18 A case in point is that of *Kane v Radley-Kane* [1999] Ch 274. The defendant, widow of the deceased, was appointed sole personal representative of the estate, and was entitled to a statutory widow's legacy of £125,000. The net estate was valued for tax purposes at £93,000, which included company shares valued at £50,000. Without the consent of the other beneficiaries under the will, she registered the shares in her name and subsequently sold them for £1,131,438. It was confirmed that the self-dealing rule applied to personal representatives. As she had sought neither the consent of the beneficiaries nor the consent of the court, she was held to be in breach of her fiduciary duty, the sale proceeds being part of the estate.

What does the duty of loyalty entail?

13.19 A personal representative's duty is the duty of loyalty and fidelity to the beneficiaries. The classic definition of fiduciary duties was stated by Millett LJ in *Bristol and West Building Society v Mothew* [1998] Ch 1:

> 'A fiduciary is someone who has undertaken to act for or on behalf of another in a particular matter in circumstances which give rise to a relationship of trust and confidence. The distinguishing obligation of a fiduciary is the obligation of loyalty. The principal is entitled to the single minded loyalty of his fiduciary. This core liability has several facets. A fiduciary must act in good faith; he must not make a profit out of his trust; he must not place himself in a position where his duty and his interest may conflict; he may not act for his own benefit or the benefit of a third person without the informed consent of his principal.'

13.20 The duty of loyalty is absolute unless:

- the will authorises the executor to act in his own interest to a limited extent; or

- the executor is from inception placed – and the testator would have appreciated that he was so placed – in a position of conflicting interest, in which case the duty may be a qualified fiduciary duty.

13.21 An important aspect of the duty of loyalty is the obligation not to profit from the fiduciary relationship. Usually the will specifically authorises the executors to charge, but less often provides for the executors to receive fees as directors if they are appointed to the board of a company which is an estate asset. If directors' fees are taken when not authorised by the will this would be a breach of fiduciary duty (*Swain v Law Society* [1982] 1 WLR 17).

13.22 A personal representative may also be a beneficiary. In those circumstances it is almost inevitable that in considering the interests of the beneficiaries he will also be considering his own personal interests, and conflict will be acute if he is considering exercising discretionary powers of appointment as between himself and other beneficiaries.

13.23 In such a situation his fiduciary duty is likely to be regarded as qualified – it can be exercised in his own favour provided that it is exercised in good faith and not contrary to the whole purpose for which it was given.

13.24 In any case of doubt arising from a conflicting interest it is preferable for the personal representatives labouring under a conflict to be substituted or to seek the blessing of the court to the decision proposed to be taken which it could be said is in conflict of interest. Avoiding dealing when in a conflicting interest position or securing the court's blessing to so doing is particularly important where it cannot be said that the conflict was authorised by the testator.

13.25 An important facet of fiduciary duty is the rule against self-dealing. A personal representative is not able to be the contracting party to a deal with the estate assets unless the will specifically authorises self-dealing or the court authorises the deal.

13.26 The result of entering into a transaction which breaches the self-dealing rule is that the beneficiaries are entitled to have it set aside, even if the transaction was demonstrably above board, unless the beneficiaries agreed to it or the court authorised it (*Ex p Lacey* (1802) 6 Ves 625). In effect the transaction is voidable, which results in considerable confusion as to title to the property and much unhappiness when the transaction is undone. It is territory not to be entered into without the fullest protection.

Action for devastavit, breach of trust or breach of fiduciary duty

13.27 An action for *devastavit,* breach of trust or fiduciary duty is a hostile step which should not be taken without full consideration of the issues.

13.28 In addition to claiming that the personal representatives should make good the loss the beneficiary/creditor will almost certainly include a claim that the personal representatives pay the cost of the action, and may seek an order that one or more of the personal representatives be removed and replaced by a 'more fit and proper person'.

13.29 It is bad practice for a personal representative in these circumstances to pay for his defence out of the estate because he may be found personally liable to make good the loss to the estate and pay the costs of the beneficiary or creditor complaining of *devastavit,* breach of trust or fiduciary duty. If he tries to pay for his defence to the proceedings out of the estate the beneficiaries/creditors may seek to prevent him from doing so by applying for an injunction or a direction that he should not do so.

13.30 It may be possible for a personal representative alleged to have committed a breach of trust/fiduciary duty/*devastavit* to seek an indemnity from another personal representative who sustained benefit from the alleged breach or who was the professional personal representative providing advice upon which a lay personal representative acted. Personal representatives can serve notices of claim between themselves and if one of them is a professional upon whose advice lay personal representatives acted it is likely that they will seek and obtain an indemnity from him. If personal representatives are exonerated from breach of duty to administer or breach of trust/fiduciary duty they are likely to be allowed one set of costs between them unless there were good reasons for them to have separate representation, as will quite commonly be the case whether there is some conflict between them on the facts or the personal interest of one of them conflicts with his duty (see *Re Spurling's Will Trusts* [1966] 1 WLR 920).

Extent of liability

13.31 The liability of defaulting personal representatives is in general to make good the loss which has been caused to the estate by their breach of duty to administer or breach of trust. Following *Target Holdings Ltd v Redferns* [1996] AC 421 it is clear that the causal link between the loss alleged and the action complained of must be established. It is unlikely to be sufficient for a beneficiary to say that there has been a breach and that loss has been incurred without proving that the loss which occurred has resulted wholly from the breach rather than wholly or partly from extraneous circumstances, such as a stock market crash.

13.32 Although restoration of the estate is likely to be appropriate where the trusts under the estate provide for successive interests, where personal representatives are found liable to a creditor whose debt has not been discharged or a beneficiary whose entitlement to claim in the estate has been ignored or miscalculated, personal representatives will be ordered to make good the loss to the creditor or beneficiary.

13.33 If a personal representative has used property in the estate for his own purposes, the beneficiaries have a choice as to whether to require him to account for the profit he actually made on the estate's property or to pay interest at such rate as the court considers appropriate. The rate may well be a commercial rate and may be compounded if the court considers that a personal representative has, in effect, acted fraudulently or otherwise in a wholly culpable manner.

Defences to claims

On the merits

13.34 A claim for *devastavit,* breach of trust or fiduciary duty can be defended on the facts in the usual way. The personal representatives/trustees may say that they did not act in the way alleged by the beneficiaries, that what they did does not constitute a breach or deny that any loss resulted. In addition they may be able to raise the following special defences.

Trustee Act 1925, s 27

13.35 Personal representatives have a defence to a claim that the estate has been distributed without regard to a debt or a claim by a person who claims to be beneficially interested if they had no notice of the claim and advertised in the *Gazette* and local newspaper for claimants in accordance with s 27 of the Trustee Act 1925. The advertisement must state that the personal representatives intend to distribute and require any claimant to send particulars of any claim within a period of not less than two months from the notice date. The effect of such an advertisement is that the personal representatives obtain the same protection as if they had distributed the estate under order of the court.

Trustee Act 1925, s 26

13.36 Where personal representatives are liable for rent, covenants or indemnities under the terms of a lease (including an underlease or agreement for a lease or underlease) or grant, they have power under s 26 of the Trustee Act 1925 to convey the property in question and distribute the estate without any personal liability for any subsequent claims under the lease or grant. However, to rely on the statutory protection, they must have satisfied all liabilities under the lease or grant which have accrued and been claimed up to the date of conveyance and, if necessary, set aside a fund sufficient to meet any future claims for fixed sums which the lessee agreed to expend on the property.

Court order

13.37 If personal representatives have distributed the estate in accordance with a direction made by the court then, provided that they have brought the full relevant facts to the attention of the court when seeking that direction, they will not be held liable to a creditor or other claimant if they acted in reliance on the court's directions. Personal representatives can seek directions of the court pursuant to CPR Part 64.2 to distribute on the footing that, all reasonable steps having been taken to trace a beneficiary, the missing beneficiary is dead (a Benjamin order after *Re Benjamin* [1902] 1 Ch 723), or to distribute on the footing that all debts have been ascertained (as in *Re Gess* [1942] Ch 37), or pursuant to an order that they should distribute without regard to a contingent liability (as in *Re Arnold* [1942] Ch 272 and *Re Yorke* [1977] 4 All ER 907).

13.38 If personal representatives are not certain how they should distribute the estate having regard to ambiguity or some difficulty of construction of the will they should apply to the court to determine the true construction of the will rather than distribute on an assumption as to its effect.

13.39 If personal representatives are unsure of their powers or consider that it is in the interests of the beneficiaries that they take steps which are beyond their powers they can apply under s 57 of the Trustee Act 1925 for the extension of their powers generally or for a specific purpose on the ground that it is expedient in the interests of the beneficiaries to exercise such powers. Further, the personal representatives may have been authorised to take steps in the administration (pursuant to the court's inherent jurisdiction with regard to the administration of estates) or the trusts of the will may have been varied by application under the Variation of Trusts Act 1958.

Trustee Act 1925, s 61

13.40 If a personal representative can satisfy the court that he acted honestly and reasonably and ought fairly to be excused not only for the breach of trust but also for failing to obtain the court's directions on the matter in question, the court has a discretion as to whether or not it should relieve him from liability either wholly or in part. The personal representative has to satisfy the court that he acted honestly and reasonably; he will have an uphill battle if he neglected to obtain proper advice. It is also clear that it is more difficult for a professional personal representative – of whom a higher standard of care is expected – to secure relief. In *Re Waterman's Will Trust* [1952] 2 All ER 1054 Harman J said 'I do not forget that a paid personal representative is expected to exercise a higher standard ... and knowledge than an unpaid personal representative and that a bank which advertises itself largely in the public press as taking charge of administrations is under a special duty'.

Limitation

13.41 Claims to any share or interest in a deceased's estate must be brought within 12 years from the date at which the right to the interest accrued. (The limitation period is shortened to 6 years for actions to recover arrears of interest in respect of any legacy or damages in respect of such arrears and time will run from the date on which the interest becomes due.)

13.42 A distinction arises between executors and administrators. An executor's title to the deceased's property dates from the testator's death. Title of an administrator, however, dates only from the grant of the letters of administration. Thus a right of action accruing after the date of an intestate's death can only accrue on grant (subject to one exception: the limitation period for actions to recover land in the possession of the deceased runs from the date of his death and not the date of the grant of letters of administration). In the case of *Green v Gaul* [2007] 1 WLR 591 Chadwick LJ went further and said *obiter* that time would not start to run against a personal representative until he/she was in a position to distribute the residuary estate (ie once all costs, funeral, testamentary and administration expenses, liabilities and pecuniary legacies had been paid out and the residuary estate of the intestate could be identified).

13.43 A breach of trust will be statute-barred if proceedings are brought more than six years after the date on which the right of action accrued (Limitation Act 1980, s 21(3)) although the right cannot accrue until the interest of the complaining beneficiary falls in. So if the complaining beneficiary is a remainderman time does not start to run until the life interest terminates. The right of action occurs when the breach is committed, not when the loss results. The 6 year time bar does not apply:

- where the trustees have deliberately concealed from the claimant his right of action in which case the limitation period does not start to run until the beneficiary has discovered the right of action or could with reasonable diligence have discovered it (Limitation Act 1980, s 32(1)). In *Cave v Robinson Jarvis & Rolf (a firm)* [2003] 1 AC 384, the House of Lords confirmed that this deprivation of a limitation defence only applies where the defendant takes active steps to conceal his own breach of duty after he has become aware of it and where he is guilty of deliberate wrongdoing and conceals it or fails to disclose it in circumstances where it is unlikely to be discovered for some time: it does not apply where the defendant does not realise that he is in error;

- where the action is for relief from the consequences of a mistake (whether of fact or law), in which case time does not start to run until the mistake is discovered or could with reasonable diligence have been discovered by the beneficiary (s 32(1) of the 1980 Act);

- where the beneficiary was under a disability (a child or lacking mental capacity) when the cause of action accrued, in which case time does not start to run until the disability ceases or the person under disability has died (s 28(1) of the 1980 Act) (the limitation for parties continues to run despite intermittent periods of disability);

- where the action is for a declaration that a particular transaction was invalid, such as where there has been a fraud on a power of appointment.

Commencement of a limitation period will be postponed in cases of deliberate concealment and mistake to the point where the beneficiary discovers it or could have done so with reasonable diligence.

13.44 Limitation cannot be pleaded where a beneficiary claims fraud, fraudulent breach of trust to which a personal representative was a party or conversion of trust property to a personal representative's own use (s 21 of the 1980 Act). However, the court may be reluctant to allow such claims if the claimant has acquiesced in the breach or has been guilty of such delay in bringing the claim that the equitable doctrine of *laches* applies.

13.45 Claims in respect of which no limitation period is prescribed by statute (such as claims arising from a breach of the self-dealing or fair dealing rules) may be prevented from being brought by the application of the equitable doctrine of *laches. Laches* may be pleaded where there has been a considerable lapse of time and the circumstances are such that either the person complaining has effectively waived the breach or his neglect of pursuing his remedy has placed the personal representative/will trustee in a position where it would not be reasonable to require him to compensate for the breach (*Lindsay Petroleum Co v Hurd* (1873-74) LR 5 PC 221 and *Nelson v Rye* [1996] 1 WLR 1378). The court will adopt a broad approach to the issue, considering whether it was unconscionable for the party concerned to be permitted to assert his beneficial rights (per Aldous LJ, in *Frawley v Neill,* (1999) *The Times* April 5, CA). If the court finds that *laches* applies, the claimant will be unable to pursue his claim: the effect is similar to that where a claim is held to be statute-barred.

13.46 If the claim is analogous to a breach of trust or breach of contract claim which is statute-barred, the claimant may not be able to pursue his claim (*Coulthard v Disco Mix Club Ltd* [2000] 1 WLR 707).

Acquiescence/release by beneficiaries

13.47 If a beneficiary consents to or acquiesces in a breach of trust he cannot subsequently complain about it. A personal representative/will trustee will not be able to defend on this basis unless the beneficiary was competent to acquiesce, knowing the facts and surrounding circumstances. Beneficiaries should be aware that trustees can exercise their right to impound the interest of any beneficiary who has instigated a breach of trust. Generally, fiduciaries are wary of exercising their equitable right to impound rather than seek a direction of the court to impound under s 62 of the Trustee Act 1925: this can be ordered only if the instigation, request or consent is in writing. A trustee is unlikely to exercise his right to impound where the beneficiary's interest is not in possession or he is a discretionary object. Acquiescence or consent on the part of one beneficiary does not prevent action being taken by others.

13.48 If a beneficiary confirms a fiduciary's actions or releases him from liability the fiduciary is protected from subsequent action by that beneficiary. A release may be inferred from conduct. A beneficiary who has consented or acquiesced in a breach of trust or released the fiduciary from liability should not be able to benefit from breach of trust proceedings brought by other beneficiaries (*Re Somerset* [1894] 1 Ch 231).

Exclusion/exoneration/exemption clauses

13.49 A will may, and commonly does, incorporate a clause seeking to cut down the liability of executors, such as providing that personal representatives are not responsible except for acts of fraud or wilful default or limiting the scope of the executor's liability in respect of his duties, eg in the case of oversight of an underlying limited company.

13.50 In any case where breach of duty to administer or breach of trust/fiduciary duty is alleged the will should be checked to see if it contains a clause attempting to exclude or limit liability or duties. It may be appropriate for the extent of the protection afforded by such a clause to be determined as a preliminary issue in a *devastavit* or breach of trust/fiduciary duty action.

13.51 Under English law exculpation clauses are valid provided that the trustees are not thereby relieved from liability for dishonesty or fraud (*Armitage v Nurse* [1998] Ch 241 and *Bogg v Raper* (1998/99) 1 ITELR 267). 'Dishonesty' means acting in a way the trustee appreciated was not in the interests of the beneficiaries or where he was reckless as to whether or not it was in the interests of the beneficiaries as a whole. An exoneration clause relieving a trustee of liability for acts, except wilful default or fraud, will not protect a trustee from acts of dishonesty, such as committing a breach of trust knowing that it is contrary to the interests of the beneficiaries or being recklessly indifferent whether it is contrary to their interests or not (*Armitage v Nurse* [1998] Ch 241 and *Walker v Stones* [2001] QB 902). An objective test will be applied to the question of dishonesty in the light of the personal representative's subjective knowledge at the time (*Walker v Stones, Twinsectra v Yardley* [2002] 2 AC 164). The recent Law Commission report recommends that testators/settlors be properly apprised of the implications of an exemption clause (Law Com 301, July 2006).

ACCOUNTS, INQUIRIES AND INVENTORIES

Application for accounts and inquiries or inventories

13.52 The court has wide powers to direct such accounts and inquiries as it considers necessary to enable the administration of the estate to be carried out. Under CPR Part 40 the court may order accounts and inquiries of its own initiative. Practice Direction 24 para 6 and Practice Direction 40 encapsulate the procedure. Accounts and inquiries are usually taken by a master.

13.53 Accounts and inquiries may be necessary:

(a)   as part of a full administration order;

(b) where directions are sought pursuant to CPR Part 64 but the court has inadequate information upon which to give directions, in which case it can order an inquiry as to a particular matter which would assist it in making its direction;

(c) where it is necessary for accounts to be taken of the administration;

(d) where an inquiry needs to be carried out to establish who the beneficiaries are (a kin inquiry).

Because the rules are not specific as to how the inquiry or account is to be dealt with, the order directing it will usually contain directions as to how it is to be carried out.

13.54 Accounts and inquiries may be sought when a claim is made by Part 7, and may be ordered pursuant to a Part 8 claim for the administration of the estate or for directions under CPR Part 64. A precedent application for an account is at Appendix 2.

13.55 If after hearing evidence on an action against a personal representative alleging wilful default the court decides that a personal representative is guilty of at least one breach of trust, and the trustee's conduct is such as to give rise to an inference that other breaches have occurred, accounts and inquiries can be ordered on the footing of wilful default (*Re Tebbs* [1976] 1 WLR 924). This means that the personal representative must account for the assets in the estate and the assets which but for the wilful default would have been in the estate.

13.56 If proceedings for an account on the footing of wilful default seek restitution of the trust fund on the basis that the trustees or their advisers have been paid excessive costs, it will be necessary for the excess (if any) to be determined. This is usually achieved by detailed assessment. The trustees' legal fees can be assessed pursuant to s 71 of the Solicitors Act 1974 without the necessity of applying for an account. In *Re Grimthorpe's Will Trusts* [1958] Ch 615 it was emphasised that expenses incurred by a fiduciary should only be reduced if the expenses were improperly incurred.

13.57 As to parties, since the proceedings are directed primarily to the personal representatives/trustees, the claimant beneficiary may not wish to join other beneficiaries. As with an application under CPR Part 64.2, all trustees should be joined as defendants.

13.58 Costs may be reserved on making an order for an account. The court can then consider how to exercise its discretion as to costs when the accounts have been prepared. If the court considers the personal representatives/trustees were at fault they are likely to be disallowed their costs from the estate/trust fund and ordered to pay the claimant's costs on the standard or indemnity basis. If the claimant fails to secure an account or wrongfully maintains that an account on the footing of wilful default should be ordered, the claimant is likely to be ordered to pay the costs of the personal representatives/trustees on the standard basis, in which case the personal representatives/trustees will be at liberty (unless the court orders otherwise) to take the balance of their indemnity basis costs from the estate/fund. Exceptionally the claimant may be ordered to pay other parties' costs on the indemnity basis. The order will usually provide that their costs should be assessed on a detailed assessment, although the court can assess them summarily if not agreed.

Application under the Non-Contentious Probate Rules 1987 (NCPR 1987)

13.59 Section 25 of the Administration of Estates Act 1925 provides that a personal representative is under a duty, when required to do so by the court, to exhibit on oath a full inventory of the estate and an account of his administration. Rule 61 of the NCPR 1987 provides that an application for an inventory and account shall be made by summons to be heard by a probate registrar or judge of the Family Division. If the summons is to be heard by a judge, it must be issued out of the Probate Department of the Principal Registry, but if by a registrar it can be issued out of the Principal Registry or the district probate registry from which the grant issued.

13.60 The summons seeking an account and inventory is supported by an affidavit setting out details of the estate, the applicant's interest in the estate and why an account and inventory is sought. If the person making the application is not a residuary beneficiary but a legatee or creditor, the judge or registrar may require some convincing that it is appropriate that he should make an order requiring the personal representatives to render an account of their administration and to exhibit an inventory of the estate. But if there is a risk that the estate is insolvent even though it is being administered as though solvent, or it is suggested that payment of a legacy will be long delayed or might need to abate, the judge or registrar may be prepared to make such an order. To comply with such an order, the personal representatives will need to swear an affidavit setting out the assets and liabilities of the estate and providing details as to how they have administered it.

13.61 No fee is payable on the issue of the summons or filing any affidavit, but two copies of the summons must be sent to the probate registry with the supporting affidavit. The summons, duly noted with the return date, must be served on the personal representatives at least two clear days before the hearing date. Summonses returnable before a probate registrar are usually heard quite quickly.

13.62 If the personal representatives, or any one of them, fail to comply with an order requiring them to provide an account and inventory their disobedience can be punished by an order of committal. If an order of committal is sought, service of an order of the registrar/judge requiring the personal representative to produce an account and inventory must be proved.

Any beneficiary or creditor wishing to enforce such an order by committal should look at the detailed provisions in RSC Ord 45 r 5 and Order 52 in Sch 1 to the Civil Procedure Rules 1998.

13.63 The procedure for an account and inventory may be used not only where the personal representatives are failing to keep the beneficiaries informed or where there is concern that the personal representatives are not acting in good faith and may be securing assets for their own benefit, but also where a grant of probate or of letters of administration has been revoked and details of the past administration of the estate cannot be obtained from the former personal representatives.

13.64 Problems between trustees and beneficiaries often concern lack of accounts. If lay trustees are really out of their depth in providing accounting information the problem may be resolved by the trustees and beneficiary agreeing that an accountant or other professional should prepare or audit the accounts.

Application to the Public Trustee

13.65 Section 13 of the Public Trustee Act 1906 provides that, unless the court otherwise orders, if an application is made to the Public Trustee (with notice to the trustees and beneficiaries) the accounts of a trust must be investigated and audited by a solicitor or accountant agreed on by the applicant and the trustees or, in default of agreement, by the Public Trustee or his appointee. This procedure can be useful if the beneficiary has queries on the accounts. The cost of the investigation and audit (which cannot be carried out at less than 12-monthly intervals) including the remuneration of the auditor will usually be borne out of the trust fund but the Public Trustee can order them to be borne by one or more of the parties on hearing both parties' submissions on costs. An appeal lies to a judge of the Chancery Division.

DISCLOSURE AND INSPECTION OF TRUST DOCUMENTS

The general position

13.66 A beneficiary of an estate and an object of a discretionary power or trust exercisable in the estate may be able to inspect and take copies of estate documents upon paying those costs incurred by the personal representatives in connection with providing copies. In general a beneficiary who has a sufficiently proximate interest (ie is not subject to discretionary power with limited chance of the power being exercised in his favour, such that he may not be regarded as appropriate to inspect documents relating to the affairs of the estate) is tempered by certain restrictions, such as that the beneficiary is not entitled to see confidential documents passing between other beneficiaries and personal representatives or other documents which evidence the reasons why the personal representatives exercised their discretion in a particular manner (see *Re Londonderry's Settlement* [1965] 1 Ch 918).

13.67 Most of the law on this subject relates to beneficiaries requesting documents from trustees of lifetime or will trusts, no doubt because of the efficacy of other remedies in estates such as under Administration of Estates Act 1925, s 25 to procure an account. Indeed some doubt has been cast on the applicability of the law relating to disclosure of trust documents to an estate, but it is generally thought that similar principles will apply.

13.68 It is trite law that a fiduciary holds assets not for his own benefit but for the benefit of the beneficiaries of the trust/estate, to whom he owes enforceable duties. These include being ready to account for the way in which he has dealt with the estate/trust assets. This means not only that the trustee must keep accounts of his dealings with the trust property and be prepared to produce them, together with supporting vouchers (*Pearse v Green* (1819) 1 Jac & W 135), but also be prepared to provide the beneficiary with up-to-date and complete information about the assets of the trust. Chitty J in *Re Tillott* [1892] 1 Ch 86 made it clear that trustees are bound to give beneficiaries proper information as to the investment of the trust and that such information must be corroborated and not merely consist of general unsupported statements. In *Re Dartnall* [1895] 1 Ch 474, it was said that a trustee must give all reasonable information as to the manner in which the fund has been dealt with and its investments and, in the absence of special circumstances, allow inspection; see also *Re Cowin* (1886) 33 Ch D 179.

13.69 If a fiduciary is to be, in any real sense, accountable for the estate's/trust's assets, the beneficiaries must be able to access information about their management and to inspect and take copies of documents relating to the estate/trust, either personally or by their solicitor (*Kemp v Burn* (1863) 4 Giff 348). It is now clear, however, from the seminal decision of the Privy Council in *Schmidt v Rosewood Trust Ltd* [2003] 2 AC 709 that the trustees' accountability and obligation to disclose is to be regarded as owed to the court and the question of whether or not documents are to be disclosed to a beneficiary, a matter for the discretion of the court. In his Withers Lecture in 2004 (see PCB 2004, 1, 23-40) Mr Justice Lightman described the position post *Schmidt v Rosewood* as follows:

> '... the right of a beneficiary is not a right to access trust documents or information but an equity incident to his beneficial interest entitling him to invoke the discretionary jurisdiction of the court to require the trustee to make disclosure.'

13.70 As the legal owner of the estate/trust property, a personal representative/trustee is entitled to custody of the trust deeds – *Evans v Bicknell* (1801) 6 Ves 174. A fiduciary is not entitled to use information acquired through his office as trustee for his own purposes and must not profit either directly or indirectly from his fiduciary position (*Boardman v Phipps* [1964]

2 All ER 187 and *Ex p Lacey* (1802) 6 Ves 625). He should keep the affairs of the estate/trust confidential and not disclose them to strangers without just cause (*Heerema v Heerema* (1985–86) JLR 293) and, as with any other fiduciary, can be restrained by an injunction from disclosing confidential information.

13.71 This does not mean that the affairs of the estate or trust should be kept confidential from the beneficiaries. It is no longer the case that beneficiaries are considered to have a proprietary right to inspect trust documents. But absent considerations which would render disclosure inappropriate in the interests of the beneficial class, a beneficiary with a real interest in the estate/trust responsibly seeking disclosure is afforded it, in appropriate cases subject to conditions.

13.72 A beneficiary can ask personal representatives/will trustees for facilities, either personally or through another such as his solicitor, to inspect the will and other relevant documents and in so doing should be permitted to inspect at least the will, accounts and supporting vouchers, documents relating to the management of the estate's assets and instructions to and the advice of the personal representatives' solicitors and counsel. Legal professional privilege cannot be claimed in this context by a personal representative against a beneficiary (except in certain circumstances where the beneficiary's interests are adverse to those of the estate/will trust).

13.73 In some cases personal representatives are reluctant to permit a beneficiary or his agent to inspect the above documents even if a beneficiary has agreed to pay the costs involved. In those circumstances a beneficiary can apply to the court for a direction under CPR Part 64 that the personal representatives make available those documents for inspection by or on behalf of the beneficiary.

13.74 Inspection by a beneficiary is a possibility irrespective of any allegation of fraud or wrongdoing on the part of the personal representatives or of the existence of litigation between the beneficiaries and the personal representatives. If proceedings for breach of duty or other proceedings involving disclosure are issued by the beneficiaries against the personal representatives then disclosure of relevant documents will take place in the usual way. Disclosure in litigation between the parties may produce different documents to the documents which the beneficiary would usually be able to inspect irrespective of litigation, such as documents usually regarded as confidential or relating to the exercise of the personal representatives'/trustees' discretion.

Disclosure in hostile proceedings

13.75 Disclosure may take place in advance of proceedings if the court considers that the parties are likely to be parties to the proceedings and that disclosure of the document is desirable to assist by, for example, resolving the matter before the proceedings (CPR, r 31.16). Otherwise, disclosure is ordered to take place in accordance with the directions given at the case management conference and will be standard disclosure unless the court orders otherwise. Standard disclosure, in accordance with CPR, r 31.6 involves disclosing documents:

- supporting the party's case or on which he relies;

- adversely affecting the other party's case; or

- supporting another party's case; and

- which the party is required to disclose by Practice Direction.

13.76 The party making disclosure must make a reasonable search for documents and must state in his disclosure statement that he understands the disclosure obligations and describe the extent of the search which has been carried out. Searches must now cover electronically stored documents as well as physical repositories (PD 31.2A). The duty to disclose extends to documents in a party's control, including if he has the right to possession or to take copies. When giving standard disclosure a party is required to make a reasonable search for standard disclosure documents (CPR, r 31.7) and the factors relevant in deciding the reasonableness of the search include matters such as the number of documents involved, the nature and complexity of the proceedings, the ease and expense of retrieval of any particular document, and the significance of any document which is likely to be located during the search.

13.77 If the court considers that the level of disclosure is inadequate, specific disclosure can be ordered pursuant to CPR, r 31.12.

13.78 In general a party to whom the document is being disclosed has the right to inspect it, although CPR, r 31.3 does impose certain restrictions on the right if the document is no longer in the possession of the person disclosing, or if the expense involved in inspection would be disproportionate to the issues in the case. Documents that are privileged are also not available for inspection in disclosure in hostile litigation, in contrast to the position which may obtain where disclosure of trust documents is sought.

13.79 The court can order specific disclosure of particular documents (CPR, r 31.12). CPR Part 18 enables the court at any time to order that a party clarify any matter in dispute or provide additional information, whether contained or referred to in a statement of his case or not. An application for further information should be preceded by written request for the information (in accordance with PD 18.1). If the recipient of the request objects to it, he must notify the requesting party within the time stipulated in the request, in which case the requesting party can issue an application notice for an order under CPR Part 18. The party against whom the order is made must file and serve a response within the time stipulated by the court and the response must be verified by a statement of truth in accordance with CPR Part 22.

Disclosure by testator's solicitor before proceedings

13.80 Following the decision in the case of *Larke v Nugus* [2000] WTLR 1033, in which it was held that the plaintiff solicitors ought reasonably to have provided a copy of the will to the defendants when asked, so as to avoid costly proceedings, the Law Society published guidance to solicitors on disclosure in situations where a will is in dispute. To avoid unnecessary litigation, the testator's solicitor should make available a statement containing his or her evidence regarding instructions for the preparation and execution of the will and the surrounding circumstances, to any person who is party to probate proceedings, or who it is believed has a reasonable claim under the will.

13.81 Although this guidance is not incorporated in the new Solicitors' Code of Conduct introduced on 1 July 2007, it is incorporated in the Law Society's best practice statement 'File retention: records management – retention and wills, deeds and documents together with supporting data' (see **12.74**).

REMOVAL AND SUBSTITUTION

Application for removal or substitution of personal representatives

13.82 The High Court has a discretionary power by virtue of s 50 of the Administration of Justice Act 1985 to appoint a substitute personal representative or to terminate the appointment of a personal representative. Section 50 does not contain a stand-alone power to appoint a new personal representative.

13.83 The procedure for applications under s 50 of the Act is set out in CPR, r 57.13. If the application is made in the course of proceedings it is by application notice; if made separately, by Part 8 claim. The application must be supported by the following:

(1) a certified sealed copy of the grant of probate or letters of administration;

(2) a witness statement setting out the circumstances in which the removal or substitution of the personal representatives or any of them is sought, particulars of the estate's assets and liabilities, those who are in possession of documents relating to the estate, names of beneficiaries and details of their interest, and who is or are proposed as substituted personal representative(s);

(3) unless the proposed substitute personal representative is the Official Solicitor, his signed or sealed consent to act;

(4)   a witness statement of the proposed substitute personal representative's fitness to act in such capacity, if he is an individual.

13.84 The court can authorise a person appointed as substituted personal representative to charge remuneration for his services on such terms as the court thinks fit. If the proposed substituted personal representative wishes to charge it is appropriate to incorporate details of the proposed charges in the witness statement in support of his application.

13.85 Applications under s 50 are usually heard by a master in chambers. A precedent application by an executor together with witness statement in support for removal of a co-executor is at Appendix 2.

Action for removal of will trustees

13.86 Disgruntled beneficiaries may wish to remove will trustees from office. If a will trustee appreciates that the relationship of trust and confidence has broken down between him and the beneficiaries he should be prepared to retire: if he does not, the court may remove him if satisfied that the breakdown is due to the manner of the administration and that the relationship is such that it will impede the proper administration of the will trust (*Letterstedt v Broers* (1884) 9 App Cas 371).

13.87 A trustee may be removed without the assistance of the court. There may be an express power in the will. The statutory powers under the Trustee Act 1925, ss 36 and 37 may provide a remedy and enable a trustee who remains out of the jurisdiction for more than 12 months consecutively, refuses or is unfit to act or is incapable of acting to be replaced. (It should be noted that the Court of Protection may be involved if a trustee lacks mental capacity – see the Trustee Act 1925, ss 36(9) and 54(2) as amended by the Mental Capacity Act 2005.) If all beneficiaries are of full age and capacity and together absolutely entitled they may direct the retirement of a trustee or trustees and the appointment of some other person either in addition to or substitution for such trustees by virtue of ss 19 and 20 of the Trusts of Land and Appointment of Trustees Act 1996.

13.88 If none of these provisions affords the dissatisfied beneficiary a remedy he will wish to look to the court's inherent jurisdiction over trustees and s 41 of the Trustee Act 1925. The court will not remove a trustee from office lightly, even if a breach of trust has been committed, unless it considers that the trust property will not be safe or that the trust will not be properly executed in the interests of the beneficiaries if the trustee remains in office.

Judicial trustees

13.89 If necessary – such as where an urgent situation arises, particularly where the trustees cannot pull together or where the trustees are about to act while labouring under a conflict of interest or duty – a beneficiary may apply to the

High Court for the appointment of a judicial trustee under the Judicial Trustees Act 1896. A judicial trustee can seek the court's directions informally and quickly without attending court. The disadvantage of having to provide security has largely fallen away, given that most judicial trustees are professionals carrying indemnity insurance. The procedure is still rather more expensive than the appointment of ordinary replacement trustees because a judicial trustee has to submit his accounts for court approval.

Removal under Trustee Act 1925, s 41 or court's inherent power

13.90 For the court to remove will trustees pursuant to a Part 8 claim under s 41 of the Trustee Act 1925 there must be no real dispute as to fact. Where facts are in dispute the beneficiary needs to issue an ordinary Part 7 claim, usually also seeking restitution/equitable compensation for breach of trust. The proceedings will be commenced in the Chancery Division of the High Court, or the county court if the trust fund does not exceed £30,000 in value (County Courts Act 1984, s 23). Evidence must be produced that the proposed replacement trustee(s) is/are willing to act. Written consents and witness statements of fitness are required in a manner similar to that where an application is made under Administration of Justice Act 1985, s 50 (see **13.83**). A document purporting to contain the written consent of a person to act as a trustee and to bear his signature, verified by some other person, is evidence of his consent to act. A witness statement of fitness (by a responsible, usually professional, person who has known the proposed trustee for a number of years and confirms that he has a good reputation and is suitable to act as a fiduciary) must be lodged and served. If a corporate trustee is proposed details of its scales of charging should be provided to the court.

13.91 The beneficiary wishing to remove the will trustee(s) will be the claimant and all will trustees will be defendants. Since this is an application which affects beneficiaries generally they should be joined, or representatives of each class of beneficiary should be joined, as defendants.

INJUNCTIVE RELIEF

13.92 While it is relatively unusual for an injunction to be sought in proceedings relating to the administration of an estate, if circumstances arise which make it necessary – such as that a personal representative is about to commit a breach of duty which would be irremediable, to distribute incorrectly, or to make away with assets belonging to the estate – an injunction could be sought against the personal representatives to restrain such action under CPR Part 25.

13.93 In such a case the personal representatives are at risk on costs in the same way as they would be in the case of a *devastavit*/breach of trust/fiduciary duty action. Since the purpose of an interim injunction is to preserve the status quo pending trial, a personal representative faced with an injunction application would be wise to offer an undertaking not to take the action complained of until the matter is determined by the court, whether in hostile proceedings brought by the beneficiaries or by the personal representatives issuing an application to the court for directions. Unless the beneficiaries consider that the estate is at imminent risk, beneficiaries may be better not seeking injunctive relief but issuing an application instead under CPR Part 64 for an order directing the personal representatives not to take a particular step in that capacity.

13.94 Circumstances may arise where personal representatives consider applying for an injunction against a third party, whether a beneficiary acting otherwise than as beneficiary or a complete stranger to the estate.

13.95 Unless action is particularly pressing and the merits are clear, personal representatives would be unwise to commence proceedings for an injunction against a third party without all the beneficiaries' agreement (if practicable) or a Beddoe order. See **13.122—13.131**.

13.96 Personal representatives should also bear in mind that they will need to give a cross-undertaking in damages: they should ensure that the consent of the beneficiaries or the Beddoe direction secures their position in relation to that undertaking. In rare circumstances, the personal representatives may either wish to make an application for a mandatory injunction requiring a third party to take particular action or a freezing order which freezes the defendant's assets so as to prevent him from dissipating or concealing his assets to make judgment against him worthless or difficult to enforce.

APPLICATION FOR DIRECTIONS

13.97 Where a difficulty arises between personal representatives themselves or personal representatives and beneficiaries as to the administration of the estate it is possible to apply for an administration order (whereby the estate is administered under the direction of the court), or more usually and economically, to make an application for directions on specific issues.

13.98 Personal representatives in doubt as to the extent of their powers, the proper exercise of their powers, caught in the crossfire between warring beneficiaries or faced with a difficult decision commonly seek guidance from the court in the form of directions pursuant to the court's ancient power to secure the proper administration of an estate or execution of a will trust (as in *Public Trustee v Cooper* [2001] WTLR 901). CPR Part 64 describes how the court can give such directions and chapter 26 of the Chancery Guide (2005) provides guidance on how to make such an application. If there is an issue of real difficulty and the personal representatives/will trustees have been unable to resolve it in discussion with the beneficiaries it should be brought to the court by the personal representatives/will trustees who may join the beneficiaries or representative beneficiaries as defendants.

13.99 A beneficiary can issue the application if he considers that the personal representatives/will trustees are being dilatory. This will probably be viewed as a hostile step with the usual costs consequences unless the court considers that, in accordance with the guidelines set out in *Re Buckton* [1907] 2 Ch 406, the proceedings could properly have been brought by the personal representatives/ will trustees. The application should be issued only if it is clear that the personal representatives/will trustees will not do so, the situation is urgent or the beneficiary perceives that the personal representatives/will trustees are labouring under a conflict of interest.

13.100 The jurisdiction to give directions is very wide ranging. Examples of situations in which an application can be made for directions include:

- any question arising as to the composition of a class of beneficiaries;

- any question relating to the rights or interests of a creditor or a person claiming to be a creditor;

- an order requiring accounts to be provided by personal representatives (see **13.52**);

- an order requiring a payment into court by personal representatives;

- an order directing personal representatives not to take a particular course of action (see **13.92**);

- as to whether a proposed exercise of particular powers of appointment is proper;

- as to the ethos and method of investment of trust/estate assets (as in *Cowan v Scargill* [1985] Ch 270, and note *Nestle v National Westminster Bank* [1993] 1 WLR 1260);

- as to whether to compromise a claim by or against the estate;

- whether doubtful debts or foreign revenue claims should be met. It has long been established that if personal representatives/will trustees pay a statute-barred debt they commit a breach of trust (see *Midgley v Midgley* [1893] 3 Ch 282). Accordingly, personal representatives/will trustees should be wary of discharging taxes levied by a foreign revenue authority which could not be enforced against them, and should seek directions before doing so, particularly where some but not all the beneficiaries would otherwise be exposed to tax claims in the jurisdiction in question;

- whether proceedings affecting the estate or trust should be prosecuted or defended at the expense of the estate/trust fund (*Re Beddoe* [1893] 1 Ch 547). Beddoe proceedings are covered in more detail in **13.122—13.131**;

- where there is perceived to be a need for a *Re Benjamin* or *Re Yorke* order. Concern over the identity of those entitled or whether there are any contingent liabilities may cause delay or indecision on the part of the personal representatives/will trustees. These matters can be resolved by an application by the personal representatives for a direction to them authorising distribution on a particular footing, eg on the footing that a beneficiary is dead (as in *Re Benjamin* [1902] 1 Ch 723), or that a contingent liability should be ignored (as in *Re Yorke* [1997] 4 All ER 907). (Note that in respect of contingent liabilities arising from a deceased's participation as a name at Lloyds, such applications have to date been governed by Practice Statement [2001] 3 All ER 765, and Chancery Guide (2005) chapter 26). However the procedure is specific to liabilities having been reinsured into the Equitas Group. At the time of writing Equitas had been bought by Berkshire Hathaway (see **17.32(6)—17.36**).

Procedure

13.101 The claimant(s) to an application under CPR Part 64 is/are almost always the personal representative(s) with the beneficiary, or some of the beneficiaries being joined as defendants. Practice Direction 64B deals with the situation where applications for directions are brought by the personal representatives/trustees. It does not provide guidance in relation to an application for directions brought by beneficiaries.

13.102 There may be concern as to which beneficiaries should be joined as defendants in which case an application can be made for directions as to who to join or to whom to give notice under CPR, r 19.8A.

13.103 If the issue concerns some only of the beneficiaries, they should be joined. Where there are numerous beneficiaries in a particular class which should be represented before the court, then a representation order should be sought. CPR, r 19.7 enables the court, if satisfied that it is expedient, to appoint one person or more to represent another person or class of people interested in the trust fund in situations where some of the class cannot readily be found or ascertained, or if the court considers that in all the circumstances it is right to appoint a representative beneficiary to save costs. If the court makes such an order, its decision is binding on those represented by the representative beneficiary. A person under disability – a child or person lacking mental capacity – must act by his litigation friend unless the court otherwise orders (CPR Part 21). It is not always necessary to join all beneficiaries or ensure that a representation order is made in respect of all beneficiaries. If they are not all joined or represented, it is the personal representatives/will trustees' duty to put before the court any matters which may affect their interests. This is not feasible if the beneficiaries' interests are adverse to those of the personal representatives/will trustees.

13.104 Where the estate/will trust is insolvent or potentially insolvent, consideration should be given to joining the creditors or a representative creditor of the estate/trust, but in general personal representatives of an insolvent estate should be applying for an order under the Insolvency Act 1986 rather than for directions (see chapter 17).

13.105 At any stage in the proceedings the court can direct that notice of the proceedings is served on those beneficiaries (or creditors) who are not parties but who will be affected by the court's decision. CPR, r 19.8A provides that notice of the claim may be served on non-parties and the recipients have 14 days in which to acknowledge service and become parties. If they fail to do so they are bound in any event by the court's decision.

13.106 Applications for directions should not be made in respect of charitable will trusts without the approval of the Charity Commission or, on appeal from a refusal by the Commission, with permission of the court (CPR Part 64). Most issues which might require the assistance of the court can be resolved by an order made by the Charity Commission under s 26 of the Charities Act 1993 or by the provision of a letter of opinion or advice under s 29 of the Act. If an application for directions is to be made in the case of a charitable will trust the Attorney-General is always the appropriate defendant and almost always the only defendant.

13.107 An application for directions is made by a Part 8 claim. The Part 8 claim form states that CPR Part 8 applies, details the question the court is to decide and the remedy sought, and sets out the legal basis relied on, including any statutory provision. If any party is in a representative capacity that must also be stated (CPR, r 8.2). The claim form must be verified by a statement of truth under CPR Part 22: this is a statement to the effect that the claimant believes that the facts stated in the claim form are true. (The statement of truth is important because without it, the claim may be struck out. It has the effect that the claim form may be relied on as evidence and, if that evidence is verified by a statement of truth without an honest belief in its truth proceedings could be brought for contempt of court by the Attorney-General or with the permission of the court (CPR, r 32.14).)

13.108 The evidence in support of the claim form must be filed and served at the same time as the claim form (CPR, r 8.5(1) and (2)). The evidence will be in the form of a witness statement, again verified by a statement of truth. The witness statement should give details of the estate or trust (appending a copy of the will and codicils and any deeds of appointment), the value of the estate/trust fund, describe the interests of the beneficiaries and set out in some detail the nature of the problem on which directions are sought. The evidence must explain what if any consultation there has been with beneficiaries and with what result. If the beneficiaries are numerous the principal beneficiaries should be consulted. If a child is a defendant to the application, the court may well expect to have put before it instructions to and the opinion of an appropriately qualified lawyer to advise as to the benefits and disadvantages of the course of action proposed from the point of view of the child.

13.109 Defendants who wish to participate in the proceedings or seek a different remedy must acknowledge service within 14 days of being served with the claim form and supporting evidence. If a defendant disagrees that Part 8 is the appropriate procedure (because, for example, there is a substantial dispute of fact) he must say so, with reasons, when acknowledging service (CPR, r 8.8(1)). The court will then give directions and can order that the claim continues as an ordinary claim. This is unusual in the case of an application for directions unless there is a major dispute of fact between the personal representative/the will trustees and the beneficiaries or there is an allegation of fraud.

13.110 The personal representative/will trustees and beneficiaries who are defendants must file and serve their evidence at the same time as acknowledging service. As with the claimant, the defendant's evidence is by witness statement verified by statement of truth. The claimant then has 14 days in which to file and serve further evidence (if any) in reply.

13.111 When the court receives the acknowledgement of service and any written evidence it will give directions as to the future management of the case (CPR, r 8.8(2)). This will involve the master deciding whether the application can be disposed of without a hearing. If directions leading to a hearing are needed, these will usually include setting a timetable, or fixing a case management conference or a pre-trial review or both (CPR, r 29.2). It is important that, if the parties are legally represented, a lawyer with sufficient knowledge of the case is present at the case management conference or the pre-trial review – if it is to take place at court – or, where appropriate, the telephone conference.

13.112 In readiness for the case management conference or pre-trial review the parties should prepare a case summary, should consider whether the parties themselves should attend and should issue any necessary applications in accordance with CPR Part 23. The parties or their legal representatives should take with them to the case management conference or pre-trial review copies of witness statements and any experts' reports.

13.113 Issues likely to be addressed at the case management conference include:

- filing and service of any further evidence;

- whether any disclosure is required;

- whether parties should attend for cross examination;

- preparation of an agreed statement before trial (if applicable); and

- if possible, fixing a date for trial.

13.114 The court will always consider whether it is possible to deal with the application on paper without a hearing. If the court would be minded to refuse to give the directions asked for on a consideration of the papers alone, the parties will be notified and given the opportunity within a stated time to ask for a hearing. Examples of applications dealt with without a hearing are applications to be permitted to distribute the estate of a deceased Lloyd's name, following *Re Yorke* [1997] 4 All ER 907 (see **17.32(6)—17.36**), and applications for a declaration as to the true construction of the will in circumstances which are not contentious, under the Administration of Justice Act 1985, s 48.

Costs implications

13.115 The costs of all proceedings are at the discretion of the court (CPR, r 44.3(1)). While the general rule is that the unsuccessful party pays the costs of the successful party (CPR, r 44.3(2)) the court can make a different order. In deciding what order (if any) to make, the court must have regard to all the circumstances including:

- the conduct of all the parties;

- whether a party succeeded only on part of his case; and

- whether an offer to settle has been made either under CPR Part 36 or otherwise.

13.116 The conduct which the court takes into account is conduct before as well as during the proceedings and includes whether the party tried to avoid the need for proceedings by settling the dispute using ADR or not, the manner in which the claim was pursued, and the success of that party's case.

13.117 Costs can be awarded on the standard or indemnity basis. Where costs are allowed on the standard basis they will only be allowed if proportionate to the matters in issue. Any doubt as to whether costs were reasonably incurred, were of a reasonable amount, or were proportionate, is resolved in favour of the paying party, (CPR, r 44.4(2)). The Court of Appeal has given guidance on proportionality in *Home Office v Lownds* [2002] 1 WLR 2450: the court looks at the costs globally. All the circumstances are to be taken into account in deciding this matter (CPR, r 44.5). Where costs are awarded on the indemnity basis any doubt as to whether the costs were reasonably incurred, or were reasonable in amount, is resolved in favour of the receiving party (CPR, r 44.4(3)). The concept of proportionality does not apply to indemnity basis costs.

13.118 If the court considers that the parties have failed to comply with any relevant pre action protocol or Section 4 of the Pre Action Protocols Practice Direction or have failed to comply with the overriding objective in CPR Part 1 and that failure has led to the commencement of proceedings or costs being incurred unnecessarily, the court can order the party at fault to pay the costs or part of them, can deprive him of costs, or can order him to pay costs on the indemnity basis.

13.119 The general principle is that, between personal representatives/will trustees and beneficiaries, personal representatives/will trustees are entitled to receive from the estate/trust fund all proper costs incurred when acting on behalf of the estate/trust (Trustee Act 2000, s 31). CPR, r 48.4 provides that where a person is party to proceedings in the capacity of trustee the general rule is that where he is entitled to be paid those costs out of the estate fund he should be reimbursed on the indemnity basis insofar as they are not recoverable from a third party but the court may order otherwise if a trustee has acted for a benefit other than that of the fund. The same principles apply to personal representatives. While it is common for the costs of all parties for directions proceedings issued by the personal representatives/will trustees to be met from the fund, if the proceedings are commenced by a beneficiary they are more likely to be construed as hostile, in which case costs usually, but not necessarily always, follow the event (CPR, r 44.3(2)).

13.120 If the court considers that the personal representatives/will trustees were at fault it may order that the personal representatives/will trustees are not entitled to take their costs from the fund. They may also be ordered to pay the beneficiaries' costs, if the personal representatives/trustees have behaved in such a way as to incur unnecessary costs. Alternatively the court might disallow the personal representatives/will trustees their costs but make no order in the defendant's favour. In recent decisions the court has made it clear that it does not regard itself as restricted from ordering costs against personal representatives/trustees or depriving them from access to the estate/trust fund. Such an order was made in the exceptional case *Breadner v Granville-Grossman* [2001] WTLR 377 where, for a number of reasons (including that the action had only been necessitated by a fault on the part of the trustees or their predecessors and that the trustees had decided to adopt a partisan approach in the course of the construction proceedings) the court ordered that the trustees should not be allowed to take their costs out of the trust fund and that they should pay the beneficiaries' costs on the indemnity basis.

13.121 The court can summarily assess any costs (usually when the hearing lasts less than one day) – except those of a child or person lacking capacity – and require a party to pay those costs, usually within 14 days. Alternatively the court can order a detailed assessment by a costs officer under CPR Part 47.

BEDDOE ORDERS: OBTAINING PERMISSION OF THE COURT TO ISSUE/DEFEND PROCEEDINGS

In what circumstances should personal representatives/will trustees apply?

13.122 If personal representatives/will trustees are contemplating taking proceedings against third parties or proceedings are issued against the estate (through the personal representatives in their representative capacity) or will trust (through the trustees) the personal representatives/will trustees are at risk as to their costs if they do not obtain the sanction of the court to their involvement in the proceedings.

13.123 The general rule is that a personal representative/will trustee who is party to third party litigation in his capacity as personal representative/will trustee (and not, for example, where proceedings are brought against him personally for *devastavit*, breach of trust or breach of fiduciary duty) is entitled to his own costs out of the estate/trust fund on the indemnity basis to the extent that those costs have not been recovered from other parties to the litigation, but the court may order otherwise if he has acted for a benefit other than that of the fund (CPR Part 48.4). The costs are incurred in the administration of the estate/execution of the will trust and are subject to the trustee's usual right of indemnity from the fund if they are properly incurred (Trustee Act 2000, s 31(2) and *Alsop Wilkinson v Neary* [1995] 1 All ER 431).

13.124 If the personal representatives'/trustees' costs are to be paid out of the estate/trust fund they are allowed on the indemnity basis. Where indemnity basis costs are ordered, any doubt as to whether they were reasonably incurred or reasonable in amount is resolved in favour of the receiving party (CPR, r 44.4(3)). However even if the trustee is entitled to his costs on the indemnity basis from the fund, those costs can be reduced on assessment if they are considered to be of an unreasonable amount or unreasonably incurred (*Re Grimthorpe's Will Trusts* [1958] 1 All ER 765).

13.125 Because of the risk of being disallowed costs personal representative/ will trustees contemplating taking proceedings against third parties (such as professional negligence claims against professional advisers or possession proceedings) or defending proceedings brought against them as personal representative/will trustees should apply to the court for a Beddoe order, unless they can secure the agreement of all the beneficiaries to their taking that action at the expense of the fund, or some of the beneficiaries are willing to give them a worthwhile indemnity. However PD 64B of the CPR envisages that if steps need to be taken quickly, and it is not possible to secure an indemnity, personal representative/will trustees should nonetheless consider litigation and take a modest element of risk, provided that they are advised by Counsel to do so.

The nature of the relief sought

13.126 A Beddoe order (after *Re Beddoe* [1893] 1 Ch 547) is a direction to personal representatives/will trustees to take or defend proceedings affecting the estate/trust at the expense of the estate/trust fund. Since the personal representative/will trustee is entitled to his costs from the estate/trust fund on the indemnity basis unless the court decides to disallow his costs, the personal representative/will trustee is inviting the court to decide at an early stage that the personal representative/will trustee is acting reasonably and in the interests of the estate/trust fund in bringing or defending the proceedings.

13.127 The beneficiaries or representatives of them may be parties to the application and may express their views as to whether the estate/trust fund should be used to meet the costs of pursuing or defending the action. If the estate/trust fund is potentially insolvent, creditors or a representative creditor may be joined and make representations. Even if not joined as parties, such beneficiaries/creditors should be consulted and their views made known to the court.

13.128 The court will consider the merits of the action proposed on behalf of the estate/trust fund on the basis of the information then available, including an opinion of a suitably qualified lawyer instructed by the personal representative/will trustee to provide a frank assessment of the merits and weaknesses of the case. The court can direct the personal representative/will trustee not to issue or defend the proceedings, to adopt a purely formal and neutral role, to issue or defend at the expense of the estate/trust fund, or to do so up to a limited stage (such as completion of disclosure or exchange of evidence) when the court will reconsider the merits of continuing with the litigation, with the benefit of a further opinion of a suitably qualified lawyer. If the court authorises the personal representative/will trustee to issue proceedings or defend at the expense of the fund it will also order that the personal representative/will trustee be entitled to be indemnified from the estate/trust fund in respect of any adverse costs order which may be made against them.

13.129 The application for a Beddoe order is made separately from the substantive proceedings giving rise to the need to seek Beddoe relief. The procedure is governed by CPR Part 64 and its practice directions and the Chancery Guide (2005) provides useful guidance on the procedure. If the personal representatives/will trustees consider that the court is likely to be able to deal with the application without a hearing then under CPR, r 8.2A they can apply to the court without naming any defendants. The court may deal with the application by a telephone hearing (PD 23.6). Any proceedings will be private. A precedent claim form and witness statement are at Appendix 2.

Beddoe proceedings involving hostile action against a beneficiary

13.130 The situation where the opponent to the third party litigation is a beneficiary is fraught with difficulty. While the beneficiary would normally be entitled (in his capacity as beneficiary) to see the evidence upon which the court is being requested to exercise its discretion, it would be inappropriate for one party to litigation to be able to see a frank assessment of the merits of the other party's case. In such cases the well-established practice detailed in *Re Moritz* [1960] Ch 251 and *Re Eaton* [1964] 1 WLR 1269 is followed. Under this procedure the beneficiary who is the potential or actual opponent in the hostile litigation receives a copy of the claim form and the personal representatives'/ will trustees' witness statement in support, but not the opinion of a suitably qualified lawyer or other sensitive exhibits. If the application is dealt with at a hearing, the beneficiary has the opportunity to make representations to the court but not to be present when the merits of the proposed action or defence are being considered. Care needs to be taken to ensure that the opponent beneficiary does not receive information about the merits or weaknesses of the personal representatives'/will trustees' case inadvertently.

Whole estate under attack

13.131 A very difficult situation arises where the personal representatives are not simply defending a contractual or debt claim to a limited amount but where the whole of the estate is under attack. This may happen where it is claimed that the deceased's estate was actually held on trust wholly for another or was contractually committed by the deceased to another who acted to his detriment in reliance on that contractual commitment. Such situations arose in *Re Dallaway* (*deceased*) [1982] 1 WLR 756 and *Evans v Evans* [1986] 1 WLR 101. Although the court may decide to permit the personal representatives to defend the claim at the expense of the estate – even though there may be no estate from which the costs could properly be paid if the attack on the estate is wholly successful – in *Alsop Wilkinson v Neary* [1995] 1 All ER 431 the court decided that where there was an attack on the whole of the fund and the dispute was in effect between rival claimants to the beneficial interest, in the absence of any direction to the contrary from the court the duty of fiduciaries is to remain neutral and offer to submit to the court's direction.

BENJAMIN ORDER

Why such an order might be needed

13.132 If all inquiries as to a beneficiary are inconclusive, an application may be made to the court for an order based on the case of *Re Benjamin* [1902] 1 Ch 723. Such an order affords the personal representatives the protection of authority from the court to distribute the estate based on certain assumptions and, if those assumptions prove subsequently to be incorrect, the personal representatives will not themselves be liable. This does not mean that a successful claimant is prevented from following assets into the hands of a beneficiary. The court has power to order that for the purpose of distributing the estate a beneficiary should be presumed to have predeceased (see *Re Green's Will Trusts* [1985] 3 All ER 455 where the judge directed that the expense and delay of a formal inquiry into whether or not the deceased's son – who went missing in action in 1943 – had died, should be avoided).

13.133 If the estate is small an application to the court may not be justified – although use of the county court is appropriate where the estate does not exceed £30,000. In practice, the personal representatives may decide to distribute to those persons whose interests are known, having obtained a missing beneficiary indemnity policy insuring against the risk of the person entitled subsequently being located. The proposed insurers will require satisfaction as to the extent of inquiries made before covering this risk. As an alternative, personal representatives could obtain indemnities from the beneficiaries.

13.134 It was held in *Evans v Westcombe, Re Evans Deceased* [1999] 2 All ER 777 that a personal representative had acted reasonably in taking out missing beneficiary insurance and making a distribution despite the absence of a Benjamin order. Insurance was held to some extent to be a better solution than an order, given the costs of the latter. The cost of obtaining insurance could come out of the estate, despite the fact that the defendant stood to benefit in her capacity as beneficiary, as the cost was incurred for the benefit of the estate as a whole.

13.135 Whether the personal representative has acted reasonably is to be assessed according to the circumstances and is an objective test. Clearly *Re Evans* means that a Benjamin order is not an absolute necessity. However, in most cases an application to the court is highly desirable since without the protection of a court order the personal representatives not only face personal liability in relation to an act which is potentially a *devastavit* but are also highly unlikely to be awarded their costs of defending the action.

13.136 Section 63 of the Trustee Act 1925 allows trustees (and by definition personal representatives) to discharge their duties by paying the trust fund into court in cases where there is doubt as to entitlement. However, unless they can show that their particular difficulty could not be resolved by an application for directions in the normal way, they may be at risk as to the costs of the application and of the beneficiaries obtaining an order for payment out.

Procedure

13.137 The application for a Benjamin order is made under CPR Part 64 by the personal representatives, joining affected beneficiaries as defendants. The witness statement in support should set out in considerable detail the extent and outcome of the inquiries and investigations made to date. In practice, unless the position has been investigated thoroughly by the personal representatives, the Chancery master may order a full kin inquiry to be made, or give other directions following which the relief sought may be given on a subsequent application.

INDEMNITIES

13.138 Personal representatives are entitled to an indemnity out of the estate in respect of administration expenses (ie not to be out of pocket). That does not require formal agreement. It is usual simply to record such expenses in the estate accounts. Beneficiaries are entitled to see supporting receipts if requested.

13.139 Personal representatives are also entitled to be protected against the consequences of a claim brought against them where they have done no wrong. It is reasonable for personal representatives to seek an indemnity where there is a dispute or there is a real risk that they are exposed to claims but decide to distribute in order to bring the administration to a close. The alternative will be for them to seek a direction from the court regarding distribution or take out insurance, which will come at some expense to the estate, or to withhold funds for as long as they are reasonably exposed to the potential claim.

13.140 In a straightforward estate it will be rare for an indemnity to be required. It is a personal representative's job to administer the estate and account to the beneficiaries for assets which are properly due to them.

13.141 If a claim against the estate arises after the administration has otherwise been completed, eg for a tax liability of which the personal representatives were previously unaware, there is an implied right for the personal representatives to recover from the residuary beneficiaries. Therefore, the personal representatives do not need an indemnity but there is little purpose in a beneficiary refusing an indemnity where personal representatives identify potential claims.

13.142 Wide indemnities that cover breaches of trust are generally unacceptable. Giving an indemnity means giving the recipient of that indemnity protection. To indemnify a personal representative against an act of devastavit (a wasting of estate assets) or a breach of trust may be to give him something to which he is not entitled, ie surrendering a right to take action against that personal representative.

13.143 A personal representative is not entitled to retain assets against the possibility that some unspecified claim might arise in the future. For this reason, there must be a reasonable basis for insistence on the protection of an indemnity. Ultimately, it is possible to go to court for a direction that the personal representative distributes the assets but clearly it is preferable to avoid that cost if agreement can be reached on the form of an appropriate indemnity.

Chapter 14

DISAPPOINTED BENEFICIARY CLAIMS: PROPRIETARY ESTOPPEL AND CONSTRUCTIVE TRUST CLAIMS

INTRODUCTION

14.1 A claim may be made against the estate in circumstances where the deceased held assets as constructive trustee for the benefit of the claimant or under the doctrine of proprietary estoppel. In recent years, there has been a proliferation of such cases.

WHY BRING A CLAIM?

14.2 Such a claim is often brought in addition to a claim under the Inheritance (Provision for Family and Dependants) Act 1975 ('the 1975 Act') (see Chapter 15); however, there is no requirement for the claimant to fall within the categories in s 1(3) of the 1975 Act or for provision to be limited to reasonable maintenance within s 1(2) of that Act. A disappointed beneficiary who is unable to dispute the validity of the deceased's will or bring a claim under the 1975 Act may nevertheless bring a successful claim subject to fulfilling the required criteria set out below.

COMPARISON

14.3 A constructive trust arises where there is an express agreement or understanding between the claimant and the deceased or a common intention (implied agreement) which can be inferred from the conduct of the parties. It is also necessary to establish that the claimant acted to his detriment in reliance upon such agreement, understanding or common intention.

14.4 A proprietary estoppel claim can arise where the claimant acts to his detriment in reliance upon a representation made by the deceased.

14.5 The success of a proprietary estoppel claim will depend to a large extent on the exercise of the court's discretion; by contrast, if an asset was held as the subject of a constructive trust then that asset must be returned to the claimant. This might produce a better result than under the 1975 Act and could also operate so as to reduce the value of the deceased's estate for inheritance tax. A successful 1975 Act claim, particularly where the main beneficiary under the will is a spouse or charity, could result in an increase in the tax otherwise payable.

PRINCIPLES

14.6   Several important principles have been established in recent cases.

There must be evidence of agreement in a constructive trust claim

14.7   In *Hyett v Stanley* [2003] WTLR 1269 the deceased left the claimant the proceeds of a substantial life policy but nothing in his will. The parties lived together at the deceased's farm which was in his sole name but subject to a mortgage in both names. This gave rise to an express agreement and the claimant had an immediate beneficial interest under a constructive trust.

Encouragement can be inferred

14.8   There must be a causal link between the promises made and the detrimental acts, although the promises need not be the only inducement. If there is an inference, the burden of proof is reversed and the defendant must show that the promises made were not relied upon.

The detriment must follow the agreement or representation

14.9   In *Churchill v Roach* [2003] WTLR 779 the detriment suffered by the claimant occurred before a common intention had been established and accordingly the constructive trust claim failed.

The detriment must be substantial

14.10   In *Jiggins v Brisley* [2003] WTLR 1141 the provision of part of the purchase price of a flat and subsequent payment of outgoings made it unconscionable to deny that property to the claimant. By contrast, if the total sum expended by the claimant (see *Churchill v Roach* above) is insufficient to be detrimental, the claim will fail.

The sum awarded must be proportionate

14.11   The claimant should not expect to receive the whole or a substantial part of the estate if this would amount to excessive compensation. In *Jennings v Rice* [2002] WTLR 1253 the court awarded £200,000 out of an estate of £1.2m even though the claimant had been promised everything. The moral for those advising claimants is to manage their expectations and adopt a realistic approach. The minimum award will be sufficient to 'satisfy the equity and do justice between the parties' – see *Evans v HSBC Trust Co* [2005] WTLR 1289.

The court must take into account a change in circumstances

14.12 In *Uglow v Uglow* [2004] WTLR 1183 the claimant and the deceased had entered into a farming partnership and at that time the deceased represented that he would leave the farm to the claimant on his death. Some years later the partnership was abandoned and the deceased changed his will, leaving the farm to another relative. The Court of Appeal upheld the judge's finding that the estoppel claim failed.

The assurances must be unequivocal

14.13 In *Murphy v Burrows* (2004-5) 7 ITELR 116 there were vague suggestions, as opposed to a specific representation, that the claimant would inherit and these were held to be insufficient for the claimant to rely upon.

PROCEDURE

14.14 The claim could be brought as part of an existing action or as a separate Part 8 claim. In the latter case, a considerable amount of work will be required at an early stage in compiling evidence in support of the claim which must be served when the claim form is issued. The claim will either seek a declaration in the claimant's favour, that certain assets of the estate should be treated as subject to a constructive trust, or that the court's discretion should be exercised for the benefit of the claimant based on proprietary estoppel. The witness statement in support will be extremely detailed, providing the court with a full history of the claimant's relationship with the deceased and highlighting important events and conversations. Details of expenditure incurred by the claimant, exhibiting receipts if possible, should also be included.

Chapter 15

DISAPPOINTED BENEFICIARY CLAIMS: CLAIMS UNDER THE INHERITANCE (PROVISION FOR FAMILY AND DEPENDANTS) ACT 1975

15.1 Disappointed beneficiaries may be able to claim under the Inheritance (Provision for Family and Dependants) Act 1975 ('the 1975 Act').

DOES THE 1975 ACT APPLY?

Domicile

15.2 Section 1 of the 1975 Act stipulates that it only applies to estates where at the time of death the deceased was domiciled in England and Wales.

15.3 In the majority of cases there will be no doubt over domicile. However, as people travel more widely and spend substantial amounts of time in second homes, it may be necessary to ascertain whether the deceased acquired a domicile of choice elsewhere before accepting that the potential applicant is entitled to bring a claim under the 1975 Act.

15.4 In *Morgan v Cilento* [2004] WTLR 457, the question for the court was whether the deceased died domicile in England and Wales, or Queensland, Australia. Unlike many other Australian states, Queensland has no equivalent to the 1975 Act. Mr Shaffer's uncontested domicile of origin was England and Wales. However, the judge concluded that Mr Shaffer acquired a domicile of choice in Queensland. Despite his intimate and loving relationship with the claimant based in London, Mr Shaffer had not abandoned his domicile of choice.

15.5 In *Agulian and another v Cyganik* [2006] WTLR 565, the Court of Appeal overturned the first instance decision that Mr Cyganik, a Cypriot who had lived in London from the age of 18 until his death aged 64 had acquired a domicile of choice in England. They found that a domicile of origin can only be replaced by 'clear cogent and compelling evidence that the relevant person intended to settle permanently and indefinitely in the alleged domicile of choice'. Mr Cyganik's girlfriend was not able to claim under the 1975 Act.

Time limit to bring a claim

15.6   Under s 4 of the 1975 Act a claim must be made within 6 months of the date of a grant of probate or letters of administration. The 6-month period runs from the date of issue of a general (as opposed to limited) grant (*Re Johnson* [1987] CLY 3882) or from the date of subsequent grant removing an earlier one (*Re Freeman* [1984] 3 All ER 906). In the former case the legislation is not clear and therefore, to be safe, it may be sensible to issue a notice of a limited grant or to clarify in writing with the other side that a claim is proposed.

15.7   If the application is not made within the prescribed time limit, it is necessary to seek the permission of the court to bring an application.

15.8   The factors applicable in the court's discretion as to whether to grant permission outside the 6-month time limit were set out by Sir Robert Megarry V-C in *Re Salmon* [1981] Ch 167 as follows:

(1)   The court's discretion is unfettered and is to be exercised judicially, in accordance with what is just and proper.

(2)   The onus lies on the claimant to establish a 'substantial case for it being just and proper for the court to exercise its statutory discretion to extend the time'.

(3)   The court will consider 'how promptly and in what circumstances the applicant has sought the permission of the court after the time limit has expired' and any notice of the claim given to the defendants of the proposed application.

(4)   Negotiations commenced within the time limit will be material.

(5)   Distribution of the estate before issue or notice of the claim will be relevant.

(6)   Whether refusal to extend the time limit will leave the claimant without redress against anybody else (for example in negligence against a solicitor for failing to apply in time) is material.

15.9   Where there is a remedy against some other person, for example a claim against the applicant's solicitors for not pursuing the claim within the time limits, leave may not be given (*Re Longley* [1981] CLY 2885*)*. However, leave may still be given in these circumstances where a financial remedy against solicitors would not be a satisfactory substitute for a successful claim (*Nesheim v Kosa* [2007] WTLR 149). In the latter case, the judge was keen to ensure that the need to discipline lawyers was not put ahead of the clear interests of doing justice between the parties.

15.10 The guidelines are not exhaustive. Brown Wilkinson J in *Re Dennis* [1981] 2 All ER 140 also suggested a further guideline; namely whether the claimant has an arguable case.

15.11 In *McNulty v McNulty* [2002] WTLR 737 the court allowed an application issued 3½ years after expiration of the 6-month time limit. The estate had not been distributed and therefore the delay 'inexcusable as it was' did not prejudice the beneficiaries. In *Garland v Morris* [2004] WTLR 797 the court allowed the claimant to issue proceedings over 30 months outside the time limit. The judge accepted the claimant's explanation that she had been unaware of her right to make a claim. She had a reasonable prospect of success and, notwithstanding distribution of the estate, there were still assets available to satisfy the claim which could be realised without undue hardship to the second defendant.

15.12 Section 20 of the 1975 Act enables the personal representatives to distribute any part of the estate without liability after the end of the 6-month period. They are not expected to take into account the possibility that the court might permit the making of an application for an order under the 1975 Act after the end of that period.

Who can apply?

15.13 An applicant must come within one of the classes set out in s 1(1) of the 1975 Act (as amended by s 2 of the Law Reform (Succession) Act 1995 and as extended by the Civil Partnership Act 2004). The categories are as follows:

(1)   the spouse or civil partner of the deceased;

(2)   a former spouse or former civil partner of the deceased;

(3)   any person living with the deceased as husband, wife or civil partner for 2 years immediately before the death;

(4)   a child of the deceased;

(5)   any person (not being the child of the deceased) who in the case of any marriage or civil partnership to which the deceased was at any time a party, was treated by the deceased as a child of the family in relation to that marriage or civil partnership

(6)   any person who immediately before the death of the deceased was being maintained, either wholly or partly, by the deceased.

Spouse or civil partner of the deceased

15.14 In order to come within s 1(1)(a) of the 1975 Act, the applicant's marriage to the deceased must have been recognised by the law of England and

Wales or by the jurisdiction in which the marriage took place. This can include polygamous marriages and marriages by cohabitation and repute or by proxy if recognised as valid by local laws.

Void/voidable marriages

15.15 If the marriage was voidable but not annulled the survivor can apply as a spouse of the deceased. If the marriage was void from the beginning, s 25(4) of the 1975 Act ensures that the applicant will qualify as a spouse if he or she entered into the marriage in good faith. For a ceremony to create a void marriage it has to at least purport to be a marriage of the kind contemplated under English law. If the ceremony does not purport to be a marriage under the law of England and Wales it is a non–marriage and no claim can be made (see *Gandhi v Patel* [2002] 1 FLR 603).

Judicial separation

15.16 If the parties were judicially separated at the time of the death then, although the surviving spouse may claim as husband or wife of the deceased, he or she will be entitled to receive only the lower level of provision which can be awarded to the other classes of applicant (see 1975 Act, s 2(a)).

Civil partners

15.17 Under the Civil Partnership Act 2004, the court has power to treat registered same sex couples in the same way as married couples for the purposes of the 1975 Act.

15.18 At the time of writing, issues of void/voidable civil partnerships and judicial separation have not yet been addressed in the courts. It can be assumed that the same principles will apply.

Former spouse or former civil partner of the deceased

15.19 Section 1(b) of the 1975 Act states that a spouse whose marriage to the deceased has been dissolved or annulled in England and Wales or terminated in another jurisdiction in a manner which is regarded as valid in England can apply for provision under the 1975 Act provided that he or she has not remarried before the death of the former spouse.

15.20 If he or she remarries subsequently, the claim will be limited to one for maintenance between the dates of death and remarriage.

15.21 It is important to establish whether the decree of divorce, nullity or judicial separation contained a section 15 or 15A order, as, if it did, the court will not be able to entertain a claim under the 1975 Act.

15.22 A section 15 order is an order, on the grant of a decree of divorce, nullity or judicial separation, that the other party to the marriage shall not, on the death of the applicant, be entitled to apply for an order for provision out of the deceased's estate under the 1975 Act.

15.23 Section 15ZA replicates the provision in relation to civil partnerships.

15.24 Section 15A creates the same restriction in relation to orders made under s 17 of the Matrimonial and Family Proceedings Act 1984 (orders for financial provision and property adjustment).

15.25 If there is a 'clean break' order which does not include a s 15 provision then it may still be difficult to make out a claim under the 1975 Act unless there has been a material change in circumstances. As above the same provisions will apply to civil partners.

Recently separated former spouses/civil partners

15.26 Where within 12 months of parties to a marriage being separated by law (whether by divorce, dissolution, judicial separation or otherwise) a party dies and an application for financial provision/property adjustment has either not been made, or proceedings not determined, the court may treat the surviving party as if the parties were not legally separated. This means the surviving party will be able to apply for treatment under the more generous provision for spouses. A similar provision exists for former civil partners (s 14A).

Any person living with the deceased as husband, wife or civil partner for two years immediately before the death

15.27 To qualify as a cohabitee it is necessary for the claimant to have been living with the deceased as husband, wife or civil partner in the same household during the whole period of 2 years immediately prior to the deceased's death.

Same household

15.28 Case law has demonstrated that it is possible to have two separate properties but one household so long as there are not two separate domestic economies (see *Churchill v Roach* [2003] ALL ER (D) 348).

As husband, wife or civil partner

15.29 The test as to whether the claimant was living with the deceased 'as husband, wife or civil partner' is set out in *Re Watson (deceased)* [1999] 1 FLR 878 and is whether, in the opinion of a reasonable person with normal perceptions, it could be said that the two people in question were living together as husband and wife bearing in mind the 'multifarious nature of relationships'. A sexual relationship is not a pre-requisite.

Whole period of two years

15.30 The provision has not been interpreted literally. In *Re Watson*, separation caused by illness did not affect the continuity of the household.

15.31 In *Gully v Dix* [2004] 1 WLR 1399 the claimant left the deceased during a dispute. The deceased died shortly thereafter while the couple were still living separately. The Court of Appeal held that the separation was transitory and did not affect the continuity of their relationship.

15.32 Section 1(1B), added as a result of the Civil Partnership Act 2004, ensures that the same provisions apply for cohabiting same sex couples.

Child of the deceased

15.33 This category is not limited to minors, and includes illegitimate children, children in utero at the date of death and adopted children. It does not include a natural child of the deceased who has been adopted by another.

Treated by the deceased as a child of the family

15.34 A claimant under this head must show that he/she was treated by the deceased as a child of the family in relation to a marriage or civil partnership to which the deceased was at any time a party.

15.35 It must first be established that there was a marriage or civil partnership and second that there was behaviour towards the child which amounts to treating the child as part of the family.

15.36 The most common claim is by step-children.

15.37 Application as a dependant (see below) is an option if a claimant fails in establishing that he/she was treated as a child of the family.

Any person who immediately before the death of the deceased was being maintained by the deceased

Immediately before the death of the deceased

15.38 The courts have interpreted 'immediately' broadly. In *Jelley v Iliffe* [1981] 2 All ER 29, Stephenson LJ applied *In re Beaumont, deceased* [1980] Ch 444, and stated that:

> 'In considering whether a person is being maintained "immediately before the death of the deceased" it is the settled basis or general arrangement between the parties as regards maintenance during the lifetime of the deceased which has to be looked at, not the actual, perhaps fluctuating, variation of it which exists immediately before his or her death'.

This was followed in *Witkowska v Kaminski* [2006] WTLR 1293 where, on appeal, the court found that the claimant continued to be maintained 'immediately before' the deceased's death despite the absence of maintenance payments in the 6 weeks before the deceased's death.

Being maintained

15.39 Section 1(3) of the 1975 Act sets out the definition of being maintained for the purposes of s 1(1)(e); namely that the deceased 'otherwise than for full valuable consideration, was making a substantial contribution in money or money's worth towards the reasonable needs of that person'.

15.40 Therefore an applicant will only be successful if he/she can show that the deceased was contributing substantially to his/her needs without a similar level of consideration in return.

15.41 In assessing whether there was full valuable consideration, and whether there was a substantial contribution, the court will consider the respective contributions of the applicant and the deceased (*Jelley v Iliffe*).

15.42 In *Re B (deceased)* [2000] Ch 662, the Court of Appeal found that a mother could be a dependant of her deceased minor child for the purposes of the 1975 Act.

THE COURTS' APPROACH

15.43 The approach of the courts in assessing claims under the 1975 Act is in two distinct stages:

(1) Whether reasonable financial provision has been made for the applicant by the deceased under the will (or through the intestacy rules).

(2) If the court finds that reasonable provision has not been made, it then considers what, if any, provision should be made.

15.44 The decision in *Robinson v Bird and Another* [2003] WTLR 529 demonstrates the two stage approach of the court. The judge initially decided to award the claimant an additional sum of £60,000 from the deceased's estate. The draft judgment was sent to counsel. Counsel for the defendant effectively reopened submissions in writing and, after considering these submissions, the judge found that he had erred by not applying his mind to the first part of the two-stage test. He changed his view when delivering the final judgment and stated that:

> 'The question that the court has to consider is not whether it might have been reasonable for the deceased to have made greater provision for the Claimant than she did but whether in all the circumstances, looked at objectively, it is

unreasonable that the deceased's will did not do so. After reflecting further on the matter, I have come to the conclusion that it is not unreasonable that the deceased's will did not do so.'

15.45 Failure by the claimant to show that the deceased had not made reasonable financial provision meant that the second stage did not need to be considered. Accordingly the claim was dismissed. The decision was upheld at appeal ([2004] WTLR 257).

Reasonable financial provision

15.46 Whether there has been reasonable financial provision is approached in a different manner according to the status of the applicant. This is the key distinction between an application by the spouse or civil partner of the deceased and an application by the other categories of applicant.

Application by spouse or civil partner of the deceased

15.47 Under s 1(2)(a) of the 1975 Act reasonable financial provision for a spouse is defined as:

'... provision as it would be reasonable in all the circumstances of the case for a husband or wife to receive, whether or not that provision is required for his or her maintenance ...'

15.48 Section 1(2)(aa) of the 1975 Act duplicates this provision in respect of civil partners of the deceased.

Other categories of applicant

15.49 The definition is contained within s 1(2)(b):

'... provision as it would be reasonable in all circumstances for the applicant to receive for his maintenance ...'

15.50 Maintenance is only defined in the 1975 Act at s 1(3), relating to dependants (see **15.39**).

Matters to which the court is to have regard in ascertaining reasonable provision

15.51 The assessment of whether the level of provision, or lack of, was reasonable and, if not, what the provision, if any, should be, is made by reference to the facts listed at s 3 of the 1975 Act namely:

(1)   the financial resources and needs (now and in the future) of the applicant (s 3(1)(a));

(2)   the financial resources and needs (now and in the future) of other applicants (s 3(1)(b));

(3)   the financial resources and needs (now and in the future) of the beneficiaries of the estate (s 3(1)(c));

(4)   the obligations and responsibilities of the deceased towards any applicant or beneficiary of the estate (s 3(1)(d));

(5)   the size and nature of the net estate of the deceased (s 3(1)(e));

(6)   the physical and mental disabilities of the applicant or any beneficiary of the estate (s 3(1)(f)); and

(7)   any other matter which the court might consider relevant, including the conduct of any party (s 3(1)(g)).

Additional factors

15.52 Section 3 sets out a number of additional factors to which the court should have regard in relation to specific categories of applicant.

(1)   *Spouse or civil partner*
       The court should have regard to the age of the applicant, the duration of the marriage or civil partnership and the contribution made by the applicant to the welfare of the family (s 3(2)(a) and (b)).
       Importantly the court is required to take into account the provision that the applicant might reasonably have expected to receive if, on the day on which the deceased died, the marriage or civil partnership, instead of being terminated by death, had been terminated by divorce or dissolution. This is often referred to as 'the divorce hypothesis' and is discussed in further detail below at **15.80–15.91**.

(2)   *Cohabitant*
       The court is required to have regard to the age of the applicant and the length of the period during which the applicant lived with the deceased as husband or wife or civil partner in the same household and the contribution made by the applicant to the welfare of the family.

(3)   *Child or person treated as a child of the family*
       The court will have regard to the manner in which the applicant was being, or might expect to be, educated or trained.
       Where the application is made by someone purporting to be treated as a child of the family the court will also have regard to whether the deceased had assumed responsibility for the applicant's maintenance and if so, the extent to which and the basis upon which that responsibility was assumed, and the length of time for which the deceased had been discharging that responsibility. The court will also have regard to whether the deceased

knew the applicant was not his own child in assuming and discharging that responsibility and to the liability of any other person to maintain the applicant.

(4)   *Dependant*
The court will have regard to the extent to which and the basis upon which the deceased assumed responsibility for the maintenance of the applicant, and to the length of time that responsibility was discharged.

Orders that can be made by the court

15.53 If the court believes that the deceased has not made reasonable financial provision for the applicant, it can make one or more of the orders provided for by s 2 of the 1975 Act:

(1)   an order for periodical payments, including providing that part of the estate is set aside to fund periodical payments;

(2)   an order for payment of a lump sum;

(3)   an order for the transfer, settlement or acquisition of property for the benefit of the applicant;

(4)   an order for variation of an ante or post nuptial settlement.

15.54 In usual circumstances, the court prefers lump sum payments to ensure a clean break, but this is not always possible.

Interim orders

15.55 The court has power under s 5 of the 1975 Act to order interim relief if it is satisfied that the applicant is in immediate need of financial assistance and part of the estate can be made available to the applicant for that purpose.

15.56 The court will take into account, 'so far as the urgency of the case admits' the matters to which the court is required to have regard under s 3 of the 1975 Act.

15.57 The relief can be ordered subject to conditions or restrictions that the court may wish to impose, for example that the interim payment is made on account of provision that may ultimately be ordered at trial.

15.58 The personal representatives should be invited by letter to make an interim payment before issuing an application. If the personal representatives receive a request for an interim payment they should consult the beneficiaries as to whether they agree that that payment should be made.

Property available for financial provision

15.59 Provision for an applicant is usually made out of residue but can be ordered out of any part of the net estate as defined by s 25(1) of the 1975 Act.

15.60 Section 25(1) defines the net estate, broadly speaking, as all property over which the deceased had power to dispose by his will or over which he held a general power of appointment, less funeral, testamentary and administration expenses and debts, and as augmented by property treated as part of the deceased's estate by virtue of ss 8–11 of the 1975 Act.

Sections 8 to 11 of the 1975 Act

15.61 Sections 8–11 effectively give the court the right to claw back property which would otherwise fall outside the estate so that it is treated as part of the net estate for the purposes of provision.

Section 8 – nominated property or property received as donatio mortis causa

15.62 Section 8 states that property nominated in accordance with any enactment or property received as donatio mortis causa (net of tax) will be treated as part of the net estate.

15.63 The provision is rarely used. Nominations under occupational schemes will only apply if the scheme is based on an enactment, which is unusual. Gifts donatio mortis causa are rare (see Chapter 1) but the value of the gift at the deceased's death (less any inheritance tax payable) can be treated as an estate asset.

Section 9 – property held on joint tenancy

15.64 Section 9 gives the court a discretionary power to treat property in which the deceased had a beneficial joint tenancy as part of the net estate in order to meet a claim.

15.65 An application under s 9 must be made within 6 months of the grant. The court has no discretion in this regard.

15.66 In exercising its power under this provision, the value of the deceased's severable share of the property is the 'value thereof immediately before death'. This wording would appear to be able to give an unjust result if the property had risen (or fallen) in value substantially between the date of death and the date of the hearing. In *Dingmar v Dingmar* [2006] 3 WLR 1183, the court addressed this injustice and interpreted the word 'value' as meaning the proportion of the property that would have been available had there been a severance before death, rather than the sum of money that that proportion would have been worth immediately before death.

15.67 If the property is subject to a mortgage, that has to be deducted in order to calculate the value of the deceased's share; but if the mortgage is protected by a joint lives insurance policy (whether term or endowment) the value of the policy will also need to be brought into account (*Powell v Osbourne* [1993] 1 FLR 1001).

15.68 The court will assume that in calculating the value of any life policy the imminent death of the deceased is known; accordingly the value of the policy immediately before death is taken to be equal to the amount which is payable on death, and the deceased will be treated as having a severable share in that amount.

Section 10 – dispositions intended to defeat applications for financial provision

15.69 Section 10 enables the court to claw back dispositions for less than full valuable consideration made by the deceased within 6 years before his death where they are made with the intention of defeating an application for financial provision under the 1975 Act, if to do so would facilitate the making of financial provision to a claimant under the Act.

Section 11 – contracts to leave property by will

15.70 Section 11 sets out similar claw back provisions in the case of a contract to leave property by will, where the contract was made for less than full valuable consideration, within 6 years before the deceased's death and with the intention of defeating a 1975 Act claim.

15.71 Where an application is made under s 11 of the 1975 Act and no valuable consideration was given or promised in respect of the contract, then it will be presumed that the deceased made the contract with the intention of defeating an application for financial provision under the 1975 Act.

Issues arising in relation to ss 10 and 11

15.72 If an application under ss 10 and 11 is contemplated, detailed consideration should be given to these sections. Broadly, the applicant can apply for an order that any donee (including a trustee) should provide property or money to enable financial provision to be made for the applicant. The court must be satisfied, on the balance of probabilities, that the deceased, when making the disposition or contract, intended to prevent an order for financial provision being made under the 1975 Act or to reduce the amount of the provision which might otherwise be granted.

15.73 An intention to defeat the claim need not have been the sole intention.

15.74 In determining whether and how to exercise discretion under these sections, the court will have regard to the circumstances in which the disposition/contract was made, and, in the case of a disposition, the circumstances of any valuable consideration given, the relationship of donee to deceased, the conduct and financial resources of the donee and all other circumstances of the case (s 10(6); s 11(4)).

15.75 An order can be made if the donee subsequently disposed of the gift. However, it cannot exceed the amount of the gift less any tax borne by the donee.

15.76 In the case of a contract to leave property by will, the personal representatives will be directed not to comply with such contract or, if they have already done so, that the contract should be set aside.

15.77 In the case of an application directed to funds received by a trustee, the repayment ordered cannot exceed the amount of the assets held by the trustee at the date of the order.

State benefits

15.78 The receipt by the applicant of benefits, whether or not means-tested, will not prevent a successful claim under the 1975 Act. In *Re Goodwin* [1969] 1 Ch 283 Megarry J awarded a widow £8 per week, backdated to her husband's death, to be charged against the assets she did not receive under the will. In *Re Collins* [1990] 2 All ER 47 a lump sum of £5,000 was awarded to a 19-year-old daughter of the deceased who received means-tested benefits; however, the court refused to disregard those benefits when assessing the claimant's financial resources under s 3.

15.79 Where the benefits are means-tested the effect of a court order or any offer that might be made on entitlement to those benefits should be considered. On current figures, every £250 of capital that the claimant has in excess of £6,000 is deemed to be notional income of £1 per week, and treated as deductible from the claimant's needs level when assessing income support. If the claimant has capital exceeding £16,000, entitlement to income support ceases. As entitlement to housing benefit may be linked to income support, it can also be affected. In certain circumstances a discretionary trust may be advantageous.

APPLICATION

Claims by spouses and civil partners

15.80 The traditional approach adopted by the court in cases such as *Re Besterman* [1984] 1 Ch 458 was that the minimum was to be done to assist the applicant widow ('provision ... should be such so as to relieve her of anxiety for the future') while ensuring that the testator's intentions were largely given effect. This was essentially a needs/reasonable requirements approach and therefore more akin to an application being made under s 1(1)(b) to (e) of the 1975 Act.

15.81 However, as noted above, provision for spouses under the 1975 Act is:

> 'Such financial provision as it would be reasonable in all the circumstances of the case for a husband and wife to receive, *whether or not that provision is required for his or her maintenance*' (emphasis added) (s 1(2)(a)).

The provision for civil partners is the same (s 1(2)(aa)).

15.82 Further, by virtue of s 3(2) the court must in addition have regard to the age of the applicant, the duration of the marriage or civil partnership, the contribution made by the applicant to the family and, importantly, the 'divorce hypothesis'.

The divorce hypothesis

15.83 The divorce hypothesis has meant that recent developments in the divorce courts have been applied in relation to 1975 Act claims. A summary of developments in ancillary relief provision since the seminal decision in *White v White* [2001] AC 596 up to the time of writing can be found at Appendix 1.

15.84 The House of Lords judgment in *White v White* [2001] AC 596 greatly impacted on what a surviving spouse might reasonably expect to receive, particularly where there has been a long marriage/cohabitation. In *White v White*, after a marriage of 30 years, the wife was awarded 40% of the assets held by the husband. The court rejected the 'reasonable needs' argument and stated that equality of division should only be departed from if there is good reason for doing so.

15.85 Post *White v White* there have been a number of cases where family lawyers have sought to argue cases for departure from equality of division, for example in *Cowan v Cowan* [2001] 2 FLR 192 where the court found that the husband's 'entrepreneurial spark' was 'a factor that ... deserved recognition'. Other arguments include illiquidity of assets (*S v S* [2001] 2 FLR 246) and that assets acquired prior to the marriage or gifted in the marriage should not be included (for example in *White v White*).

15.86 Following *Charman v Charman* [2007] 1 FLR 1246 the presumption of equality may be departed from, for example where there is a stellar contribution such as in *Cowan v Cowan*, or where assets are inherited.

Impact of ancillary relief cases on 1975 Act claims

15.87 *White v White* has had a significant impact on surviving spouse 1975 Act claims. In *Adams v Lewis* [2001] WTLR 493, whilst noting that the amount a widow(er) would receive on a divorce is only one factor, Judge John Behrens stated that it was 'a most important factor' reasoning 'the observations of

Lord Nicholls in *White v White* ... apply just as much to an inheritance claim by a widow or widower as to an application for financial provision after a divorce'.

15.88 His Honour Judge Behrens cited four points from Lord Nicholls' judgment in *White v White*:

- 'If in their different ways a husband and wife each contributed equally to the family then in principle it follows that it matters not which of them earned the money and built up the assets. There should be no bias in favour of the money earner as against the house maker and the child carer.'

- 'A judge should check any tentative view he forms against the yardstick of equality of division. As a general guide equality should only be departed from if and to the extent that there is a good reason for doing so.'

- The test of 'reasonable requirements' referred to in the authorities was a departure from the statutory requirements in s 25 of the Matrimonial Causes Act 1973.

- In assessing the amount of a lump sum it is permissible to take into account the wife's wish to be in a position to make provision by will for her adult children. Such a wish would not normally fall within s 25(2)(b) as a financial need but that did not mean 'this natural parental wish is irrelevant to the s 25 exercise'. In principle a wife's wish to have money so she can pass some on to her children is every bit as weighty as a similar wish by a husband.

In making his judgment His Honour Judge Behrens found there were sufficient assets in the estate to have provided for both spouses on divorce and found that, on a divorce, the widow would have been awarded half the estate. He concluded that there was no reason to depart from the principle of equality whether or not there is a presumption of equal division. Accordingly, he made an award that effectively gave the claimant spouse half the value of the assets.

15.89 Other cases demonstrate the increasingly sympathetic approach that the courts appear to have towards widow(ers) in 1975 Act claims:

(1) In *McNulty v McNulty* [2002] WTLR 737 the District Judge carried out a *White v White* cross check to demonstrate what an equal division of family assets would produce and held that a balance of £105,000 was required to achieve equality. However, the widow was awarded £175,000. It will often be appropriate to award a higher sum than the spouse would have obtained on a notional divorce.

(2) In *P v G (Family Provision: Relevance of Divorce Provision)* [2007] WTLR 691 the judge held that the analogy with divorce was the minimum that a widow should be awarded in a 1975 Act claim.

15.90 In *Cunliffe v Fielden and Others* [2006] Ch 361 the widow of a year-long marriage was awarded £800,000 from a £1.4m estate by the first instance judge. The Court of Appeal reduced the award made by the first instance judge to £600,000 and criticised the way in which the first instance judge had applied *White v White*, stating that he appeared to think he was required to presume a 50:50 split of the estate. The correct approach following *White v White* is to apply the statutory provisions to the facts of the individual case with the objective of achieving a result which is fair and non-discriminatory and, having undertaken that exercise, to cross check it against the yard stick of equality of provision. The Appeal Court also criticised the judge's application of the principles in *White v White* given the brevity of the marriage in this case. The award is considered to be unusually high, given that it was a short marriage.

15.91 Many judges comment on how difficult it is to apply the analogy with divorce on death (see *Stephanides v Cohen* [2002] WTLR 1373; *P v G (Family Provision: Relevance of Divorce Provision)* [2007] WTLR 691; *Moody v Stevenson* [1992] Ch 486) as the situation arising on death is so different from that arising on divorce. In *Singer v Isaac* [2001] WTLR 1045, Master Bowles reiterated that the divorce hypothesis is only one of the considerations to be taken into account by the court. Justifying why divorce should not be given permanent consideration he referred to the fact that:

(1) on divorce resources inevitably have to be split between two spouses and that is inherently not the case in a 1975 Act application;

(2) death may significantly alter the balance of available resources; and

(3) competing interests differ on divorce from an application under the 1975 Act.

Claims by other categories of applicant

15.92 As set out at **15.49** reasonable financial provision for categories of applicant other than a surviving spouse and civil partner is limited to what is 'reasonable in all circumstances for the applicant to receive for his maintenance'.

15.93 Maintenance is only defined as regards dependants under s 1(3) of the 1975 Act:

'... a person shall be treated as being maintained by the deceased ... if the deceased, otherwise than for full valuable consideration, was making a substantial contribution in money or money's worth towards the reasonable needs of that person.'

15.94 The courts have a wide discretion when considering what constitutes maintenance. There is often a factual dispute as to the level of maintenance that was provided by the deceased, particularly in cases involving cohabitees and dependants.

15.95 If the deceased provided a roof over the head of the applicant, it is usually the case that a court will want to provide the applicant with accommodation (although not necessarily the accommodation that the applicant shared with the deceased – see *Saunders v Garrett* [2005] WTLR 749).

Claims by former spouses

15.96 Claims by former spouses are rare. Whilst *Re Farrow* [1987] 1 FLR 205 showed that a former spouse receiving substantial maintenance payments is likely to have a good claim under the 1975 Act, the clean break has become the preferred arrangement on divorce. *Barrass v Harding* [2002] WTLR 1071 shows that a former spouse may find it difficult to get over the first hurdle of the two-stage test (was provision for the deceased unreasonable?) if the divorce was some years ago and arrangements had been made at the time that settled their affairs.

Claims by cohabitees

15.97 Developments as to eligibility to apply are set out at **15.27–15.32**.

15.98 *Churchill v Roach* has developed the concept of maintenance in relation to cohabitation. The court confirmed that the relevant question is not whether the applicant could have survived without the deceased's support but whether the deceased made a 'substantial contribution'. The provision of accommodation, cash advances, and joint domestic bills was sufficient to show 'a substantial contribution' and although the applicant's income was sufficient to cover her 'financial needs' it was insufficient for her housing needs. Norris J in that case awarded the applicant a property from the deceased's estate.

Claim by a child or someone treated as a child of the family

15.99 Children of the deceased are eligible to claim under the 1975 Act whether or not they were dependent upon or being maintained by the deceased at the time of death. However, traditionally claims by able-bodied adults capable of earning their own living have been discouraged by the court.

15.100 The traditional position is set out in *Re Coventry* [1980] Ch 461, where it was held that:

> 'It cannot be enough to say "here is a son of the deceased; he is in necessitous circumstances; there is property of the deceased which could be made available to assist him but which is not available if the deceased's dispositions stand; therefore those dispositions do not make reasonable provision for the applicant." There

must, as it seems to me, be established some sort of moral claim by the applicant to be maintained by the deceased or at the expense of his estate beyond the mere fact of a blood relationship, some reason why it can be said that, in the circumstances, it is unreasonable that no or no greater provision was in fact made.'

15.101 The question raised by Browne-Wilkinson J in *Re Dennis* [1981] 2 ALL ER 140 exemplifies the traditional approach to claims by adult children under the 1975 Act:

'Why should anyone else make provision for you if you are capable of maintaining yourself?'

15.102 Subsequent cases suggested a need for the adult child to show that the deceased had a 'moral obligation' in order to bring a successful claim.

15.103 Butler-Sloss LJ in *Re Hancock* [1998] 2 FLR 346 and *Espinosa v Bourke* [1999] 1 FLR 747 took the opportunity to review the post *Re Coventry* cases, noting in the latter:

'There may have been some confusion in the minds of trial judges that the appellate court was placing a gloss upon the words of section [s 2] and putting some special emphasis on the requirements of sub-section 1(d) so as to elevate moral obligation of moral circumstances to some threshold of requirement ... an adult child is, consequently, in no different position from any other applicant who has to prove his case.'

15.104 This represented a shift in the court's view of claims by adult children, and has led to a number of cases bought in recent years by adult children under the 1975 Act.

15.105 In *Myers v Myers* [1999] 1 FLR 747, the judge found that the deceased's will had not made reasonable financial provision for his daughter and, of an £8m estate, she was awarded £275,000 to be held on trust together with a lump sum of £20,000 to equip her new home and a further £45,000 to discharge credit card debts and pay for a single premium for health cover.

15.106 In *Gold v Curtis* (unreported) 4 August 2004 (Ch), the judge found that the deceased had not made reasonable provision for her adult son and, of an estate worth approximately £870,000, the son was awarded £220,000 to augment his income and £30,000 as a capital sum. The adult son was still far less well off than his sister who received everything under her mother's will, but the judge reiterated that the basis of the court's jurisdiction is the relief of financial need and not the achievement of equality or fairness between two competing children.

Estrangement

15.107 In *Garland v Morris* [2007] WTLR 116, the claimant's 15-year estrangement from her father prior to his death led the judge to conclude that the claimant 'no longer had any reasonable claim on [her father's] bounty'. The judge made no award to the claimant, despite the fact that she lived in significantly more difficult financial circumstances than the deceased's other daughters who took the whole estate under the will.

Treated as a child of the family

15.108 This claim is usually brought by step-children. Slade LJ in *Re Leach deceased* [1986] Ch 226 held that the treatment must be in relation to the relevant marriage, but does not need to be effected during that marriage (or now also civil partnership). He also stated that treatment as a child of the family must involve more than the 'mere display of affection, kindness or hospitality by a parent towards a step-child'. The deceased must have 'expressly or impliedly, assumed the position of a parent towards the applicant, with the attendant responsibilities and privileges of that relationship'.

Claim by dependant

15.109 Developments as to eligibility to apply are outlined at **15.38–15.42**.

15.110 In *Jelley v Iliffe* the Court of Appeal observed that maintenance will generally raise a presumption of assumption of responsibility, as required under s 3(4) of the 1975 Act.

PRACTICE AND PROCEDURE

Pre-claim investigations

15.111 The initial client interview is an opportunity to gather as many pertinent facts as possible to establish if there are adequate grounds to bring a claim under the 1975 Act and to enable you to form a view as to the likely size of any award. A checklist of pertinent questions can be found at Appendix 2.

15.112 A 1975 Act claim is not a challenge to the validity of a will. Therefore lodging a caveat is not appropriate even if it might buy time to make investigations (see *Parnall v Hurst & Others* [2003] WTLR 997).

15.113 A standing search may be lodged to establish whether a grant has already been issued in the estate or to notify one of the issuing of a grant in due course. This will ensure that necessary action is taken within 6 months of the grant issuing in accordance with s 4 of the 1975 Act (see **15.6**). If the 6-month time limit has expired the applicant will need to apply for leave to issue the claim out of time.

15.114 Where an application is to be made under s 9 of the 1975 Act requesting the court to treat the deceased's severable share of a joint tenancy as part of the net estate, the application must be made within 6 months of the date of the grant. The court has no discretion to extend this time limit.

Collating evidence

15.115 There are a number of issues which should be considered before embarking on 1975 Act claim.

(1) Was the deceased domiciled in England and Wales? If not, there can be no claim under the 1975 Act, but there may be some entitlement to assets under a forced heirship, matrimonial property or community property regime (see Chapter 9).

(2) Is the potential applicant within, or likely to be within, one of the classes of applicants set out in s 1(1)(a) to (e) of the 1975 Act?

(a) Spouse or civil partner – was the marriage or civil partnership recognised in England and Wales or in the jurisdiction in which it took place? Was there a judicial separation?

(b) Former spouse or civil partner – check the marriage certificate, decree of dissolution, nullity or separation or equivalent documents relevant to civil partnerships, and obtain copies of any ancillary relief orders or agreements regulating financial provision. It is important to establish that the decree does not contain a provision which, under s 15, 15ZA or 15A of the 1975 Act, prevents the other party to the divorce or separation from bringing a 1975 Act claim. In any event, if there is a clean break order it may be difficult to make out a claim under the 1975 Act unless there has been a material change in circumstances.

(c) Cohabitant – what evidence is there showing cohabitation for a continuous period of at least 2 years (telephone bills, utility bills etc)? Where both parties retained their own property, consider whether it can be argued that there were two separate domestic economies. Can the couple can be said to have been living together as 'husband/wife or civil partners'?

(d) Child – it may be necessary to establish the child's paternity. Obtain a certified copy of the child's birth certificate if this is likely to be an issue. Was there a period of estrangement likely to affect the child's claim on the deceased's bounty (*Garland v Morris* [2003] WTLR 797)?

(e) Treated by the deceased as a child of the family – consider obtaining statements/affidavits from those who knew the family to establish whether the criteria are satisfied.

(f) Dependent – steps should be taken to establish the relationship between the applicant and the deceased, the period over which the deceased made provision for the applicant, the form of provision and the level of contribution. Was there any contractual arrangement such that it could be said that maintenance was for full valuable consideration? Did the deceased say or write anything which indicated that he did not assume responsibility for the applicant during his lifetime and/or after his death.

(3)   Consider at an early stage the size and nature of the estate to establish whether it is worth making or resisting the claim. Is there enough in the estate for provision to exceed legal costs in obtaining that provision? An estate which may at first appear to be quite substantial may be burdened with debt, inheritance tax and/or heavy administration expenses such that ultimately there may be little to litigate about.

If acting for a potential claimant, obtain a copy of the grant (which will give an indication of the size of the estate), any testamentary documents and details (from the personal representatives if need be) of the assets in the estate, the debts, likely administration expenses and whether the executors are aware of any jointly held property or other property which could be treated as part of the net estate of the deceased. The client may be able to provide this information which can be double checked with the personal representatives. Bear in mind ss 8–11 of the 1975 Act which enable property that would normally pass outside the estate to be brought back in for the purposes of making provision.

(4)   The Association of Contentious Trust and Probate Specialists Guidance Notes for the Resolution of Trust and Probate Disputes (known as the ACTAPS Code) applies to claims under the 1975 Act. Accordingly it may be possible to use the code to seek disclosure of the will file in accordance with the reasoning in the Court of Appeal decision in *Larke v Nugus* [2000] WTLR 1033 (see **12.72—12.75**). The will file may contain relevant information, although personal representatives should ensure that any waiver of privilege is exercised carefully.

(5)   Consider whether the effect of the intestacy rules or the provision which the deceased made under his will and any codicils does in fact make adequate provision for the potential claimant, or make some provision for him which will be taken into account in assessing an award in his favour. Are there any other assets passing outside the estate (joint property, pension provision, life assurance) that would affect the level of provision obtainable?

Where under the terms of the will and any codicil, the potential applicant is to receive a pecuniary legacy, it is usually possible to find out at a fairly early stage from the executor's solicitors whether the legacy might have to abate. If the potential applicant takes a share of or a life interest in residue it may be difficult to assess the extent of the benefits he is likely to receive until the administration is reasonably well advanced.

A particular difficulty arises where the potential applicant is one of a number of discretionary objects, and there are few (if any) indications as to how the trustees propose to exercise their discretion. Where there is a discretionary will, then whether acting for the executors, residuary beneficiaries or potential applicant, it is necessary to establish whether the deceased gave any indication of his wishes as to the way in which the discretion should be exercised.

In all cases of uncertainty, suggest that the potential applicant commences proceedings for protective purposes and then try to secure the agreement of the other parties to the litigation that the application should not proceed until after the trustees have indicated how they propose to exercise their discretion.

(6)   Consider the s 3 factors:
    (a)   What are the financial resources and needs of the applicant now or in the future and those of any other applicant or beneficiary of the estate?
    (b)   Are there any obligations that the deceased had towards the applicant or towards any beneficiary?
    (c)   Does the applicant suffer from any physical or mental disability? This does not need to be easily apparent. In *Myers v Myers* [1999] 1 FLR 747 the fact that the adult child claimant suffered from depression (which was not overtly emphasised in the course of the trial), was a factor taken into account by the judge. Also consider whether any other member of the applicant's family has a disability. In *Gold v Curtis* (unreported) 4 August 2004 (Ch), the fact that the adult child applicant herself had a daughter suffering from a disability, was taken into account by the judge in making an award to the applicant.
    (d)   Consider whether any other factors can be brought into account under s 3(1)(g), the catch all provision. Specifically is there any significant conduct issue on the part of the applicant or any other party, which the court should consider?

(7)   If the grant has already issued more than six months previously, consider whether the court is likely to be influenced by any of the factors set out in *Re Salmon* [1981] Ch 167 (see **15.8**) and whether there might be a claim for professional negligence against the potential applicant's solicitors in the event that leave is not granted. As at **15.9**, leave may still be given in these circumstances where a financial remedy against solicitors would not be a satisfactory substitute for a successful claim (*Nesheim v Kosa* [2007] WTLR 149).

A precedent letter of advice in response to a claim under the 1975 Act, checklist when taking instructions and list of documents to be collated, are at Appendix 2.

PROCEEDINGS

Time limit

15.116 As discussed above, at **15.6**, claims should be issued within 6 months of the date of grant.

Jurisdiction

15.117 A claim may be issued in the High Court or the county court. Both courts have jurisdiction to hear claims under the Act. Article 7(3) and (4) of the High Court and County Courts Jurisdiction Order 1991 (SI 1991/724) which stated that claims to the value of less than £25,000 should be tried in the county court, while those worth more than £50,000 should be tried in the High Court, has been repealed.

15.118 Claims in the High Court may be commenced in the Chancery or the Family Division. The approaches of the divisions vary somewhat and solicitors advising should consider carefully where a client's best interests are served. For example, a surviving spouse or civil partner may wish to claim in the Family Division, where judges may be more familiar with the generous provision on ancillary relief claims.

Commencement and proceedings

15.119 A claim under the 1975 Act is dealt with under CPR Part 57.

15.120 It is made by issuing a Claim Form in accordance with CPR Part 8 with the following modifications:

- The written evidence filed and served by the claimant with the Claim Form must exhibit an official copy of the grant of probate or letters of administration and every testamentary document in respect of the grant or letters of administration.

- The time within which a defendant must file and serve an Acknowledgment of Service and any written evidence is not more than 21 days after the service of the Claim Form on him.

If the Claim Form is served out of the jurisdiction, the period for filing the Acknowledgement of Service and written evidence is 7 days longer than that specified in the CPR, r 6.22 or the relevant practice direction. An example of a claim form and, separately, a witness statement in support of claim, can be found at Appendix 2.

15.121 A defendant who is personal representative of the deceased must file and serve written evidence including a statement to the best of his/her ability with:

- full details of the value of the deceased's net estate;

- the persons beneficially interested in the estate and the names and addresses of all living beneficiaries together with the value of their interests in the estate;

- whether any living beneficiary is a client or patient within the meaning of CPR, r 21.1(2); and

- any facts which might affect the exercise of the court's powers under the Act.

In addition, any defendant who is a personal representative and who wishes to remain neutral in relation to the claim must state this in the Acknowledgment of Service. An example of a witness statement by a personal representative can be found at Appendix 2.

Parties and joinder

15.122 The deceased's personal representatives must be joined to the claim as defendants (unless of course the personal representative is a claimant).

15.123 Beneficiaries of the estate should be joined, as they are interested in the estate and may be affected by any order ultimately made. It is not necessary to join those benefiting from small pecuniary legacies.

15.124 Where applications are to be made under ss 8–11 of the 1975 Act, those affected should be joined.

15.125 If there are a number of beneficiaries, a representation order can be made under CPR Part 19. The court can also order that notice of the claim be served on any person not a party to the claim but who may be affected by the claim. If the person served with the notice files an Acknowledgment of Service within 14 days, he/she will become a party. If no Acknowledgment of Service is served, he/she will be bound by the ultimate judgment as if he/she were a party.

15.126 Under the Practice Direction to CPR Part 57, if a claim is made jointly by two or more claimants and any conflict of interest arises, a claimant may choose to be represented by separate solicitors or counsel or may appear in person and, if the court considers that claimants ought to be separately represented, it may adjourn the application until they are. There are obvious costs implications to having several sets of representation. The authors' experience is that modest differences in applicants' circumstances should not stand in the way of the costs benefit of joint representation.

Role of personal representatives

15.127 Where a personal representative is not a claimant or actively interested in the estate, he/she should adopt a neutral role. Failure to do so may result in a costs penalty in the ultimate outcome.

Service of Claim Form

15.128 Once proceedings are issued, the Claim Form should be served within 4 months. The Claim Form should identify under which sections of the 1975 Act the claimant applies (for example, under s 2 for reasonable provision and where relevant under s 4 for permission to apply out of time, s 5 for an interim order, ss 8–11 for claims to property outside the estate).

Compromise

Who can compromise

15.129 Claimants and defendants who are not under any legal disability may settle claims without approval from the court.

15.130 CPR, r 21.10 requires the court's consent to be obtained for compromises affecting minors or protected parties. Under CPR Part 21, a child is defined as a person under 18 and a protected party is defined as a party, or an intended party, who lacks capacity under the Mental Capacity Act 2005 to conduct the proceedings. A party will not have capacity under the Mental Capacity Act 2005 if 'at the material time he is unable to make a decision for himself in relation to the matter because of an impairment of, or disturbance in the functioning of, the mind or brain'. The procedure is different depending on whether agreement has been reached prior to the issue of proceedings or post the issue of proceedings.

15.131 Where a claim by or on behalf of a minor or protected party has been agreed prior to proceedings, the approval of the court must be sought by application under the Part 8 procedure. The application must contain the information set out in the practice direction to CPR Part 21 including the age and occupation (if any) of the minor or protected party, the litigation friend's approval of the compromise and a copy of counsel's opinion as to the merits of the compromise. The application is usually made to a District Judge or Chancery Master.

15.132 Charity trustees may approve a compromise under s 15 of the Trustee Act 1925. They are also able to agree compromises under the Charities Act 1993, s 26.

15.133 If the Attorney General is involved in the proceedings, his consent must also be obtained.

How to compromise

15.134 If settlement of a 1975 Act claim is agreed on before the application is issued, perhaps as a result of entering a caveat, the terms can be recorded in a Deed of Variation. If, however, proceedings are discontinued where the parties reach a compromise, the following methods may be used:

- Notice of Discontinuance;

- Deed of Variation;

- Consent Order.

15.135 The latter two are to be preferred, particularly if there are inheritance tax and/or capital gains tax advantages (see **15.137**).

15.136 The Consent Order is usually drafted on a 'Tomlin' basis; it recites that the proceedings are stayed on the basis of the terms set out in the schedule with liberty to reapply in the event that any of those terms is not adhered to. A general form of Tomlin Order can be found at Appendix 2.

Taxation issues

15.137 Section 19 of the 1975 Act provides that an order made under s 2 shall for all purposes relate back to the date of death and be treated as a disposition by will or on intestacy. This includes consent orders but not notices of discontinuance. Section 146(1) of the IHTA 1984 states that, for inheritance tax purposes, assets in the deceased's estate shall devolve subject to the terms of the order. This is extended by s 146(8) to include orders staying or dismissing proceedings. The capital gains tax legislation, now found in the Taxation of Chargeable Gains Act 1992 ('TCGA 1992'), does not contain a similar provision. The effect of this is that, unless HMRC agrees otherwise, there may be a chargeable disposal for capital gains tax by the personal representatives or beneficiaries. This could be avoided by the parties entering into a separate instrument of variation under s 62 of the TCGA 1992 within two years of death.

15.138 Orders made under the anti-avoidance provisions (ss 10 and 11) of the 1975 Act requiring recipients of assets to account for their value will have the effect of increasing the value of the estate of the deceased for inheritance tax (IHTA 1984, s 146(2) and (8)). If the tax on the estate is significant, it may be better to avoid obtaining an order under s 2, and simply to treat the transfer as a gift by the recipient to the claimant. This will be treated as a potentially exempt transfer for inheritance tax purposes, such that no IHT will be payable provided the original recipient survives 7 years from the date of the transfer. It may be necessary to make provision in the compromise agreement for the payment of IHT in the event that the original recipient does not survive the full 7 years from the date of the transfer.

15.139 The words *'for all purposes'* in s 19 of the 1975 Act include references to income tax. An instrument of variation under IHTA 1984, s 142 is effective for income tax only from the date of the document. A consent order under s 2 of the 1975 Act should be insisted upon to prevent the original beneficiary suffering an unnecessary tax liability on income already paid over by the personal representative.

Costs

15.140 Under CPR, r 44.3(2) the general rule is that the unsuccessful party will be ordered to pay the costs of the successful party. This is subject to the court's discretion (CPR, r 44.3(2)(b)).

15.141 If the parties have acted reasonably and the estate is sufficient, the court may order costs to be payable from the estate (whether or not the claim succeeds).

15.142 An applicant bringing a claim unreasonably is at risk of paying his costs and those of the respondents. Claims for provision from small estates are discouraged since the beneficiaries may end up with little or nothing (see *Re Fullard* [1981] 2 All ER 796).

15.143 Beneficiaries who defend claims against overwhelming evidence may similarly be out of pocket (see *Millward v Shenton* [1972] 2 All ER 1025, a claim by a disabled child defended by the charity beneficiary).

15.144 A successful party which has refused to enter into negotiations or pursue alternative dispute resolution, may be penalised in costs. The Part 36 procedure can be useful because, if, for example, an offer is made by for example the defendant which the claimant fails to beat at trial, the claimant whilst successful can be ordered to pay the defendant's costs since the date of the offer. Conversely a claimant who beats his/her own Part 36 offer (which the defendant rejected) should see in addition to the usual rule that the loser pays the winner's costs, the imposition of additional cost penalties, for example, punitive interest rates.

15.145 If the claim settles, each party may agree to bear its own costs, although provision is likely to be made for the personal representatives.

Personal representatives' costs

15.146 Personal representatives will usually recover costs on an indemnity basis although they may be denied the usual indemnity or be made liable for costs on the basis of conduct, if they have acted inappropriately.

15.147 Since the procedural rules require the personal representatives to file a witness statement in answer to a claim within 21 days of service, a Beddoe application is rarely appropriate. If the claim obviously cannot be substantiated

or the estate is illiquid, personal representatives should obtain directions at an
early stage and the application might include reference to costs.

Chapter 16

DISAPPOINTED BENEFICIARY CLAIMS: FATAL ACCIDENT CLAIMS

16.1 In the event of a wrongful death, the deceased's estate may bring a claim against the tortfeasor pursuant to the Law Reform (Miscellaneous Provisions) Act 1934. In addition, a claim may be brought against the tortfeasor by the dependants and relatives of the deceased pursuant to the Fatal Accidents Act 1976. We will address these in turn.

LAW REFORM (MISCELLANEOUS PROVISIONS) ACT 1934

Heads of claim

16.2 Examples of pre-death items which may be claimed for pursuant to this Act include:

- the deceased's pain, suffering and loss of amenity;

- the deceased's loss of earnings; and

- the cost of caring for the deceased and the deceased's medical expenses.

In addition, funeral and probate expenses may be claimed for.

Recoverable benefits

16.3 A compensator (generally the tortfeasor's insurers) will be obliged to report any claim pursuant to the Act to the Compensation Recovery Unit of the Department for Work and Pensions and then to repay any recoverable benefits received by the deceased prior to their death upon the settlement of any claim. The compensator may be entitled to reduce the amount payable to the deceased's estate by some or all of the amount repaid.

Contributory negligence

16.4 To the extent the deceased's negligence contributed to the accident, then there may be a reduction in the damages awarded.

FATAL ACCIDENTS ACT 1976

Claimants

16.5 The classes of potential claimants are set out in s 1(3) of the Fatal Accidents Act 1976. They include:

- the wife or husband or former wife or husband of the deceased;

- the civil partner or former civil partner of the deceased;

- any person who:
  - – was living with the deceased in the same household immediately before the date of the death; and
  - – had been living with the deceased in the same household for at least 2 years before that date; and
  - – was living during the whole of that period as the husband or wife or civil partner of the deceased;

- any parent or other ascendant of the deceased;

- any person who was treated by the deceased as his parent;

- any child or other descendant of the deceased;

- any person (not being a child of the deceased) who, in the case of any marriage to which the deceased was at any time a party, was treated by the deceased as a child of the family in relation to that marriage;

- any person (not being a child of the deceased) who, in the case of any civil partnership in which the deceased was at any time a civil partner, was treated by the deceased as a child of the family in relation to that civil partnership;

- any person who is, or is the issue of, a brother, sister, uncle or aunt of the deceased.

Heads of claim

16.6 The following may be claimed for:

- bereavement (the amount that may currently be awarded in this respect is £10,000);

- funeral expenses; and

- loss of dependency.

Loss of dependency

16.7 Claims may be made in respect of the loss of dependants' financial dependency on the deceased and in respect of any loss of services dependency, ie in respect of services such as gardening, decorating and DIY, which the dependants would have expected to be undertaken by the deceased were it not for the death.

16.8 In calculating the dependency claim as a whole, it is usual first to calculate the dependants' annual dependency on the deceased (called the multiplicand), and then to apply to the multiplicand a multiplier, which is calculated in accordance with statistical tables that take account of accelerated receipt and mortality.

16.9 When assessing the annual financial dependency of a surviving non-working spouse, the conventional approach (*Harris v Empress Motors* [1984] 1 WLR 212) is to assume as a rule of thumb that the deceased would have spent one third of the couple's net income on himself, one third on the surviving spouse, and one third jointly. This produces a two-thirds figure for the financial dependency. Where there are children, this increases to three-quarters.

Disregard of benefits

16.10 If as a result of the death the dependants receive pecuniary benefits, such as pursuant to the deceased's will or a life insurance policy, then by virtue of s 4 of the Act those benefits are required to be ignored for the purposes of calculating their financial dependency on the deceased. Practitioners should be aware that this requirement has led to much case-law, particularly in relation to pension arrangements.

Contributory negligence

16.11 To the extent the deceased's negligence contributed to the accident, then there may be a reduction in the damages awarded. Further, if a particular dependant contributed to the accident, then there may be a reduction in that dependant's award.

Interaction with Inheritance (Provision for Family and Dependants) Act 1975 claims

16.12 The receipt of damages by a person with a claim under the 1975 Act may constitute a financial resource to be taken into account under s 3 of the 1975 Act. Accordingly, in some cases it may be appropriate for the 1975 Act claim to be issued within the 6-month time-limit as a protective measure, and then adjourned by consent pending the outcome of the Fatal Accidents Act 1976 claim.

Chapter 17

CREDITOR CLAIMS AND INSOLVENT ESTATES

PAYMENT OF DEBTS

17.1 Personal representatives have a duty to pay the deceased's debts with reasonable due diligence having regard to the available assets (*Re Tankard* [1942] Ch 69).

17.2 Debts incurred by the deceased must be fully investigated by the personal representatives. If they are in doubt as to the validity of any claim, they can:

(a) rely on the discretion to compromise claims given to them by the Trustee Act 1925, s 15. If so, they should, if possible, arm themselves with an indemnity from the beneficiaries;

(b) ask the Chancery Master to determine the matter under CPR Part 64.

Personal representatives may ignore a debt if it is unenforceable or statute barred. (The issue was considered in *In the Matter of the Estate of K Deceased* [2007] WTLR 1007.)

Order of payment of debts

17.3 Unless the will directs otherwise, the Administration of Estates Act 1925, Sch 1, Part 2, determines the order in which assets are to be applied for payment of debts. In practice, the consent of the beneficiaries ought to be obtained where the personal representative's task is not straightforward.

17.4 Despite the order set out in the Administration of Estates Act 1925, Sch 1, Part 2, a creditor who obtains judgment can enforce his debt against any available asset in the estate. Adjustments must be made by the personal representatives and, if they fail to 'marshal' assets in favour of the beneficiary whose entitlement was depleted by the creditor's debt, out of property which ought to have been used for that purpose, they will be liable to account, subject to a right of reimbursement from overpaid beneficiaries.

17.5 If a debt is secured on a property that property will bear the debt unless repayment of the mortgage is provided for elsewhere in the will (Administration of Estates Act 1925, s 35).

INSOLVENT OR POTENTIALLY INSOLVENT ESTATES

17.6 Section 421(4) of the Insolvency Act 1986 sets out that the estate of a deceased person is insolvent 'if, when realised, it will be insufficient to meet in full all the debts and other liabilities to which it is subject'.

17.7 Personal representatives may be faced with substantial but unquantified liabilities which if enforced will render the estate insolvent. Where there is an insolvency, personal representatives have a duty to both beneficiaries and creditors.

Methods of administration

17.8 The Administration of Insolvent Estates of Deceased Persons Order 1986 (SI 1986/1999) applies the relevant parts of the Insolvency Act 1986 to the estates of deceased persons.

17.9 When insolvency has been established the estate may be administered in one of the following ways:

(1) Informally by the personal representatives, along bankruptcy lines.

(2) By the personal representatives but under the jurisdiction of the court, an administration order having been made.

(3) Formally, under an Insolvency Administration Order (see Insolvency Act 1986, ss 264 and 267). Anyone who would have been entitled to apply for bankruptcy during the deceased's lifetime but where death has occurred before presentation of a bankruptcy petition, may apply for an Insolvency Administration Order. The effect of an order is that the estate vests in the Official Receiver until a trustee in bankruptcy is appointed; the latter will then administer the estate. If death occurs after presentation of a petition, the estate is administered by the Official Receiver or a trustee in bankruptcy in the normal way.

17.10 The personal representatives may themselves petition for an Insolvency Administration Order if they have ascertained by inquiry that the estate is insolvent. Alternatively, executors appointed by the will may renounce and leave it to the creditors to take a grant or petition for an order.

Order for payment of debts on insolvency

17.11 If an estate is insolvent there is a statutory order for payment of debts (which is effectively the same as the order on bankruptcy, namely: secured creditors; bankruptcy expenses; preferential creditors; ordinary creditors; statutory interest; deferred debts, for example debts due to the bankrupt's spouse or civil partner).

17.12 If assets are distributed without taking this hierarchy into account, the personal representatives can be personally liable for any loss.

17.13 There will be no bankruptcy expenses where the personal representative is administering the estate informally (see **17.9(1)** above).

17.14 Funeral and administration expenses have priority over preferential debts but not over secured debts (Administration of Insolvent Estates of Deceased Persons Order 1986, art 4(2)).

17.15 Despite this provision, personal representatives and solicitors should be careful of incurring costs in relation to an insolvent estate following *Re Vos (deceased)* [2005] WTLR 1619.

17.16 In *Re Vos*, for nine years following the deceased's death, DJ Freeman, the solicitors for the executor of Mr Vos's estate, carried out work on a number of matters for the estate, including negotiations with Lloyd's to try to settle the deceased's liability for losses at Lloyd's. The negotiations were protracted and ultimately unsuccessful. Lloyd's eventually issued proceedings to recover sums due and obtained judgment. Following judgment Lloyd's presented their petition for an Insolvency Administration Order. A trustee in bankruptcy was appointed and sought to reclaim the administration fees DJ Freeman had charged for the administration.

17.17 Section 284 of the Insolvency Act 1986 provides that dispositions made between the date on which a bankruptcy petition is presented and the date on which assets vest in the trustee are void unless made with the consent of the court or subsequently ratified by the court. Paragraph 12 of the Administration of Insolvent Estates of Deceased Persons Order 1986 modifies s 284 so that is has effect as if the petition had been presented on the date of death. On this basis, repayment of DJ Freeman's fees was ordered on the basis that the payments were void, had not been made with the consent of the court and could not be ratified by the court as there had been no benefit to the estate as a result of incurring the fees.

17.18 On this basis practitioners should, before taking on an estate that is or may be insolvent, consider asking the personal representative or beneficiaries to underwrite the work. If they are not prepared to do so, they should consider advising the personal representatives to apply to the court for an order validating costs.

Formal or informal administration

17.19 The Administration of Insolvent Estates of Deceased Persons Order 1986 disapplies s 292(2) of the Insolvency Act 1986, which means that the estate does not have to be administered by a qualified insolvency practitioner. If the personal representatives administer the estate without an insolvency practitioner, the additional charge to the estate is reduced.

17.20 However, in certain circumstances a trustee in bankruptcy can recover property not available to the personal representatives administering an estate outside bankruptcy. In deciding whether to administer the estate informally themselves or whether to apply to the court for an Administration Order, personal representatives should consider for example the impact of s 421A of the Insolvency Act 1986 as inserted by the Insolvency Act 2000.

17.21 Prior to the existence of s 421A, an Insolvency Administration Order could not be used to claw back property held by the deceased as beneficial joint tenant with another co-owner. The deceased's share will have passed by survivorship on death, and could not be recovered by creditors.

17.22 Section 421A enables a trustee appointed under an Insolvency Administration Order to apply to the court, on certain conditions, to recover the value of the deceased's former beneficial interest from the survivor. The application for an Insolvency Administration Order must have been made within 5 years of the date of death. The court will have regard to the circumstances of the survivor in deciding the matter.

17.23 The application can only be made by a trustee under an Insolvency Administration Order and not by a personal representative. Similarly, a trustee in bankruptcy may be able to apply to the court for a transaction to be set aside where there has been a transaction at an undervalue or a preference (Insolvency Act 1986, ss 339, 340). This application is not available to personal representatives.

17.24 The personal representatives may find themselves held accountable if they fail to petition for an Insolvency Administration Order where it would benefit the creditors to do so. For example, in the case of a s 421A application, if the personal representative has not applied for an Insolvency Administration Order within 5 years of death, the creditor will find that they cannot get their hands on assets passing outside the estate by survivorship. The situation becomes particularly complicated if a personal representative is also the survivor as clearly he/she will be in a position of conflict and the creditor may be able to seek his/her removal under the Administration of Justice Act 1985, s 50 (see **13.82–13.85**).

PROTECTION FOR PERSONAL REPRESENTATIVES

17.25 Personal representatives are personally liable for the deceased's debts (whether they had notice of them or not) where there were sufficient assets in the estate to meet those debts (*Ministry of Health v Simpson* [1951] AC 251).

17.26 If there are contingent liabilities personal representatives will be personally liable to creditors when the contingency falls in even though the contingency is remote.

Trustee Act 1925, s 27

17.27 Section 27 of the Trustee Act 1925 provides protection for personal representatives where appropriate advertisements have been made before distributing the estate and where personal representatives have no prior knowledge of debts.

Administration of Estates Act 1971, s 10(2)

17.28 Section 10(2) of the Administration of Estates Act 1971 protects a personal representative who has paid a debt to a creditor not realising that the estate is insolvent, so long as the personal representative acted in good faith. This section will not protect where the unpaid creditor is superior to the paid creditor. If the personal representatives have paid inferior debts or legacies, they will be taken to have admitted that there are sufficient assets in the estate to meet the creditor's claim.

Plene administravit

17.29 Personal representatives can seek to rely on the defence of *plene administravit*, ie that the personal representatives have fully administered the estate and have no assets left in their hands. Such a defence will not be effective if the personal representatives knew of the debt and chose to ignore it, even if it was a contingent liability and the likelihood of the contingency occurring was remote. If the defence of *plene administravit* is effective, the creditor can enter judgment against the estate to be enforced if any assets fall in in the future.

17.30 If there are insufficient assets remaining in the estate in consequence of maladministration by the personal representatives or they have chosen to ignore a creditor's entitlement, the creditor may proceed against the personal representatives on a *devastavit* claim (see Chapter 13). If the claim of maladministration is substantiated, personal representatives faced with such a claim cannot defend on the basis of plene administravit.

APPLICATIONS TO THE COURT

17.31 Where the estate is complex or substantial the personal representatives who have administered out of court would be well advised to complete their debt inquiries so far as possible and then seek the protection of the court. If this is done reasonably the costs of such an application should be treated as an administration expense.

17.32 Applications to court should also be considered in the following situations:

(1) Even though the personal representatives have placed the usual advertisement under the Trustee Act 1925, s 27, there may still be some

doubt about whether the totality of the deceased's debts have been ascertained, such as where the personal representatives have some notice of an alleged debt but inadequate details to enable them to deal with it, or of stale claims as in the case of *In the Matter of the Estate of K Deceased* [2007] WTLR 1007. In the latter, the judge said that whilst the court had to consider what protection should be afforded to potential creditors, it should also be sympathetic towards the administrators' desire to be immunised from personal liability and the beneficiaries' desire not to be kept from their inheritance for longer than necessary. There had to come a time when distribution without reference to the potential claims could be sanctioned by the court and without the administrators incurring risk of personal liability. If personal representatives distribute pursuant to such a direction they are protected from claims by disappointed creditors provided that the personal representatives brought the full relevant facts to the attention of the court.

An alternative may be to take out an indemnity policy to cover the risk of creditors arising at a later stage. In *Evans v Westcombe* [1999] 2 All ER 777 a similar policy, used to protect the personal representative in the event of a missing beneficiary transpiring, was held to be a proper expense of the administration.

(2)   When the personal representatives are considering whether or not to take or defend proceedings at the expense of the estate. Beddoe applications are dealt with in more detail in Chapter 13. If Beddoe proceedings are being issued in a potentially insolvent estate, the creditors or a representative of the creditors should be joined in addition to beneficiaries or a representative of them.

(3)   Difficulties will be encountered where the estate may be solvent if a disputed claim by a creditor is unsuccessful but insolvent if his claim succeeds. In such circumstances, the creditor is unlikely to wish the estate to be depleted by the costs of defending his action against the estate. While the creditor in question is a necessary party to any Beddoe summons, it may be appropriate to adapt the practice set out in *Re Moritz* [1960] 1 Ch 251 and *Re Eaton (Shaw v Midland Bank Executor and Trustee Company Ltd)* [1964] 1 WLR 1269 whereby, broadly speaking, the person whose claim is against the estate is excluded from the hearing when the merits of the defence to his action are being considered by the court.

(4)   Various difficulties may arise during the course of the administration of the estate; there may, for example, be a dispute between the beneficiaries and creditors or between any of them and the personal representatives as to the best method of selling assets. If the personal representatives consider that they need the protection of a direction of the court on such an issue, they can apply for guidance under CPR 64.

(5)   Personal representatives can seek protection under the Trustee Act 1925, s 61 which provides that personal representatives can be relieved from the

consequences of a breach of trust where they acted 'honestly and reasonably, and ought fairly to be excused for the breach of trust and for omitting to obtain the directions of the court'. An example might be where the personal representatives have given the creditor an opportunity to prove his claim or issue proceedings and he has failed to do so. Although personal representatives often act honestly and reasonably it may be more difficult for them to satisfy the court that they should be excused for failing to obtain the court's directions.

(6)   Contingent liabilities may arise as a result of the deceased's membership of loss-making syndicates at Lloyd's. Personal representatives acting in such potentially insolvent estates need to consider the consequences of the company into which Names' losses have been reinsured being unable in the future to meet all obligations. Equitas was the company into which Names' losses for 1992 and earlier years were reinsured, but in 2007 its liabilities were reinsured by National Indemnity Company, a member of the Berkshire Hathaway Group (see **17.36** below). If it were to fail, the question of continuing liability may resurface several years after the estate has been wound up. If substantial funds are held, pressure from beneficiaries for personal representatives to distribute may make an application for a *Re Yorke* order a necessity. In *Re Yorke deceased* [1997] 4 All ER 907 the court sanctioned a distribution to legatees without the executors keeping a retention from the estate, and stated that a court order in these circumstances would give the executors protection from personal liability. However, a *Re Yorke* order will protect executors but not the beneficiaries to whom assets have been distributed.

17.33 The procedure concerning the estates of deceased Lloyd's names is governed by a Practice Statement [2001] 3 All ER 765, which can be found the Chancery Guide at 1A-200. (NB see **17.36**.)

17.34 In these circumstances personal representatives (and, if applicable, trustees) may apply for permission to distribute the estate by a Part 8 Claim Form plus supporting witness statement or an affidavit substantially in the form set out in Appendix 11 to the Chancery Guide. Costs can be agreed or the claimants can invite the court to make a summary assessment by submitting a statement of costs in the form specified in the Costs Practice Direction.

17.35 The application will be considered on paper in the first instance by the Master who, if satisfied that the order should be made, will make the order. If not satisfied, the Master will give directions as to how to proceed.

17.36 The procedure is specific to liabilities having been reinsured into the Equitas Group and therefore, since the liabilities of Equitas were reinsured by National Indemnity Company, it has not been clear whether the *Re Yorke* procedure will still work. However the position at the moment appears to be that until Equitas actually transfers its undertakings to National Indemnity Company the procedure should remain effective.

Chapter 18

TAX EVASION, FOREIGN TAXES AND CRIMINAL MATTERS

DISCLOSURE TO REVENUE AUTHORITIES (INCLUDING FOREIGN REVENUE AUTHORITIES)

18.1 From time to time, personal representatives will be requested by revenue authorities (whether within or outside the home jurisdiction of the trust) to provide information about the will, the deceased or the estate beneficiaries. Where further information is requested which seems to be a prelude to a full-scale investigation, or revenue authorities seek facilities to inspect documents, personal representatives and will trustees are placed in a very difficult position. The Revenue has considerable powers to require production or to search and seize documents.

18.2 Under s 19A of the Taxes Management Act 1970 (TMA 1970), HM Revenue & Customs (HMRC) can require the taxpayer to produce 'such documents' and 'such accounts' as may be relevant to the investigation. TMA 1970, s 20 empowers the inspector to require delivery up of any document (calculations, accounts and other particulars) which may contain information relevant to the taxpayer's liability. Under s 20(3), virtually any third party within the jurisdiction can be required to supply access to such documents in its possession or power, provided that the inspector reasonably believes they may contain information relevant to any tax liability to which any taxpayer is or may become subject, except material covered by legal professional privilege (*R v Special Commissioner of Income Tax, ex p Morgan Grenfell* [2002] 2 WLR 1299); such disclosure does not include material covered by legal professional privilege, such as Counsel's advice).

18.3 Although HMRC can, under TMA 1970, s 20C, conduct search and seizure operations where serious tax fraud is suspected, it seems that the effect of the Finance Act 2000 will be that HMRC will first ask the taxpayer to volunteer the documents and that the provisions of s 20C will be used only if the taxpayer does not want to co-operate.

18.4 The issue for personal representatives/will trustees is therefore whether they should comply with a request for information or insist that the requisite procedures are followed, in which case further suspicion and more rigorous implementation of HMRC's powers may follow. It is likely to be in the personal representatives' and beneficiaries' interest to consult the principal beneficiaries and encourage them to agree to the provision of limited information.

18.5   The personal representatives'/will trustees' position is more difficult if the revenue authority seeking the information is a foreign revenue authority, to which the personal representatives do not have an obligation to provide returns. It has been a long-established principle that one state will not enforce the revenue laws of another (*Government of India v Taylor* [1955] AC 491, and the *QRS 1 ApS v Frandsen* [1999] STC 616).

18.6   However, in certain instances the English courts have provided assistance to foreign states obtaining evidence regarding the beneficial ownership of assets in support of a foreign revenue claim, as in *Re State of Norway* [1990] 1 AC 723 and the position may be covered by Finance Act 2000, s 146 (for serious non compliance of which see **18.8**). Furthermore, where the deceased had an irregular foreign tax position, consideration must be given to whether that stemmed from ignorance or culpable tax evasion; if the latter, money laundering issues may also arise, as to which see **18.14**.

FOREIGN REVENUE CLAIMS

18.7   It has long been established that if trustees pay a statute-barred debt they commit a breach of trust (see *Midgley v Midgley* [1893] 3 Ch 282). Accordingly, trustees have historically been advised to be wary of discharging taxes levied by a foreign revenue authority which could not be enforced against them and that they should not comply with requests by foreign revenue authorities for the provision of information and documentation without a court order. According to a Jersey authority (*Re Tucker* (1987–88) JLR 473), trustees should seek directions before doing so; if they do not propose to do so a beneficiary might wish to seek such a direction, but it should be noted that in *Re Lord Cable* [1976] 3 All ER 417 beneficiaries who sought to restrain trustees by injunction from paying foreign taxes failed because on the facts of that case it was no breach of trust for the trustees to do so. Trustees may, in particular, wish to seek directions to do so when beneficiaries or some of them would otherwise be exposed to tax claims in the jurisdiction in question. Historically trustees have been directed to pay foreign taxes with good reason, such as where certain beneficiaries or the trustees themselves would be at jeopardy of enforcement measures (*Re Lord Cable* [1977] WLR 7; *Re Marc Bolan Charitable Trust* (1981) JJ 117). This reasoning is likely to apply to personal representatives.

18.8   However it should be noted that the position adopted in *Government of India v Taylor* and *QRS 1 ApS v Frandsen* may not apply if treaties are in place which enable the collection of taxes between states. Following the work of the Organisation of Economic Co-operation and Development there are now a considerable number of arrangements for co-operation between states in the provision of information to enable tax assessments to be raised and revenue collected; for example, the Millennium Convention on Mutual Administrative

Assistance in Tax Matters. This provides for exchange of information, recovery of tax claims and service of documents. It has now been signed up to by Belgium, Denmark, Finland, Iceland, the Netherlands, Norway, Poland, Sweden, the United States, France, Italy and Azerbaijan. The Finance Act 2002, s 134 provided for the UK to implement the Mutual Assistance Recovery Directive between EU member states in relation to the recovery of tax debts. While it was unclear which taxes it covered it appears that pursuant to the Finance Act 2006, ss 173–176 the scope of the UK's power to enter into arrangements relating to mutual recovery of taxes and exchange of information will be extended. Further, the Finance Act 2000, s 146 enables service of a notice under TMA 1970, s 20 in respect of foreign taxes, which have been clarified as referring to serious non-compliance with the tax laws of another state.

18.9 The collection of information for fiscal affairs is easier for revenue authorities if there is an allegation that fiscal crime has been committed: it has always been an exception to the non-enforcement principle if criminal conduct is an issue. In that case, the range of international treaties for co-operation in criminal matters will come into effect and, in such circumstances, it should be borne in mind that information relating to the deceased's failure to comply with foreign revenue laws may come to the attention of the relevant foreign revenue authority as a result of obligations arising under the anti-money laundering legislation and mutual co-operation provisions (see **18.25** and **18.28**).

BENEFIT FRAUD/TAX EVASION

18.10 It is not uncommon for personal representatives to conclude that the deceased had too much capital or income to have been able to claim the allowances he or she claimed from the state.

18.11 In such a situation, whether or not a claim is made by the state, the personal representatives should clear up the position with the relevant authority and reach agreement on paying a sum by way of settlement of liability for overpaid benefits.

18.12 A similar problem arises when the personal representatives discover a source of income – such as a Swiss bank account – which appears unlikely to have been disclosed to HMRC. The position should be checked against the deceased's past income tax returns and if it is clear that there has been a non-disclosure, the position remedied with HMRC.

18.13 In each case, consideration should also be given to whether or not overclaimed benefit or underpaid tax was overclaimed or underpaid mistakenly or culpably. If the latter, money laundering issues may also arise, as to which see below.

MONEY LAUNDERING AND TERRORIST FINANCING ISSUES

18.14 The law in relation to money laundering is now principally contained in Part 7 of the Proceeds of Crime Act 2002 (POCA 2002), whereas that in relation to terrorist financing is principally contained in the Terrorism Act 2000. POCA 2002 was enacted in the UK to give effect to the Second EU Money Laundering Directive and similar legislation to that in the UK exists in many other jurisdictions.

18.15 Under POCA 2002, ss 327–329, a person who transfers or converts 'criminal property', who becomes concerned in an arrangement under which it may be transferred, converted, used or enjoyed by another, or who acquires, uses or has possession of 'criminal property' otherwise than for valuable consideration may commit an offence if he does not first obtain the consent of the Serious Organised Crime Agency (SOCA). The Terrorism Act 2000, s 18 contains a similar offence in relation to unauthorised dealings with 'terrorist property'. Each of these offences carries a maximum of 14 years' imprisonment, a fine or both.

18.16 The offences under POCA 2002, ss 327–329, together with:

- attempting or conspiring to commit, or inciting the commission of, such an offence;

- aiding, abetting, counselling or procuring the commission of such an offence; and

- acts which would, had they been done in the UK, have constituted an offence of the type described above in this paragraph

are referred to in that Act as 'money laundering'.

18.17 Under POCA 2002, s 330, if a person acquires knowledge, suspicion, or grounds for suspicion of money laundering in the course of carrying on a business in the Regulated Sector (which is defined in Sch 9 to POCA 2002 and includes the provision of trust and company formation and administration services and tax advice) he is under a duty to disclose his knowledge or the grounds for his suspicion to SOCA (where appropriate via his or her Money Laundering Reporting Officer), as soon as is reasonably practicable. Terrorism Act 2000, s 21A contains a similar offence in relation to failure to report knowledge or grounds for suspicion in relation to dealings with 'terrorist property'. These offences can be punished by a maximum of five years' imprisonment, a fine or both.

18.18 There are specific defences to these offences where legal professional privilege applies. However, one of the key requirements for privilege to exist is that the information should have been communicated to the legal adviser without the intention of furthering a criminal purpose. Therefore, if a legal adviser is consulted in order to assist in, for example, making a transfer of 'criminal property' it is likely that the client will have no privilege because of his purpose.

18.19 It is to be hoped that practitioners and trustees will rarely come across 'terrorist property' (which includes property likely to be used for the purposes of terrorism as well as the proceeds of terrorist activity, including rewards received for its commission); similarly, it may be hoped that they will rarely come across what might ordinarily be considered to be 'criminal property'. However, the definition of 'criminal property' under POCA 2002 includes any person's benefit from 'criminal conduct' (which need not necessarily be their own criminal conduct and which is, broadly, anything which is criminal under the law of any part of the UK, or which would have been criminal were it to have been done in the UK, including fiscal crime).

18.20 Thus, POCA 2002 is in issue not only where the estate or trust property includes the proceeds of serious organised or violent crime, but also where tax evasion (whether in relation to UK or foreign tax) or culpable overclaiming of benefits is concerned: for these purposes, tax evasion and benefit fraud are crimes on a par with drug trafficking and armed robbery.

18.21 The effect of POCA 2002, ss 327–329 is that a person wishing to be involved in any way in the conversion, transfer, use or possession of 'criminal property' (including funds which have been enhanced by a culpable failure to pay tax in any jurisdiction or culpably overclaimed benefits) will generally need to make a report to SOCA in order to seek its consent. Similarly, where 'terrorist property' is concerned a report would have to be made under the Terrorism Act.

18.22 Secondly, a person engaged in a business in the Regulated Sector who becomes aware of, or who has grounds to suspect that someone else is in possession of or dealing with criminal property (not to mention terrorist property) may have to make a report to SOCA even if he does not himself take any part in the relevant activities.

18.23 Where tax (whether UK or foreign) has been underpaid or benefit has been overclaimed, consideration must therefore be given to whether or not there may be knowledge or suspicion (or even grounds for suspicion) that the deceased acted culpably. Clearly in some cases, a failure to disclose a tax liability or claiming benefits where they were not due may have been inadvertent, in which case although the position should be addressed, as described above, no obligation to report to SOCA should arise. However, if the personal representatives do suspect that the non-disclosure or overclaiming was deliberate they should report, making it clear (at least where UK matters are concerned) that they are taking steps to remedy the matter, otherwise they risk committing one or more of the offences in POCA 2002, ss 327–330. In such circumstances it is unlikely that SOCA will take the matter further unless it appears that there was significant non-disclosure in which case HMRC or the Benefits Agency might launch an enquiry; however, given that the personal representatives will themselves have disclosed the position to the relevant UK authorities, the additional risk in such circumstances is limited.

18.24 A complication arises in relation to foreign tax, however. The UK has ratified conventions designed to further international co-operation in relation to criminal matters, such as the 1959 European Convention on Mutual Assistance in Criminal Matters and its Additional Protocol, the 1990 European Convention on Laundering, Search, Seizure and Confiscation of the Proceeds of Crime, and the 1988 United Nations Convention Against Illicit Traffic in Narcotic Drugs and Psychotropic Substances (the Vienna Convention).

18.25 Under the Criminal Justice (International Co-operation) Act 1990, the English courts will co-operate with other jurisdictions in the fight against money laundering without requiring dual criminality.

18.26 Since the establishment of the Financial Action Task Force (FATF), the introduction of legislation aimed at combatting terrorism and, in particular, at ensuring that terrorists and those who support them are denied access to the international financial system, has increased rapidly. Members introduce measures requiring intermediaries and service providers to identify beneficial owners before business relationships are established and to be obliged to report suspicious transactions in accordance with FATF's 40 recommendations. FATF currently has 33 member states. India and China are hoping to join. FATF works with other regional anti money laundering and anti terrorist groups to combat money laundering and terrorist financing.

18.27 As such measures are introduced, the duty of confidentiality of trustees in respect of fiduciary business will be severely undercut if suspicion of money laundering is present. Further, it has been held (in *Barclays Bank plc v Taylor* [1989] 1 WLR 1066 and in *Acturus Properties Ltd v Attorney General for Jersey* (2000–01) 3 ITELR 360) that the bank, fiduciary or other intermediary which is requested, by due process, to provide information or documentation to assist a criminal investigation does not have standing to challenge that request, although the person or entity to whom the bank/trustee owes duties of confidentiality does. In *Acturus Properties Ltd v Attorney General for Jersey* the Royal Court of Jersey also held that such a notice did not breach either Art 1 or Art 6(1) of the European Convention on Human Rights on the grounds that neither of these could be involved during a criminal investigation and/or that any interference with Convention rights was justified in the public interest.

18.28 Another consequence of the mutual co-operation between states is that where the non-payment of foreign tax is reported to SOCA, there is a strong likelihood that the information will be passed, via HMRC, to the relevant foreign revenue authority. The consequence is, therefore, that even where it might otherwise be appropriate on trust principles not to disclose information to a foreign revenue authority, at least some information may reach it as a result of the international anti-money laundering co-operation process; in those circumstances, this will be a factor which trustees and personal representatives will wish to take into consideration in considering whether the foreign tax should be paid on the principles discussed above.

Part VI

CLAIMS AGAINST PROFESSIONAL ADVISERS

Chapter 19

CLAIMS AGAINST PROFESSIONAL ADVISERS

WHAT CLAIMS MAY BE MADE?

19.1 Claims may be made against professional advisers in various situations but broadly come under the following:

(1) against those drafting and advising in relation to wills, trusts and estate planning, where that advice later transpires to be negligent;

(2) against professionals acting as personal representatives/trustees;

(3) against professionals for negligent advice to executors/trustees;

(4) in relation to costs.

CLAIMS AGAINST THOSE DRAFTING AND ADVISING IN RELATION TO WILLS, TRUSTS AND ESTATE PLANNING

19.2 There are two main areas where professionals may come under attack for their performance:

(1) will drafting and estate planning; and

(2) estate administration.

To claim successfully in negligence it is necessary to prove:

(a) that the professional had a duty of care;

(b) that the duty was breached; and

(c) that the breach caused loss.

This chapter does not attempt to deal with aspects of the law of negligence exhaustively, but simply to pick out key aspects relevant in the context of probate disputes. Practitioners should refer to specialist texts when considering negligence claims against professional advisers.

Will drafting

19.3   *White v Jones* [1995] 2 AC 207 established that a duty of care is owed to the beneficiary of a will. This was a radical departure from the previous position that as a beneficiary under a will was not party to the contract between the testator and the will draftsman he/she could not sue on it.

19.4   Will draftsmen have faced negligence claims involving the following (non exhaustive) list of scenarios:

- Failure to prepare a will within an acceptable timescale before the death of the testator. In *White v Jones* [1995] 2 AC 207 the House of Lords upheld the Court of Appeal's view that the deceased's solicitor, who had delayed for 44 days in drafting a will benefiting the claimants, was negligent, the deceased having died before a new will was executed.

- Failure to give adequate directions on how to execute a will. In *Ross v Caunters* [1980] Ch 297 the solicitor had simply warned the testator that he should have the will witnessed 'in the presence of two independent witnesses' but had failed to advise that the will should not be attested by a beneficiary's spouse.

- Failure to supervise execution of a will. In *Esterhuizen v Allied Dunbar Assurance plc* [1998] 2 FLR 668 a representative of Allied Dunbar took instructions for a new will. Once the will had been engrossed the representative took steps to ensure execution but, not being able to find anyone to witness the will and the testator refusing to be driven to a local garage to find witnesses, the representative left the will with the testator. The will was witnessed by only one witness and was therefore invalid. The court held that the duty of care owed to a beneficiary as established in *White v Jones* applied equally to a company holding itself out as a will making service to that of a solicitor and that it was not enough to merely inform the testator about execution of the will – the personal representative should have taken reasonable steps to assist his client.
  The draftsman has a duty to check for correct execution if the will is signed away from the office (*Gray v Richards-Butler* [2000] WTLR 143) and to store the original carefully if asked to do so.

- Failure to carry out the testator's intentions. In *Carr-Glynn v Frearsons* [1999] Ch 326 the court held that the solicitor who failed to check that a jointly owned property was held as tenants in common when amending a will so as to provide for the deceased's half share in the property to go to the deceased's niece, was liable when the half share automatically passed to the survivor on death. The *Corbett v Bond Pearce* [2006] WTLR 967 litigation arose out of a solicitor's negligent advice to the testatrix that she could execute a will but leave it undated on the basis that it would be effective after she had made subsequent lifetime gifts. The will was executed in September, the gifts effected in December, and the will dated on 26 December 1989. It is contrary to the Wills Act 1837 for a will to be subject to an unstated condition which has to be proved by extrinsic evidence, therefore the will was successfully set aside by the beneficiary of a previous will.

Estate planning

19.5 Negligent estate planning advice is a common cause of complaint. Complaints may arise over loss of a tax planning opportunity through negligent advice or omission; for example *Daniels v Thompson* [2004] WTLR 511, in which a solicitor failed to advise that the transfer of the deceased's house to her son during her lifetime would only be an effective potentially exempt transfer if she moved out of the property. In fact, the claim failed because it was advanced on the basis that liability to inheritance tax was a loss that the testatrix was capable of suffering and the Court of Appeal held that the testatrix never had a cause of action. An application to amend the pleadings to allege a breach of duty to the personal representative was refused as the personal representative had suffered no loss in that capacity.

19.6 In *Cancer Research Campaign and others v Ernest Brown & Co* [1998] PNLR 592, the court held that a solicitor's duty is confined to the terms of his retainer. The deceased, herself a beneficiary of the bulk of her brother's estate (who had predeceased approximately 18 months before), died leaving her residuary estate to seven charities. The claimant charities alleged breach of duty on the part of the solicitors for failing to vary the brother's will so as to avoid a charge to inheritance tax. The court held that the duty owed to the beneficiaries was confined to the terms of the retainer, which in this case was to draw the deceased's will. As such the solicitors had a duty to ensure that the beneficiaries received the benefit intended, but the duty did not extend to requiring them to advise the testatrix on how to increase the potential benefit to the claimants by means of a deed of variation. After the death of the testatrix the solicitors owed no duty to the residuary beneficiaries: any duty was owed solely to the executors of the estate.

Can an intended beneficiary of a lifetime gift bring a claim?

19.7 Whilst *White v Jones* [1995] 2 AC 207 conferred a remedy on a disappointed beneficiary of a will, this principle has not yet been extended to lifetime transactions. In *Hemmens v Wilson Browne* [1995] Ch 223, it was suggested that there may be circumstances in which a solicitor owes a duty to the intended beneficiary of a lifetime gift. However, in *White v Jones* it was stated that the intended beneficiary of a lifetime gift would not be owed a duty. In *Daniels v Thompson* [2004] WTLR 511, the question of whether a beneficiary could claim for such loss was not considered. The Court of Appeal held that the deceased did not suffer loss as the inheritance tax was only payable on death and therefore not her liability. As set out at **19.5** above, permission to amend the claim so that the solicitor owed a duty to the personal representative was refused because the personal representative had suffered no loss in his capacity as such.

Limitation period

19.8 The limitation period for a negligence claim is 6 years from the date that the cause of action accrues; namely when damage occurs. In *Bacon v Howard Kennedy* [1999] PNLR 1, instructions to solicitors to prepare a will were ignored. The judge held that the damage was not suffered until death, as at any point until death, the testator could have remedied the defect.

19.9 In cases where damage has occurred but the fact of the damage does not become known to the potential claimant until after the 6-year limitation period, the claimant can rely on s 14A of the Limitation Act 1980, which provides for a limitation period to run for 3 years from the date of knowledge.

19.10 Section 14B of the Limitation Act 1980 provides that a negligence claim will be time-barred after 15 years from the date on which the act or omission constituting negligence occurred. This is the case even if the cause of action has not yet accrued. Therefore although the authors are aware of no authority on this point it would appear that a negligently drafted will cannot be attacked more than 15 years after the date of the negligent act, even if death only occurs after 16 years.

CLAIMS AGAINST PROFESSIONALS ACTING AS PERSONAL REPRESENTATIVES OR TRUSTEES

19.11 Claims may be brought against personal representatives or trustees in their capacity as such. For more information see Chapter 13. A professional will owe a higher duty of care than a lay trustee (*Bartlett v Barclays Bank Trust Company Ltd (No 1)* [1980] 2 WLR 430). Trustee Act 2000, s 1 states the following:

'(1) Whenever the duty under this subsection applies to a trustee, he must exercise such care and skill as is reasonable in the circumstances, having regard in particular –

(a)   to any special knowledge or experience that he has or holds himself out as having, and

(b)   if he acts as trustee in the course of a business or profession, to any special knowledge or experience that it is reasonable to expect of a person acting in the course of that kind of business or profession.'

CLAIMS AGAINST PROFESSIONALS FOR NEGLIGENT ADVICE TO EXECUTORS/TRUSTEES

19.12 See **19.2–19.11** above. The claims will be brought by the executors/trustees against their professional advisers. There may be pressure from residuary beneficiaries to bring such claims. Failure to do so could result in actions for breach of trust/devastavit, as to which see Chapter 13.

CLAIMS IN RELATION TO COSTS

19.13 Claims may be made in relation to the professional costs of trusts and estate administration.

19.14 Where the professional is a solicitor, costs will usually be disputed through one of two routes:

(1) by seeking a remuneration certificate under the Solicitors' (Non Contentious Business) Remuneration Order 1994;

(2) by seeking a Solicitors Act taxation under the Solicitors Act 1974.

Remuneration certificate

19.15 Article 3 of the Solicitors' (Non Contentious Business) Remuneration Order 1994 (the 'Order'), states that a solicitor's costs should be 'such sum as is fair and reasonable to both solicitor and entitled person having regard to all the circumstances ...' The article refers specifically to other factors that should be taken into account, for example the complexity of the matter and the specialised knowledge required.

19.16 Under the Order, where the costs do not amount to more than £50,000, entitled persons may require a solicitor to obtain a remuneration certificate from the Council of the Law Society in relation to the fees charged.

19.17 An entitled person is a client or an entitled third party. An entitled third party is defined in art 2 of the Order as:

> 'a residuary beneficiary absolutely and immediately (and not contingently) entitled to an inheritance, where a solicitor has charged the estate for his professional costs for acting in the administration of the estate, and either (a) the only personal representatives are solicitors (whether or not acting in a professional capacity) or (b) the only personal representatives are solicitors acting jointly with partners or employees in a professional capacity;'

Therefore, for the purposes of costs, a residuary beneficiary is treated as if he/she were a client in challenging the costs of a solicitor acting in the administration of an estate.

19.18 The remuneration certificate will state what sum in the opinion of the Council would be a fair and reasonable charge for the business covered by the bill. The Council's view of what is fair and reasonable is often lower than that charged.

Solicitors Act taxation

19.19 Under s 70 of the Solicitors Act 1974, the party chargeable with a solicitor's bill (usually the client) can apply to have the bill assessed. If the application is made within one month from the delivery of the bill the court will order that the bill be taxed. If the application is made after one month but within 12 months from the delivery of the bill, the court has a discretion as to whether to order that the bill be assessed. As a general rule, the court will make no such order under the Act if the application is made after 12 months from delivery of the bill (although, the court still retains its inherent jurisdiction to order detailed assessment (*Re A Solicitor* [1961] Ch 591).

19.20 The general rule is that if more than 20% is deducted from the bill, the solicitor will have to pay the costs of detailed assessment. If less than 20% is deducted the client or third party must pay the costs of the detailed assessment (Solicitors Act 1974, s 70(9)). The court can, however, make a different order in special circumstances having regard to the conduct of the parties, the amount of reduction made and whether it is reasonable for the third party to dispute an item (see CPR, r 47.18).

19.21 The same rules apply in relation to persons other than the party chargeable with the bill, where said persons have paid or are/were liable to pay the bill.

Action for an account

19.22 Where the costs of a professional other than a solicitor (for example an accountant) are being disputed, the claimant can apply for an account under CPR Part 64 and ask the court to refer the file to the Supreme Court Costs Office for determination of costs.

19.23 There are no specific rules as to who is responsible for the costs incurred in the action. The court therefore has complete discretion as to what order for costs should be made, taking into account all the factors as set out in CPR 44.3. These include conduct of the parties (including whether it was reasonable for a party to raise or pursue a particular issue), degree of success and settlement offers.

Appendix 1

ANCILLARY RELIEF CASES SINCE
WHITE V WHITE

INTRODUCTION

As set out in Chapter 15, by virtue of s 3(2) of the Inheritance (Provision for Family and Dependants) Act 1975, where a spouse or civil partner is applying for provision under the Act, the court must have regard to what is known as the 'divorce hypothesis'; namely the provision that the applicant might have expected to receive if, on the day on which the deceased died, the marriage or civil partnership, instead of being terminated by death, had been terminated by divorce or dissolution.

The divorce hypothesis has meant that developments in the divorce courts have been applied in relation to 1975 Act claims. The following is a summary of developments since the seminal case of *White v White* [2001] AC 596, which may be useful to practitioners in assessing the level of provision awarded to a surviving spouse or civil partner under the Inheritance (Provision for Family and Dependants) Act 1975.

WHITE V WHITE [2001] AC 596

The House of Lords' judgment in *White v White* [2001] AC 596 greatly impacted on what a spouse might reasonably expect to receive on divorce, particularly where there was a long marriage/cohabitation. It is worth considering the facts in *White v White* briefly.

- marriage of 30 years;

- husband and wife had established a dairy farming business worth approximately £4.6m;

- at first instance, the wife received £980,000; and

- on appeal she was awarded £1.5m.

The House of Lords awarded the wife 40% of assets. The significance of the decision is summarised in the following points:

(1) the Lords reiterated that the s 25 factors (Matrimonial Causes Act 1973) remained the basis of assessing a claim;

(2) that there should be no favour towards the 'money maker' against the 'home maker'; and

(3) equality of the division should only be departed from if there was good reason for doing so, essentially rejecting the 'reasonable needs' argument. In big money cases the court essentially asks 'why should the surplus belong solely to the husband': the yardstick of equality is a guide and not a presumption.

POST WHITE V WHITE

Post *White v White* there have been a number of cases where family lawyers have striven to argue cases for departure from equality of division. Examples include:

- Cases where the husband has argued he has made a 'stellar contribution' to the wealth of the couple; examples include *Cowan v Cowan* [2001] 2 FLR 192 where the court found that the husband's degree of entrepreneurial spark was 'a factor that … deserved recognition'.
  H v H (Financial Provision: special contribution) [2002] 2 FLR 1021 established that a partner in a city law firm did not make a stellar contribution.

- Illiquidity of assets (*S v S* [2001] 2 FLR 246).

- Premarital acquired assets or assets gifted in the marriage (for example *White v White*).

However, in cases such as *H-J v H-J* [2002] 1 FLR 415 and *Lambert v Lambert* [2003] 1 FLR 139, where there were long marriages terminated by divorce, the courts have awarded a 50/50 division of assets between the husband and wife.

Lambert v Lambert [2003] 1 FLR 139

The facts of *Lambert v Lambert* were:

- marriage of 23 years with 2 children;

- husband sold his company for £20m and claimed that he had made a 'stellar contribution' and that the company's success was due to his excellent skills; and

- the wife argued that as a mother, she had contributed to the company's success.

The Court of Appeal held that the wife should receive 50% of the assets and in doing so confirmed that there should be no discrimination between the money maker and the home maker. Equality should only be departed from if there was a good reason for doing so. The Court of Appeal did not accept the husband's argument that he had made a 'special (stellar) contribution' and should therefore receive the lion share of the assets.

Despite those cases the law continued to develop reasons to depart from equality.

GW v RW [2003] 2 FLR 108

In 2003, Nicholas Mostyn QC gave judgment sitting as a deputy judge of the High Court in *GW v RW* [2003] 2 FLR 108. The facts were:

- marriage of 12 years. The husband was aged 44 and the wife aged 43. They had two children aged 5 and 2;

- at the time of the divorce the assets were worth £12m of which £473,000 had been brought into the marriage by the husband and he had built up the rest entirely from his remuneration.

The wife was awarded 40% of the total assets. Two reasons for departure were given. First, although the equality of contribution from *Lambert* was obvious in a long marriage, it did not apply to a marriage of 12 years' duration. The second was that there was an inequality of contribution in the form of the assets the husband had established prior to the marriage and his assets had grown significantly during a 2-year period of separation during the marriage.

Foster v Foster [2003] 2 FLR 299

Only a month later, the Court of Appeal gave its decision in *Foster v Foster* [2003] 2 FLR 299. In this case:

- the marriage lasted only 3 years and there were no children;

- the wife earned more than the husband but the bulk of the assets were properties that the parties owned for development.

The Court of Appeal held that when the assets were generated from joint efforts, the length of the marriage becomes less relevant and they should both share in them. However, it was justifiable to treat the assets which the parties had built up prior to the marriage differently (on the basis that these were contributions made by each of the parties without assistance from the other).

McFarlane v McFarlane and Parlour v Parlour [2004] 3 WLR 1480

In 2004, the Court of Appeal gave its judgment in *McFarlane v McFarlane and Parlour v Parlour* [2004] 3 WLR 1480. Mrs McFarlane went on to appeal to the House of Lords and that decision will be dealt with below.

The facts of *Parlour* were:

* marriage of 3 years with 8 years of cohabitation prior to marriage;

* there were three children aged 8, 6 and 4;

* the wife was aged 34, the husband aged 31. He was a professional footballer and at the time was earning £1.2m net playing for Arsenal, but his contract was due to expire. The wife had worked previously as an optician's assistant but gave up work to be a home maker.

The capital division was agreed at 37%. The dispute related to income. The wife was awarded £444,000 per annum (37% of the husband's net income) for a period of 4 years at which stage there would be a review to see whether or not a clean break could be effected or an extension for further maintenance but at a lesser sum.

The court took into account the role the wife had played in the husband's successful career and felt that she should not be limited to her needs. The court re-emphasised the overriding objective for there to be fairness.

M v M [2004] 2 FLR 236

Later that year, Baron J heard the case of *M v M* [2004] 2 FLR 236. The facts were:

* the wife was aged 42 and the husband was aged 44;

* it was a 12-year marriage;

* there were three children aged 14, 11 and 9. One child had special needs;

* the husband was an accountant and devised sophisticated tax saving financial vehicles. The wife gave up her career as a statistician to care for the children;

* the assets were £12.4m.

The wife sought:

(a) 50% of £5.43m which had built up since separation;

(b) 40% of the husband's future income that he expected to earn by way of bonuses in the next 7 years; and

(c) 50% of the £6.97m assets which had accumulated prior to separation.

The husband accepted that the wife should have a share of the post-separation assets. He offered just over 30%. He offered 50% of the assets accumulated prior to separation and no share of future income.

The wife received £6.2m which was an equal division of the assets (including the accruals post-separation) but excluding the husband's future earnings. The court held that each party had made an extraordinary contribution to the marriage and that there was no distinction between periods of cohabitation and marriage. The financial resources had increased significantly since separation and would continue to do so but it was impossible to predict the husband's future earnings. Those future earnings required real effort and were not certain. The future earnings were not considered to be marital assets which would fall for division.

The assets that had built up since separation were included because the parties had continued to be financially linked throughout and the litigation had not been unduly delayed.

Sorrell v Sorrell [2006] 1 FLR 497

In *Sorrell v Sorrell* [2006] 1 FLR 497 Bennett J departed from equality on the basis that the husband had made a special contribution in exceptional circumstances.

The facts:

•   it was a 32-year marriage and the parties had three adult sons;

•   the husband was aged 60 and wife aged 59;

•   the assets were in excess of £73m net;

•   the husband had built up a business which was worth £7billion (from his original stake of £250,000). The wife had maintained the home and looked after the children.

The wife received 40% of the assets on the basis of the husband's exceptional contribution. Bennett J at paragraphs 112 and 114, stated:

'The husband has achieved in his business career what few others have done and he is regarded within his field and the wider business community as one of the most exceptional and most talented businessmen ... The husband does possess the "spark" or "force" or "seed" of genius.'

Miller v Miller; McFarlane v McFarlane [2006] UKHL 24

Miller v Miller; McFarlane v McFarlane [2006] UKHL 24, involved appeals by Mrs McFarlane and Mr Miller which were heard together by the House of Lords on 24 May 2006. The *McFarlane* appeal concerned the judgment of the Court of Appeal in July 2004 (which was heard with the *Parlour* case). The facts of *McFarlane* were:

- the husband was a high earning accountant and the wife was a former solicitor. They were both in their mid-forties. They had three children;

- marriage of 18 years;

- on divorce they agreed an equal division of capital (approximately £3m);

- there was insufficient capital for an immediate clean break but the husband's net annual income of £750,000 far exceeded the combined needs of the parties.

The wife said she needed £128,000 per year but claimed a maintenance order of £275,000. The District Judge awarded her £250,000 to reflect her needs and the contributions she had made over the years of the marriage. On appeal, Bennett J reduced the annual maintenance figure to £180,000 per year. The Court of Appeal reinstated the District Judge's figure of £250,000 but imposed an extendable term of 5 years rather than allowing the order to continue on a joint lives basis. This meant that the wife would have to apply to the court before the expiry of the 5 years' term to extend maintenance. The House of Lords allowed the appeal and reinstated the order of the District Judge, namely periodical payments at the rate of £250,000 per annum for joint lives or until remarriage.

The facts of *Miller* were:

- the wife was aged 35 and the husband aged 42;

- there were no children and the marriage lasted just under 3 years;

- the husband was worth in the region of £17.5m, plus his shares in New Star, which were estimated at between £12m–£18m (but a value was not formally attributed to them);

- prior to the marriage, the wife was earning £85,000 a year which she gave up a year into the marriage.

The wife was awarded £5m and the award was upheld by the Court of Appeal. The husband's appeal to the House of Lords was dismissed on the basis that the award was fair against the value of the assets built up during the marriage.

Although the House of Lords did not give a unified judgment, three main strands were identified and they agreed that the court had to give consideration to:

(a)   the financial needs of the parties;

(b)   compensation; and

(c)   sharing.

It confirmed that the approach of fairness pronounced by the House of Lords in *White v White* was of universal application to all marriages whether long or short. Each spouse will be assumed to have made a full contribution in their own sphere, whether it be domestic or breadwinning, and there is to be no discrimination. However, the source and nature of the parties' property are matters to be taken into account in determining fairness. The yardstick of equality will be applied more readily to 'matrimonial assets' although they were divided as to what would constitute such assets. The concept of special contribution remained alive.

In most cases the quest for fairness would begin and end with their needs because the available assets were insufficient to meet their needs.

The judgment is complicated and has resulted in further test cases, in particular in respect of how and in what circumstances the concepts of sharing and compensation should be applied, and how to define matrimonial assets.

Charman v Charman [2007] 1 FLR 1246

One of the first cases to be heard after *Miller and McFarlane* was the first instance decision in *Charman v Charman* [2007] 1 FLR 1246. This summary deals with the decision at first instance and the appeal. The facts were:

- the parties separated after 27 years of marriage. The husband had relocated to Bermuda and the wife had remained in England;

- there were two children of the marriage;

- during the marriage the husband had made a fortune in the insurance market;

- the wife alleged that the wealth generated by the husband was to the tune of £150m–£160m of which £6m was in her name, £25m–£30m held in a trust for the parties' children and the remaining £125m or so was either in the husband's ownership (approximately £56m) or in a trust called 'Dragon Holding Trust' (£68m). One of the key issues in the case was whether the husband had 'immediate access to the funds' of the trust so as to enable them to be considered a financial resource.

The court stated that on the facts the sizeable trust assets in the Dragon trust should not be excluded from the 'marital pot'. The court confirmed the husband's claim that his 'wholly exceptional' and 'remarkable abilities in the insurance world' entitled him to a greater share of the assets than his wife. The wife received a total of approximately £48m including assets already in her name which represented just under 37% of the total assets.

In May 2007, the Court of Appeal rejected the husband's appeal. It held that it was open to the judge to find a likelihood of advancement to the husband from the trust and therefore attribute the trust assets to him. General guidance regarding the principles of asset division on divorce following the House of Lords' decision in Miller were given:

- the 'sharing principle' identified by the House of Lords in *Miller* means property should be shared equally unless there is a good reason for departure;

- the court's starting point should be the financial position of the parties but the discretionary exercise undertaken by the court has two stages – computation and distribution;

- the 'sharing principle' applies to all types of property but where property is 'non matrimonial', there is likely to be better reason for departure from it;

- where there is conflict between needs, compensation and/or sharing, whichever gives the greater outcome out of needs and sharing will prevail, but sharing can subsume needs;

- the doctrine of special contribution was still alive. It could be financial or non financial;

- even where special contribution existed, the departure in favour of one party was unlikely to extend beyond one-third:two-thirds; and

- it was not correct in big money cases to deduct the parties' joint needs and divide any surplus assets.

The husband's application for permission to appeal to the House of Lords was refused.

In between the first instance judgment on *Charman* and the Court of Appeal decision, there was a run of cases dealing with the treatment of post separation assets.

Rossi v Rossi [2007] 1 FLR 790

The first was the case of *Rossi v Rossi* [2007] 1 FLR 790 which was heard by Nicholas Mostyn QC, sitting as a Deputy High Court Judge. The facts were unusual because the husband brought ancillary relief proceedings against the wife over 10 years after the wife had obtained a divorce and he explained the delay by reason of his 7-year detention in India.

Apart from the question of the relevance of delay, a critical question was whether the assets which had been acquired post separation formed part of the 'marital pot'. The judge held that each party's claims against the other should be dismissed on a clean break basis in life and death. He was of the view that all the assets represented non-matrimonial post separation accrual and even if the husband's claim had been mounted timeously, it would have been tenuous.

S v S [2007] 1 FLR 2120

There then followed two cases of *S v S* [2007] 1 FLR 2120.

The facts were:

- 18-year marriage with no children and 7 years of separation.

- The husband owned a share of a business and argued that he had developed the business without the formal support and contribution of the wife. There was a significant disagreement between experts as to the correct value of the husband's company. The husband's expert suggested £3.73m and the wife's suggested £27.2m. The company had been in difficulties and a flotation or sale would only be possible with considerable effort by the husband.

- The husband had two pension schemes with a combined CETV of £2.1m. Excluding shares and pensions, the couple's assets are worth £1.9m. The husband's income was in the region of £287,500.

- The wife was awarded the former matrimonial home, with a net value of £970,000, a lump sum payment of £200,000 and a further payment of £900,000 to be secured against the husband's preference shares, plus periodical payments of £75,000 and mortgage payments until the mortgage was redeemed.

The court held that it should consider available assets (their value actual or potential) as at the date of the hearing. In these exceptional circumstances, that could only be a starting point.

The wife's wish to remain in the matrimonial home seriously limited the options available with regard to the structure and quantum of the division. It was not unfair that in return for conceding that the wife retain current tangible wealth to enhance her pension fund so as to achieve equality, whilst also taking the whole of the not insignificant risk in relation to the company, the husband should retain the whole of any award if the company was sold which would be as a result of his future endeavours.

As the years had passed since separation, it had become less and less fair that the wife should be entitled to ask for a share in the potential of the husband's company. The wife could have instituted proceedings earlier.

S v S [2007] 1 FLR 1496

Shortly afterwards there was a second case reported as S v S [2007] 1 FLR 1496. The case was heard by a judge outside the Family Division due to a conflict. The judge considered the different types of assets and the treatment of non-matrimonial property. He referred to *Rossi v Rossi* and carried out an analysis of the different opinions of Lord Nichols and Baroness Hale in *Miller*. He concluded that it is premarital or extra marital property plus 'income or fruits' which are non-matrimonial. However, such assets could not be excluded if they were required to meet needs.

H v H [2007] 2 FLR 548

H v H [2007] 2 FLR 548 was heard by Charles J just before the Court of Appeal decision in *Charman*. The court held that the House of Lords' decision in *Miller* should not be adhered to as if it were statute.

The wife was awarded £13.7m comprising half the assets at separation plus one-third of income earned in 2005, one-sixth of income earned in 2006 and one-twelfth of income earned in 2007. This represented a 'run-off' to independent living for the wife because the size of the husband's income would create a disparity of economic positions and the wife had contributed to his greater earning capacity. Although the husband had a significant earning capacity, the wife could not lay claim to it beyond this as a fruit of the marital partnership.

The income award generously covered the wife's needs and reflected the level of expenditure of the parties and their standard of living. It could be classified as either compensation or sharing.

It confirmed *Charman*, that the guidance given by the House of Lords in *Miller* should not be treated as if it were a series of statutory tests, the passing or failing of which would lead to a particular and set result. The more sensible approach was to have regard to the particular circumstances considering concepts such as matrimonial property and the application of the yardstick of equality and thus the arrangement of reasonable possibilities in their application.

S v S (2007) 151 SJLB 1165

In a remarkable third case reported as S v S (2007) 151 SJLB 1165, Baron J, on appeal, held that the District Judge had erred in regarding assets provided to a wife by her parents as non-matrimonial and ring fencing them when making an order on the basis of needs.

CR v CR (2007, All ER (D) 33 (Oct))

CR v CR (unreported) 19 June 2007 (Bodey J) also involved a long marriage, where the wife had supported the husband's career and looked after the children. Again, the issue was the treatment of post separation assets.

It was held that all available assets were to be considered in the same way and valued as at the date of the hearing and not to the date of separation. The wife was awarded 50% of the assets and in addition an extra £1m to be paid by way of instalments for recognition of her contribution to the domestic infrastructure. The wife's needs were generously assessed.

Vaughan v Vaughan [2007] 3 FCR 533

The case of *Vaughan v Vaughan* [2007] 3 FCR 533, heard by Ward LJ, Mummery LJ and Wilson LJ is a good example of the principles in big money cases being adopted in mid-range value cases. It was held that the District Judge's order did not infringe the sharing principle by imposing a division which represented a departure from equality, 57%:43% in favour of the wife in circumstances where there was a good reason for that inequality, such as the desirability of a clean break. The departure from equality represented a fair quid pro quo. The Circuit Judge's order, which was based on new evidence, was set aside as he should have attempted to discern the extent to which his proposed order departed from equality in the division of all of the parties' assets and whether there was good reason to do so.

P v P [2007] EWHC 2877 (Fam)

In *P v P* [2007] EWHC 2877 (Fam), Moylan J held that the application of the sharing principle could not be used to justify an award which does not meet needs. The wife's position had failed to recognise that some of the assets in the schedule could not be valued with any certainty and that assets in employee benefit trusts set up by the husband's employers could not be treated as having the same value as assets held in other forms.

The wife received £8.4m and the husband retained £8.3m. Moylan J acknowledged that the wife received a significant proportion of the resources which had accrued since separation. However, the wife had no further claim to a share of the husband's wealth.

Appendix 2

PRECEDENTS AND MATERIALS

Precedent 1: Subpoena Requiring Production of a Testamentary Document

IN THE HIGH COURT OF JUSTICE
FAMILY DIVISION
[THE NOMINATED REGISTRY]

IN THE ESTATE OF [*deceased's full name*] **DECEASED**

Elizabeth the Second, by the Grace of God of the United Kingdom of Great Britain and Northern Ireland and of Our other realms and territories Queen, Head of the Commonwealth, Defender of the Faith:

To [*holder of document*]

It appears by an affidavit of [*name of applicant/applicant's solicitor*] sworn on [*date*] and filed in [*the Nominated Registry*] that a certain document, being or purporting to be testamentary, namely the last will purported to be made and executed on [*date*] of [*name of deceased*] late of [*address of deceased*] who died on [*date of death*] is now in your custody or power.

We command that you within eight days after service hereof on you inclusive of the day of service do bring into and leave with the proper officer of [*the Nominated Registry*] aforesaid the said document together with any other testamentary document relating to the estate of the late [*name of deceased*] now in the possession, custody or power of you the said [*name of holder of document*].

Witness, [   ], Lord High Chancellor of Great Britain the [*date*] day of [*date*].

Signed [   ]
District Probate Registrar

Subpoena issued by [*solicitors*], of [*address*].

You the within named [*name of holder of document*] are warned that disobedience to this subpoena by the time therein limited would be a contempt of court punishable by imprisonment.

Precedent 2: Affidavit in support of an application under Supreme Court Act 1981 s 123 for the issue of a subpoena requiring the production of a testamentary document

IN THE HIGH COURT OF JUSTICE
FAMILY DIVISION
[THE NOMINATED REGISTRY]

IN THE ESTATE OF [*deceased's full name*] DECEASED

I, [*full name and address of deponent*], Solicitor of the Supreme Court, MAKE OATH and say as follows:

1.   I have the conduct of this matter on behalf of [*name of client*]. I make this affidavit of my own knowledge except where otherwise expressly appears where I make this affidavit on information and of belief. The source of my information is from [*explain source of information*].
2.   This affidavit is sworn in support of an application under s.123 of the Supreme Court Act 1981 for the issue of a subpoena requiring [*name of the person to be subpoenaed*] to produce the purported Will dated [*date of will*] and any other testamentary documents he may have of [*name and address of deceased*] who died on [*date of death*].
3.   I have caused enquiries to be made as to the whereabouts of the last will of the deceased and as the result of those enquiries I believe it to be in the possession of [*name of the person to be subpoenaed*].The grounds of my belief are [*state grounds of belief and exhibit any relevant correspondence*].
4.   It appears that without being compelled to do so [*name of the person to be subpoenaed*] will not produce the purported will. I have written to [*name of the person to be subpoenaed*] on [*insert relevant*] occasions requesting [*him/her*] to deliver up possession of the Will and have received no response. There is now produced to me marked [   ] copies of the relevant correspondence.
5.   I therefore request this Court to grant the application for the issue of a subpoena requiring the production of the purported will.

Sworn etc

Precedent 3: Affidavit in support of application for appointment of administrator

Claim No [   ]

IN THE HIGH COURT OF JUSTICE
[FAMILY DIVISION]

IN THE ESTATE OF [*deceased's full name*] DECEASED

I [*Claimant's name*] of [*Claimant's address*] MAKE OATH as follows:

1.   [*deceased's full name*] deceased late of [*deceased's address*] died on [*date of death*] [intestate/leaving as his purported last will the document now produced and shown to me and dated the [*date*]. He died domiciled in England and Wales.

[2.   [[*If there is a will*] Notwithstanding that by his purported last will the deceased appointed [*name*] as his executor [*insert reason for s116 application*].]

2.   [*If intestacy*] The Deceased is survived by [*give details of those entitled on intestacy including the ages of any infant children*].[*Names of those entitled on intestacy*] are together the only persons entitled to share in the deceased's estate. [*Go on to detail circumstances in which a problem has arisen between those entitled on intestacy such that it is not considered appropriate that they take out a grant*].

3.   Proceedings have not yet commenced but in view of the likelihood of proceedings in due course the executor appointed by the last purported will and [*name*] the residuary beneficiary under that will and [*name of residuary beneficiary under previous will/names of those entitled on intestacy*] have agreed that [*name, address and occupation of proposed administrator*] should be appointed to administer the estate of the deceased. There is now produced and shown to me marked 'A' a true copy of a letter from [*name*] dated [*date*] confirming that he is willing to act (and providing details of his charging rates).There are also produced and shown to me in a bundle marked 'B' letters from [*name*] supporting the appointment.

4.   From information provided to me by [*name*] I believe that the estate is worth £[*value*] gross and approximately £[*value*] net.

5.   No minority or life interest arises [*or give details of these with such interests and the nature of their interests*].

6.   I therefore apply for an order that letters of administration [with the will annexed] of the estate of [*deceased's name*] deceased be granted to me under s116 of the Supreme Court Act 1981.

Sworn etc

Precedent 4: Caveat

IN THE HIGH COURT OF JUSTICE
FAMILY DIVISION
THE PRINCIPAL REGISTRY[1]

IN THE ESTATE OF [*deceased's full name*] DECEASED

Let no further grant be sealed in the estate of [*deceased's full name and any other names by which s/he was known*] deceased of [*deceased's last address including postcode*] who died on the [*date of death*] at [*deceased's place of death*], without notice to [*name of client*] c/o [*name of partner*] of [*name and address of firm*] (ref : [   ]).

---

[1]   There is no nominated Registry, ie all Caveats can be filed at the Principal Registry

Dated this   day of   200[ ].

Signed

[*Solicitors*]

Solicitors for the said [*client name*]

Whose address for service is:

[*address*]

(Ref : [   ])

Precedent 5: Warning to caveat

IN THE HIGH COURT OF JUSTICE
FAMILY DIVISION
[THE NOMINATED REGISTRY]

IN THE ESTATE OF [*deceased's full name*] DECEASED

To [*caveator*] of [*address*] who has entered a caveat in the estate of [*deceased's full name*] deceased.

You have eight days (starting with the day on which this warning was served on you):

1.   to enter an appearance either in person or by solicitor or probate practitioner at the [*name and address of nominated registry*] setting out what interest you have in the estate of the above-named of deceased contrary to that of the party at whose instance this warning is issued; or

2.   if you have no contrary interest but wish to show cause against the sealing of a grant on such party, to issue and serve a summons for directions by a District Judge of the Principal Registry or a Registrar of a District Probate Registry.

If you fail to do either of these, the Court may proceed to issue a grant of probate or administration in the said estate notwithstanding your caveat.

Dated the [   ] day of [   ] 200[ ]

Issued at the instance of [*name and address and interest including date of will, if any, under which interest arises*] by [*solicitors*] of [*address*].

Precedent 6: Affidavit of service of warning

Caveat No: [   ]

IN THE HIGH COURT OF JUSTICE
FAMILY DIVISION
[THE NOMINATED REGISTRY]

IN THE ESTATE OF [*deceased's full name*] DECEASED

I, [*solicitor's name*], of [*name and address of firm*], solicitor, make oath and say:

1. That on [*date*] I duly served [*name of caveator*] with a true copy of the warning now produced and marked by me [   ], by [*select the appropriate option below*]

    [delivering it to and leaving it with [*an employee of*] [*name of caveator*] at their office that being the address for service of the caveator given in his caveat].

    [sending it by pre-paid [*ordinary post/registered post/recorded delivery*] to [*name of caveator*] that being the address for service of the caveator given in his caveat].

    [leaving it at the document exchange address for box number [   ] included in the address for service of the caveator given in his caveat].

2. Annexed to this affidavit marked 'A' is a true copy of the warning referred to above.

Sworn etc

Precedent 7: Appearance

**IN THE HIGH COURT OF JUSTICE
FAMILY DIVISION
[THE NOMINATED REGISTRY]**

IN THE ESTATE OF [*deceased's full name*] DECEASED

Caveat No: [   ] dated the [   ] day of [   ] 200[ ]

Full name and address of deceased	: [	]
Full name and address of person warning	: [	]
Interest in the Estate of the person warning	: [	]
Full name and address of Caveator	: [	]
Caveator's interest in the Estate and date of will under which the interest arises	: [	]

Enter an appearance for the above-named Caveator in this matter

Dated this [   ] day of [   ] 200[ ]

Signed

[*Solicitors*]

Solicitors for the said [   ]

[address]

(Ref: [   ])

Precedent 8: Application for Standing Search

IN THE HIGH COURT OF JUSTICE
FAMILY DIVISION
[THE NOMINATED REGISTRY]

IN THE ESTATE OF [*deceased's full name*] DECEASED

We apply for the entry of a standing search so that there shall be sent to us an office copy of every grant of representation in England and Wales in the estate of:

Full name of deceased   :   [

Full address   :   [

Exact date of death   :   [

which either has issued not more than 12 months before the entry of this application or issues within six months thereafter

Signed: ....

[*solicitors' firm*]

Address: [*address of firm*]

Reference: [   ]

Precedent 9: Affidavit in support of application for grant ad colligenda bona

IN THE HIGH COURT OF JUSTICE
FAMILY DIVISION
[THE NOMINATED REGISTRY]

IN THE ESTATE OF [*deceased's full name*] DECEASED

I, [*solicitor's name*], of [*name and address of firm*], solicitor, make oath and say:

1.   I make this statement in support of an application for a grant ad colligenda bona by [*name of applicant*].

2.   There are now produced and shown to me Exhibits marked [   ] to which I shall refer in the course of this Affidavit. My knowledge of the matters referred to is derived from [the papers referred to and from my involvement in this matter or from my firm's conduct of this matter on behalf of [*name of applicant*]].

Background

3.   [set out details of background to application including that:

      [The Deceased executed a will [and codicils] on [*insert date of will*]. A copy of these documents (together the '**Will**') are at Exhibit '[   ]'.

[Under the Will the Deceased appointed [*insert name of executor*] as executor].

[explain relevant clauses of will]

[The Deceased died on [*insert date of death*]. A copy of the Deceased's death certificate is at '[   ]'].

Dispute regarding [   ]

4.   [*Outline nature of the substantive dispute*]

Administration of the Deceased's estate

5.   It has now been over [*insert number*] months since the Deceased died.
6.   [*Insert name of applicant(s)*] wish the Deceased's estate to be administered. [*Set out why the estate needs to be administered*]
7.   [At '[   ]' is a copy of a letter on behalf of [*insert name of other parties*] agreeing to this application.]

Application

8.   In the circumstances, [*insert name of interim administrator*] applies for a grant ad colligenda bona so that the assets of the Estate can be collected in and preserved, pending resolution of the dispute [*insert details as necessary*].
9.   I therefore request the Registrar to make an order for a grant ad colligenda bona to [*insert name of interim administrator*] in the estate of the Deceased [and in particular to take such steps as are necessary for the upkeep repair and maintenance of the Property but not to sell the said property without an order of the District Registrar].

Sworn etc

Precedent 10: Brief details of claim for rectification of will

IN THE HIGH COURT OF JUSTICE
[CHANCERY DIVISION][2]

IN THE ESTATE OF [*deceased's full name*] DECEASED

Details of Claim

The Claimants' claim as executors of the last will dated [*date of will*] of [*deceased's full name*] of [*deceased's address*] who died on [*date of death*] and whose will was proved in the [*insert relevant registry*] by the Claimants on [*date of grant*] for rectification of the Deceased's will under s20(1)(a) of The Administration of Justice Act 1982 [by the inclusion of a legacy of £5,000 in

---

[2] An application may be made under the Non-Contentious Probate Rules to a Registrar of the Principal Registry Family Division or to a District Probate Registrar unless a probate action has been commenced.

clause 6 this gift having been inadvertently omitted from the Deceased's will *or insert relevant details*] and for the will to be pronounced for in solemn form reflecting the rectification.

Precedent 11: Witness statement in support of rectification application

Claim No [   ]

IN THE HIGH COURT OF JUSTICE
[CHANCERY DIVISION[3]]

IN THE ESTATE OF [*deceased's full name*] DECEASED

I [*Solicitor's name*] of [*address of firm*] state as follows:

1.   I am a partner in the firm of [*solicitor's firm*]. Save where I have stated otherwise, I make this witness statement from the facts within my own knowledge.

2.   On [*date*] I attended [*deceased's name*] ('the testator') at [*deceased's address*] for the purpose of taking instructions for his will. The new will was to be substantially in the same form as his previous one, which was also prepared by my firm. In addition, he now wished to leave various legacies to his grandchildren and to friends he had known for many years.

3.   I prepared a draft will which I sent to the testator for approval on [*date*]. He instructed me to proceed with preparation of the engrossment which was sent to him for signing on [*date*]. The completed document was returned to me by the testator duly executed and dated [*date*]. This original will is now produced and shown to me marked 'A'.

4.   Following the testator's death on [*date of death*] it was pointed out to me that his previous will had included a legacy of £5,000 in favour of [*Joe Bloggs*] but that this gift had been inadvertently omitted from the later document. I have no doubt that the testator intended this gift to be included in his last will since his instructions to me were to include all dispositions set out in his previous will together with the additional legacies referred to above. There is now produced and shown to me marked 'B' a copy of my file note detailing the testator's instructions.

5.   All of the residuary beneficiaries entitled under the testator's will agree to the will being rectified to reflect the inclusion of the legacy referred to and copies of their written consents are produced and shown to me in a bundle marked 'C'.[4]

6.   I am informed and believe that the omission of the legacy in favour of [*Joe Bloggs*] was a clerical error within s 20(1)(a) of the Administration

---

3   An application may be made under the Non-Contentious Probate Rules to a Registrar of the Principal Registry, Family Division or to a District Probate Registrar unless a probate action has been commenced.

4   Only include where agreed.

of Justice Act 1982 and in the circumstances I respectfully ask the District Judge to make an order accordingly.

[*Statement of truth*]

Precedent 12: Application for construction of a will

Claim No [   ]

IN THE HIGH COURT OF JUSTICE
CHANCERY DIVISION

IN THE ESTATE OF [*deceased's full name*] DECEASED

Details of claim

By this application, the Claimant, who is the executor of the will dated [*insert date*] of [*deceased's full name*] deceased seeks determination of the following questions and the following relief:

1.   that it may be determined, on the true construction of the deceased's will and in the events that have happened, whether the net estate is held by the Claimant as executor:

    (a)   on trust as to one half share for the first defendant and as to the remaining half share for the second defendant; or

    (b)   on trust as to the entirety for the first defendant alone; or

    (c)   on trust as to one half share for the first defendant and as to the remaining half share for the statutory next of kin of the deceased, on the basis that he shall be deemed to have died intestate in respect of such remaining half share; or

    (d)   on some other, and if so which, trusts;

2.   that the third defendant [*or as the case may be*] be appointed to represent for the purposes of this application the next of kin of the deceased;

3.   all necessary accounts, inquiries and directions;

4.   further or other relief; and

5.   that provision may be made for the costs of this application.

Precedent 13: Witness statement in support of an application for construction of a will

Claim No [   ]

IN THE HIGH COURT OF JUSTICE
CHANCERY DIVISION

IN THE ESTATE OF [*deceased's full name*] DECEASED

I [*Claimant's name*] of [*Claimant's address*] state as follows:

1.   I am the executor of the will of [*deceased's full name*] dated [*date of will*] probate of which was granted to me by the [*insert registry*] on [*insert date of grant*].

2.   The deceased's will left [one half of his estate to [*Joe Bloggs*]] subject to the condition that [*insert details of condition*].

3.   There is now produced and shown to me marked [   ] a schedule of the assets and liabilities in the estate.

4.   Through my solicitors I obtained the opinion of [   ] a Chancery counsel of [   ] years' call. A copy of my solicitors' instructions to counsel and of counsel's opinion are now produced and shown to me in a bundle marked [   ]

5.   Counsel advises that on a true construction of the deceased's will the condition attaching to the gift is incapable of being fulfilled and the half share of the estate passes to [   ] absolutely.

6.   A copy of counsel's opinion has been sent to [   ] as the beneficiary entitled to the other half share of the estate and to [   ] and [   ] who are the statutory next of kin of the deceased. All of these persons agree to the half share in the estate passing to [   ] in accordance with counsel's opinion and copies of their written consents are now produced and shown to me in a bundle marked [   ].

7.   In the above circumstances, I request the court's authority to distribute the estate in reliance on counsel's opinion and on the terms set out in the draft order now produced and shown to me marked [   ].

[*Statement of truth*]

Precedent 14: Claim form requesting court to decree probate of a will in solemn form in the context of a validity dispute

Claim number [   ]

IN THE HIGH COURT OF JUSTICE
CHANCERY DIVISION

IN THE ESTATE OF [*deceased's full name*] DECEASED

Details of claim/particulars of claim

The Claimant is [*residuary beneficiary/legatee*] under the last will (the 'Will') dated [*date*] of [*deceased's full name*] (the 'Deceased') who died on [*date of death*] and claims probate in solemn form of the Will.

The First Defendant is [*the executor named in the Will*].

The Second Defendant is the [*residuary beneficiary/legatee*] under an earlier will of the Deceased dated [*date of earlier will*][*beneficiary on intestacy*].

The Claimant claims that the court shall decree probate of the will in solemn form of law.

[*Statement of truth*]

Precedent 15: Claim form requesting court to pronounce against the purported last will of the deceased in favour of an earlier will on grounds of lack of validity

Claim number [   ]

IN THE HIGH COURT OF JUSTICE
CHANCERY DIVISION (PROBATE)

IN THE ESTATE OF [*deceased's full name*] **DECEASED (PROBATE)**

Details of claim

The Claimant is [*explain relationship to deceased*] who died on [*date of deceased's death*] and [*explain entitlement under the earlier will*] dated [*date of will*].

The Defendant is [*explain relationship to deceased*] and [*explain entitlement under purported will*] under a purported will of the deceased dated [*date of purported will*].

[*insert either/or together as appropriate*].

[the purported will] was not executed by the deceased in accordance with the provisions of the Wills Act 1837 as amended.

[further or in the alternative] at the time of the purported execution of the [purported will], the deceased [did not have capacity to make a will].

[further or in the alternative] at the time of the purported execution of the [purported will], the deceased did not know and approve the contents thereof [and the circumstances in which it is alleged that the same was executed were such as to excite the suspicion and vigilance of the court].

[further or in the alternative] the execution of the [purported will] was obtained by undue influence].

The Claimant claims:

1.   that the court shall pronounce against the [purported will];
2.   that the court shall pronounce for the [earlier will] in solemn form of law;
3.   that a Grant of Probate of the [earlier will] to issue to the Claimant or to such proper person as the court thinks fit.

[*Statement of truth*]

Precedent 16: Witness Statement of Testamentary Scripts

IN THE HIGH COURT OF JUSTICE
CHANCERY DIVISION (PROBATE)

IN THE ESTATE OF [*deceased's full name*] **DECEASED**

I, [*name of Claimant/Defendant*], of [*address of the Claimant/Defendant*] in this claim state that I have no knowledge of any document:

1.   being or purporting to be or having the form or effect of a will or codicil of [*deceased's full name*] deceased whose estate is the subject of this claim;

2.   being or purporting to be a draft or written instruction for any such will or codicil made by or at the request of or under the instructions of the deceased; or

3.   being or purporting to be evidence of the contents or a copy of any such will or codicil which is alleged to have been lost or destroyed.

EXCEPT:

1.   [*insert details of wills/codicils/instructions for wills/drafts of which you have knowledge*].

Sworn etc

Precedent 17: Letter requesting Larke v Nugus Statement

Dear Sirs

[*Deceased's full name*] deceased

We have been asked to advise [*insert name of client/s*], residuary beneficiaries [under [*insert name of deceased*]'s will dated [*insert date of will*] (the 'Will')] [on intestacy].

Larke v Nugus Statement

You may be aware that since 1959 the Law Society has recommended that where a dispute arises as to the validity of a will the testator's solicitor should make available a statement of his or her evidence regarding instructions for the preparation and execution of the will and surrounding circumstances. This recommendation was endorsed by the Court of Appeal in *Larke v Nugus* [2000] WTLR 1033.

Please provide statements from all appropriate members of your firm on the following points in relation to the Will:

1.   How long had you known the deceased?
2.   Who introduced you to the deceased?
3.   On what date did you receive instructions from the deceased?
4.   Did you receive instructions by letter? If so please provide copies of any correspondence.
5.   If instructions were taken at a meeting please provide copies of your contemporaneous notes of the meeting including an indication of where the meeting took place and who else was present at the meeting.
6.   How were the instructions expressed?
7.   What indication did the deceased give to you that he/she knew that he/she was making a will?

8.   Did the deceased exhibit any signs of confusion or loss of memory? If so please give details.

9.   To what extent were earlier Wills discussed and what attempts were made to discuss departures from his/her Will making pattern?

10. What reasons if any, did the deceased give for making any such departures?

11. When the Will had been drafted how were the provisions of the Will explained to the deceased?

12. Who, apart from the attesting witnesses, was present at the execution of the Will?

13. Where, when and how did the execution take place?

Please provide a copy of all documents and correspondence on your will file.

Please provide a copy of all previous testamentary documents and all documents on any previous will files.

Please provide any additional information that you consider will assist the court in the event that this dispute is unresolved. [Please provide a schedule of costs and liabilities/copy of the IHT200].

Please do not hesitate to call the writer, [*name of solicitor*], on [*telephone number of solicitor*] if you have any queries on the above.

Yours faithfully

Precedent 18: Letter requesting medical records

Dear [*name*]

[*deceased's full name*] deceased
[*date of birth*]
[*date of death*]
[*address*]

I act for [*name(s) of client(s)*] who are beneficiaries under a Will dated [*insert date of will*] (the 'Will'), executed by the late [*deceased's full name*] deceased. I enclose a copy of the Will.

Under the [*insert deceased's name*]'s Will [*insert executor name(s)*] are appointed as executor.

Concerns have been expressed about the validity of the Will [*insert further details as relevant*].

In accordance with Section 3(1)(f) of the Access to Health Records Act 1990, a copy of which is enclosed, please provide copies of [*insert deceased's name*]'s medical records. Section 3(1)(f) provides that an application for the health records of a deceased patient may be made by the deceased's personal representative or by any person who may have a claim arising out of the patient's death. As beneficiaries under the Will our clients fall within that category of entitled parties.

We will, of course, pay your reasonable copying charges in producing copies of these reports. Alternatively, if you wish to send us the originals, we can copy them here and return them to you by Special Delivery.

Yours faithfully

Enc: Copy Will

s 3(1)(f) of the Access to Health Records Act 1990

Precedent 19: Letter to GP requesting views on capacity

Dear [*name*]

[*name*] deceased
[*address of deceased*]
[*date of death*]

I act for [*name(s) of client(s)*], the residuary beneficiaries of the deceased's will dated [*date*].

[The deceased also appears to have signed a will on [*date*] under which [*his/her*] residuary estate passes to [*name*]. [Under both wills] [*executor name(s)*] [*is/are*] appointed executor(s).]

I note [*insert source of information*] that you were the deceased's GP. As such, I should be grateful for your views on the deceased's testamentary capacity on [*dates on which instructions were given and date of creation of will*].

Guidelines when assessing capacity (contemporaneously or retrospectively)

The BMA and Law Society have written a book in association entitled *'Assessment of Mental Capacity: Guidelines for Doctors and Lawyers'*. I enclose a copy of chapter 14, which sets out practical guidelines for doctors in such matters.

Testamentary capacity

I enclose a copy of chapter 5 of *'Assessment of Mental Capacity: Guidelines for Doctors and Lawyers'* which sets out the legal test for testamentary capacity; namely that [*insert name of deceased*] must have had, at the time [*he/she*] gave instructions for the [*will/codicil*] and at the time [*he/she*] executed it, understood:

1.   the nature of the act of making a [*will/codicil*];
2.   the effect of making a [*will/codicil*];
3.   the extent of [*his/her*] property;
4.   the claims of others.

Framework of report

I would be grateful if you could provide us with a report setting out:

1.   Your professional qualifications and any relevant experience in assessing mental states and capacity.

2. How long you had known [*the deceased*] and in what capacity.
3. Details of [*the deceased*]'s state of health in the period leading up to [*dates*].
4. Changes in [*the deceased*]'s condition in recent years or months which you regard as significant.
5 The effect on [*the deceased*]'s capacity of any treatment or medication being administered.
6. Please provide an opinion to the best of your ability as to [*the deceased*]'s testamentary capacity as at [*dates*].

Retrospective report

I am aware that it is always a difficult exercise to make a retrospective assessment of capacity. However, it is quite common, indeed the norm, in disputes of this nature, for doctors to be asked for a retrospective report on capacity. Should this matter proceed to trial, the court will take this into consideration when reviewing your opinion. Ultimately, they will require your view, with the knowledge you now have, as to whether, on the balance of probabilities, the deceased had testamentary capacity on the day the [*will/codicil*] was executed.

Please do not hesitate to contact me if I can be of assistance.

We will be responsible for your reasonable fee in preparing this report.

I look forward to hearing from you.

With kind regards

Yours sincerely

Precedent 20: Application for an account by executor under CPR Part 64

Claim No [   ]

IN THE HIGH COURT OF JUSTICE
CHANCERY DIVISION

IN THE ESTATE OF [*deceased's full name*] DECEASED

Details of claim

The Claimants seek the following relief pursuant to CPR Part 64 paragraph (2)(a), namely:

[*Insert as appropriate*]

1. that the Defendant, the executor of the Will dated [*date*] of [*deceased's full name*] deceased (the 'Deceased'), may be ordered to furnish proper particulars and accounts of the [real and personal] estate of the Deceased [and the investments thereof];

2.   that the balance of funds retained by the Defendant be distributed forthwith;
3.   that the Defendant account to the estate for any sums deducted by way of fees;
4.   if necessary, that the administration of the estate of the Deceased [and/or the execution of the trusts of the Will] may be carried out under the direction of the court and all necessary and proper accounts, directions and inquiries;
5.   that the Defendant may be ordered to pay the cost of this claim personally;
6.   further or other relief.

Precedent 21: Application under the Administration of Justice Act 1985, s 50 by executor for removal of co-executor[5]

Claim No [   ]

IN THE HIGH COURT OF JUSTICE
CHANCERY DIVISION

IN THE ESTATE OF [*deceased's full name*] DECEASED

Details of claim

The Claimant pursuant to section 50 of the Administration of Justice Act 1985 as one of the executors of the will dated [*date*] (the 'Will') of [*deceased's full name*] deceased who died on [*date*] (the 'Deceased') seeks an order:

1.   that, pursuant to section 50 of the Administration of Justice Act 1985, the appointment of the Defendant as one of the executors be terminated forthwith;
2.   that all of the property in the estate do vest forthwith in the Claimant as the continuing personal representative and trustee of the Deceased;
3.   that the Defendant deliver up to the Claimant's solicitors [*name and address of firm*] within [*14 days*] all and any papers relating to the estate of the Deceased; and
4   that the cost of this application be borne by the estate in the due course of administration.

Precedent 22: Witness statement in support of application under Administration of Justice Act 1985, s 50 by executor for removal of co-executor[6]

Claim No [   ]

---

[5]   This can be adapted as appropriate for an application by beneficiaries to remove an executor/executors.
[6]   This can be adapted as appropriate for an application by beneficiaries to remove an executor/executors.

IN THE HIGH COURT OF JUSTICE
CHANCERY DIVISION

IN THE ESTATE OF [*deceased's full name*] **DECEASED**

I [*Claimant's name*] of [*Claimant's address*] state as follows:

1.   I am [*insert occupation*]. I am one of the executors of the will dated [*date*] (the 'Will') of [*deceased's full name*] deceased (the 'Deceased'), late of [*deceased's address*] who died on [*date*].

        This witness statement is signed in support of an application made under section 50 Administration of Justice Act 1985 for, among other things, the termination of the appointment of [*defendant*], my co-executor, as one of the executors of the Deceased.

2.   I have provided at pages [   ] of the numbered bundle of papers exhibited to this statement and marked [   ] copies of the Will and of the Grant of Probate issued on [*date*] out of the [*nominated registry*].

3.   The reason for this application is [*details of background to claim*].

4.   I have written to my co-defendant requesting an explanation of [*details*]. My letters to the First Defendant remain unanswered and copies of these are now produced and shown to me in a bundle marked [   ]. [The Defendant agrees that it is proper for him/her to step down as an executor. I have provided a copy of a letter by which he/she agrees to the order sought at page [   ] of [   ].]

        In the above circumstances I request the court to grant me the relief sought in the form of the attached draft order.

[*Statement of truth*]

Precedent 23: Beddoe Application

Claim No [   ]

IN THE HIGH COURT OF JUSTICE
CHANCERY DIVISION

IN THE ESTATE OF [*deceased's full name*] **DECEASED**

Details of claim

1.   The Claimant is the Executor ('the Executor') under the will dated [*date of will*] of [*deceased's full name*] deceased.

2.   The Executor seeks the following relief pursuant to CPR Part 64.2(a):

        2.1   an order that the Executor may be at liberty to defend an action which has been begun against [him/her] in the Chancery Division of the High Court as executor of the above named deceased for the following relief, namely payment of £[*insert value*] or such other amount as the court shall find due to the Executor in such action pursuant to an alleged oral agreement for services made between him and the deceased together with interest thereon;

2.2   that the Executor may be indemnified against all costs arising out of, and incidental to, the said action out of the estate of the said deceased;

2.3   if, and so far as may be necessary, administration of the estate of the said deceased; and

2.4   that provision may be made for the costs of this application.

CPR Part 8 applies to this claim.

Precedent 24: Witness Statement in support of Beddoe Application

Claim No [   ]

**IN THE HIGH COURT OF JUSTICE
[CHANCERY DIVISION]**

IN THE ESTATE OF [*deceased's full name*] DECEASED

I [*Claimant's name*] of [*Claimant's address*] state as follows:

1.   I am the above named claimant and I make this application in support of my application for a Beddoe order. Save where otherwise appears the facts and matters that I state are within my own knowledge.

2.   By her last will dated [*date of will*] the above-named deceased appointed the partners at the date of her death in the firm of [*name of firm*] to be her executors and trustees. The deceased died on [*date of death*]. I am and was at that date a partner in the firm of [*name of firm*]. On [*date of grant*] probate of the deceased's will was granted to me by the Principal Registry, power being reserved to the other executors. True copies of the will and grant are now produced and shown to me in a bundle marked [ ]

3.   It will be seen that by clause [*insert clause number*] of the will the deceased divided her estate between various members of her family and others. Those beneficiaries are the defendants named in the application.

4   Within a few days of the deceased's death my firm received a letter from [*Joe Bloggs*] dated [*date*] by which he should receive payment of £[*value*] by way of wages for services allegedly rendered to the deceased between [*insert relevant dates*]. [*Joe Bloggs*] is a beneficiary under the deceased's will and one of the above-named defendants. While I have no personal knowledge of the matter my inquiries of those acquainted with the deceased suggest that [*Joe Bloggs'*] claim is without any merit and ought to be rejected on behalf of the estate. On [*date*] my firm wrote to [*Joe Bloggs*] accordingly and he subsequently instructed solicitors. Copies of the letters to which I have referred together with other correspondence up to the issue of proceedings are now produced and shown to me in a bundle marked [ ]

5. A copy of the application issued by [*Joe Bloggs*] is now produced and shown to me marked [ ]. The nature of the claim will be seen from the [*claim form/particulars of claim*] and the sum claimed is now £[*value*], or such other amount as may be found due, together with interest.

6. I have obtained statements from various sources in relation to the claim of [*Joe Bloggs*] of which true copies are now produced and shown to me in a bundle marked [ ]. In accordance with what I consider to be the correct practice it is not intended to serve that exhibit on the defendants.

7. I subsequently obtained a written opinion from [*name of counsel*] and copies of that opinion and of my instructions are now produced and shown to me in a bundle marked [ ].

8. I attach a schedule showing the likely costs of the proceedings.

9. In the light of the statements and of counsel's opinion referred to above I consider that the proceedings instituted by [*Joe Bloggs*] ought to be defended on behalf of the deceased's estate. In the circumstances I ask the court to make the order sought by the Claim Form in these proceedings.

[*Statement of truth*]

Precedent 25: Application by surviving spouse under the Inheritance (Provision for Family and Dependants) Act 1975

Claim No [   ]

IN THE HIGH COURT OF JUSTICE
[CHANCERY/FAMILY DIVISION]

IN THE ESTATE OF [*deceased's full name*] DECEASED

Details of claim

1. The Claimant applies under the Inheritance (Provision for Family and Dependants) Act 1975 as the widow of [*deceased's full name*] deceased who died on [*date*] (the 'Deceased').

2. The Defendants are the executors [and trustees] of the will dated [*date of will*] pursuant to a grant dated [*date of grant*] issued from the [*registry*].

3. The Deceased died domiciled in England and Wales.

4. The Claimant seeks the following relief:

    4.1 An order that such reasonable financial provision as the Court thinks fit be made for the Claimant out of the net estate of the Deceased.

    4.2 Such further or other relief.

    4.3 An order that the costs of this application be paid out of the said estate.

CPR Part 8 applies to this claim.

Precedent 26: Witness Statement in support of claim under Inheritance (Provision for Family and Dependants) Act 1975

Claim No [   ]

[IN THE HIGH COURT OF JUSTICE]
[CHANCERY/FAMILY DIVISION]

IN THE MATTER OF THE ESTATE OF [*Deceased's full name*] DECEASED AND IN THE MATTER OF THE INHERITANCE (PROVISION FOR FAMILY AND DEPENDANTS) ACT 1975

I, [*Insert name*] of [*address and occupation*], state as follows:

1.   I am the above-named Claimant and I am the [*state relationship or connection with the Deceased*]

        [*insert as relevant/appropriate*]

        [widow of the above-named [*Deceased's full name*] ('the Deceased'), to whom I was married on [*date*]. There is now produced and shown to me marked [   ] a certificate of our marriage].

        [I am a person who, immediately prior to the death of the Deceased was being maintained either wholly or partly by [him/her] [*or give details of dependency for example*] [The Deceased used to pay me the sum of £[   ] per month by standing order. [He/She] also on various occasions paid me sums in cash and paid for petrol for my car. [He/She] also paid for holidays].

        [I met the Deceased in [month] [year] and shortly thereafter [he/she] left [his/her] [wife/husband] and came to live with me. Prior to [his/her] death [he/she] and I lived together at [*insert address*]. We continued to live as man and wife until his death.]

2.   The Deceased died on [*date*] being then domiciled in England and Wales. A certificate of [his/her] death is now produced and shown to me marked [   ].

3.   [By [his/her] Will dated [*date*] the Deceased bequeathed [*state provision in Will*] and appointed the [   ] and [   ] Defendant[s] as executor[s]] [The Deceased died intestate]. [A Grant of Probate/Grant of Letters of Administration] in relation to the estate of the Deceased was taken out on [*date*] and the Defendant[s] [is/are] the personal representative[s]. There is now produced and shown to me marked [   ] Office Copy [Grant of Probate/Grant of Representation] and all testamentary documents as required by CPR 57.16 3(b).

4   The net value of the Deceased's Estate for Probate purposes is £[*insert value*].

5.   The disposition of the Deceased's estate [effected by [his/her] Will][the law relating to intestacy] is not such as to make reasonable financial provision for me. The provision made [in the Will][under intestacy] is as follows: [*Give full details*].

6. To the best of my knowledge and belief the person[s] or class[es] of person[s] interested in the estate and the nature of their interest[s] are as follows: [*Set out the legacies to the Will*]

7. My means are as follows: [*Set out all present and foreseeable financial commitments, resources and expenses*]

8. [*Set out all other facts and matters which the Claimant intends to place before the court relevant to the factors to which the court is required to have regard under s 3 of the Act. Also set out particulars of any known previous proceedings relevant to the application. Such proceedings will often be material to the question whether the application ought to be transferred from the Family Division to the Chancery Division or vice versa. Transfer of the proceedings might also be appropriate in other circumstances eg insufficient grounds being shown by the parties or where the application involves the taking of complicated accounts for which special facilities exist in the Chancery Division.*]

9. [*Where permission to apply out of time is sought*] I ask the Court's permission to make this application notwithstanding that the period of six months has expired from the date on which representation in regard to the estate of the Deceased was first taken out and the grounds of my request are as follows [*set out grounds – Re Salmon factors: the delay has been minimal and was the result of the efforts made to settle the matter between us without having recourse to legal proceedings. The administrators and all persons who have a contrary interest were made aware of my claims at the earliest opportunity. The estate has not been distributed and therefore no prejudice is caused. On the other hand injustice and hardship will result to me and to my children if permission is refused to make the application*].

10. I ask that financial provision be made for me out of the Deceased's estate by way of [*state nature of provision applied for, eg periodical payments, and/or lump sum and/or transfer to me of the property known as [   ]*] out of the Deceased's estate.

[*Statement of truth*]

Precedent 27: Witness statement of personal representative in reply to application under Inheritance (Provision for Family and Dependants) Act 1975

Claim No [   ]

IN THE HIGH COURT OF JUSTICE
[CHANCERY/FAMILY DIVISION]

IN THE MATTER OF THE ESTATE OF [*deceased's full name*] DECEASED AND IN THE MATTER OF THE INHERITANCE (PROVISION FOR FAMILY AND DEPENDANTS) ACT 1975

I, [*insert name*] of [*address and occupation*] state as follows:

1. I am the [*First/Second*] Defendant and [*the sole/one of*] the Executor(s)/Administrator(s) of the estate of [*deceased's name*] who died on [*date*] (the 'Deceased') [*and*] was appointed by [*his/her*] [*will/codicil*], probate of which was granted to me on the [*date of grant*] out of [*registry*].

    There is now produced and shown to me marked [ ] an Office Copy of the Grant of Probate and a copy of the Deceased's last Will dated [*insert date*] and [*describe any codicils*]. [Letters of Administration to the estate of the above named Deceased were granted to me on [*date*] out of the [*registry*].]

2. The net estate of the above named [*name of deceased*] was sworn for probate purposes at £[*value*] and consists of [the following assets: (list all of them) or if the assets are numerous: the assets are set out in the list now produced and shown to me marked [   ]].

3. [*Give further details of the assets, particularly those which are not readily realisable*].

4. [*Give details of any other matters which should be drawn to the attention of the court, such as that the deceased left a memorandum to the effect that the applicant should not benefit*].

5. [*Give full particulars of the names and addresses of all persons beneficially interested in the Estate and the value of their interests insofar as it is possible to ascertain them, explaining which, if any, of the beneficiaries are children or patients*].

6. [*If the Defendant is also a beneficiary in the estate such as a widow, she (or he) is not obliged to give details of his or her means but if he or she wishes the court to take into account his or her financial circumstances, details will have to be given both as to capital income needs and likely resources and needs for the foreseeable future, together with details of any disability*].

7. [*Add a suitable concluding paragraph*].

[*Statement of truth*]

Precedent 28: Advice letter regarding response to claim under the Inheritance (Provision for Family and Dependants) Act 1975

Dear [*name*]

[*deceased's full name*] deceased

I write further to [   ] and enclose copies of the following:

1. [   ];
2. [   ]; and
3. [   ].

Background

[*insert full name of deceased*] ('[A]') executed [*his/her*] last will on [*date*] (the 'Will').

Under the Will [*explain relevant provisions of Will*].

[A] died on [*date of death*] and grant of probate was issued to [*executor name(s)*] on [*date of grant*] out of [*registry*].

[A]'s net estate for probate purposes was £[*value*].

[B]'s Claims

[*Insert the claimant's name*] ('[B]') claims that the provision made in the Will for [*him/her*] was not reasonable and therefore [*he/she*] has a claim under the Inheritance (Provision for Family and Dependants) Act 1975 (the '1975 Act').

In summary [B] claims [   ].

Economics

From the information contained in [   ], the assets are:

Asset	£
[Real estate]	
[Bank accounts]	
[Policy(ies)]	
[Household goods]	
Total estate	

The sum at issue is potentially £[*value*].

1975 Act claim

Court's approach

When the court is faced with a claim under the 1975 Act it will ask two questions:

1. whether the level of provision (here [*insert provision*]), under the Will was unreasonable; and, if so,
2. what 'reasonable financial provision', if any, should be made?

The first question addresses whether [B] has a claim. If [*he/she*] does, the court will consider the question of quantum.

That issue, of quantum, is always very difficult to assess.

The provision that the court can make depends on the status of the applicant. Here, [B] is [A]'s [[*wife/husband/civil partner*] and therefore the court can make provision which is reasonable in all the circumstances for [B] to receive whether or not it is for their maintenance (s 1(2)(b))]

or

[[*Former wife/husband/civil partner/child/dependant/cohabitee*] and therefore 'reasonable provision' means provision which is reasonable for [B] to receive for his/her maintenance only – *may want to expand regarding definition of maintenance*].

FACTORS THE COURT CONSIDERS

The court's approach to both questions is by reference to the factors listed at s 3 of the 1975 Act as follows:

1. The financial needs and resources (now and in the future) of the Applicant – s 3(1)(a)

    [Commentary]

2. The financial needs and resources (now and in the future) of other applicants – s 3(1)(b)

    [Commentary]

3. The financial needs and resources (now and in the future) of the beneficiaries – s 3(1)(c)

    [Commentary]

4. The obligations and responsibilities of the deceased to any applicant – s 3(1)(d)

    [Commentary]

5. Size and nature of the estate – s 3(1)(e)

    [Commentary]

6. Disabilities of any party – s 3(1)(f)

    [Commentary]

7. The other factors the Court thinks are relevant – s 3(1)(g)

    Conduct is of limited relevance.

    However, we would want to draw to the Court's attention in our concerns regarding [   ].

8. Additional factors

    [use below as appropriate]

    [As [B] is [A]'s [wife/husband/civil partner] the court will also have regard to:

    (a)   [B]'s age – s 3(2)(a)

[Commentary]

(b)   Length of the marriage – s 3(2)(a)

[Commentary]

(c)   [B]'s contribution to the welfare of [A]'s family – s 3(2)(b)

[Commentary]

(d)   the award if [A] and [B] had divorced – s 3(2)

[Commentary]]

or

[As [B] is [A]'s cohabitee the court will also have regard to:

(a)   [B]'s age

[Commentary]

(b)   the length of time [A] and [B] lived together – s 2(2A)(a)

[Commentary]

(c)   [B]'s contribution to the welfare of [A]'s family] – s 2(2A)(b)

[Commentary]]

or

[As [B] is [A]'s child the court will also have regard to [*education of B if relevant*]

[Commentary]

or

[As [B] was treated by [A] as a child of the family the court will also have regard to:

(a)   [education of B if relevant] – s 2(3)(a)

[Commentary]

(b)   whether [A] had assumed responsibility for maintaining [B] and to what extent and for how long – s 2(3)(b)

(c)   the liability of any other person to maintain [B] – s 2(3)(c)

[Commentary]]

or

[As [B] alleges [he/she] was dependent on [A] the court will also have regard to whether [A] had assumed responsibility for maintaining [B] and to what extent and for how long – (s 2(4))

[Commentary]]

CONCLUSION ON [B]'S CLAIM UNDER THE 1975 ACT

[Commentary]

WAY FORWARD

[Commentary]

–   Further information/evidence

        [Commentary]

–   Potential terms of compromise

        [Commentary]

Conclusion

Please confirm whether you agree to:

1.   [   ];
2.   [   ]; and
3.   [   ].

Yours sincerely

Precedent 29: Checklist when taking instructions regarding claims under the Inheritance (Provision for Family and Dependants) Act 1975

(1)   Claimant's personal details
(2)   Status/interest within s 1(1) of the Act as amended by s 2 Law Reform (Succession) Act 1995 (NB domicile of deceased)
(3)   Basis of claim:

        –   no provision in will/on intestacy

        –   provision made is inadequate

        –   joint property within s 9 of the Act

        –   anti-avoidance provisions (s 10)
(4)   Obtain copy of grant/standing search (NB leave to apply out of time)
(5)   Obtain will/details of disposition of estate on intestacy or otherwise
(6)   Consider s3 factors:

        –   Financial background, available resources, needs and current standard of living of applicant/ other applicants/ beneficiaries of the estate

        –   General background and history of relationship(s)

        –   Obligations and responsibilities of deceased towards other beneficiaries/applicants

        –   Size and nature of estate and types of asset:

      (i)   possible effect on success of claim

      (ii)   effect if already distributed

  –   position of party under physical/mental disability

  –   other relevant matters/conduct

(7)   Statement or memorandum by testator
(8)   Consider choice of jurisdiction and interaction with other claims
(9)   Explore possibility of compromise before proceedings
(10)   The position of personal representatives

Precedent 30: List of Documents to be Collated for 1975 Act Claim/Defence

General (bringing or defending a claim)

– Death Certificate
– Grant of probate/letters of administration/details of next of kin
– Will (and codicils)/former wills
– Note of instructions/letter of wishes/note of instructions to make fresh will/other documentary evidence of deceased's reasons
– Statement of deceased's assets and liabilities
– Marriage/civil partnership certificate
– Papers re divorce/nullity/judicial separation/foreign divorce or separation
– Ancillary relief/child maintenance orders
– Birth certificate/evidence of paternity
– Office copies of Land Registry entries/title deeds re any property

If acting for applicant

– Evidence of relationship with deceased, eg letters, photographs, notes and diary
– Bank statements/building society passbooks
– Portfolio/property valuations
– Documentary evidence of other assets
– Wage slips or accounts if self-employed
– Credit/debit card statements/mortgage/loan account statements/other evidence of debt
– Tax assessments
– Details of state benefit/child benefit
– Child maintenance order
– Accounts for: school fees/extra tuition fees/school uniform/school holiday costs/university fees
– Household bills:

    – gas/electricity/telephone/water rates/council tax

    – house/contents insurance

    – rent/service charges/sinking fund

-     repair bills

-     cleaning/garden assistance

– Other personal expenditure eg:

-     car bills

-     travel bills

-     medical/dental/optician bills

-     invoices evidencing other special expenditure

Precedent 31: Heads of Agreement on Settlement of Claim

AGREEMENT

THE PARTIES

1.   [   ] of [   ] (the 'Executor');
2.   [   ] of [   ] [('A');
3.   [   ] of [   ] ('B'); and

RECITALS

A.   [*deceased's name*] (the 'Deceased') of [*deceased's address*] (the 'Property') executed his/her Will on [*date of will*] (the 'Will').

B.   The Deceased died on [*date of death*].

C.   Grant of Probate was issued to the Executor out of [*registry*] on [*date of grant*].

D.   By virtue of clause [*clause number*] of the Will, [*insert details of will as relevant*].

E.   [*Outline nature of claim or intimated claim*].

F.   The parties hereto have decided to compromise [*insert details of claim*] against or arising out of the Deceased's estate on the terms set out below.

OPERATIVE PROVISIONS

The parties have agreed the following:

1.   [   ].
2.   [   ].
3.   [*costs*].
4.   That this Agreement is in full and final settlement of [   ] against or arising out of the Deceased's estate.

Signed etc

Precedent 32: Tomlin Order (to which attach Heads of Agreement)

UPON the parties having agreed the terms of settlement

BY CONSENT IT IS ORDERED that:

1. All further proceedings in this action shall be stayed upon the terms set out in the attached Schedule, except for the purpose of carrying such terms into effect.
2. Each party shall have liberty to apply to the court if the other party does not give effect to the terms set out in the Schedule.

. . . .

[   ]   [   ]   [   ]

Solicitors for   **Solicitors for**   **Solicitors**

. . . .

Date   **Date**   **Date**

INDEX

References are to paragraph numbers.